We have long awaited *The Humanitarian Machine*. Here it is with all the misgivings, dilemmas, contradictions and rewards that are such lives. Read and cherish these experiences because they reflect a truth and humanity that screams from the pages.

– Phil O'Keefe, Professor, Northumbria University, UK

# The Humanitarian Machine

As the world reels from the impact of a global pandemic and increasing intensity of climate-caused hazards, the humanitarian sector has never been more relevant. But providing aid to those affected by disasters and crises is more complex than ever.

In *The Humanitarian Machine* aid workers reflect on their own experiences of working in crisis. As they write about their work and the ways in which they each approach the challenges of helping people, they comment on some of the most vexing issues facing the humanitarian sector. Each speaks from their own perspective, asking tough questions, sharing thoughtful reflections about their ongoing work, and unpacking what it really means to be a humanitarian worker. The stories they tell, whether recounting a specific experience or reflecting on years of practice, reveal the dilemmas they face and demystify the overly romanticized aura that sometimes surrounds humanitarian practice.

Complementing the candid accounts that humanitarian leaders contribute in this book, the editors examine how their stories, perceptions, and understandings align with similar conversations that take place in other settings. Viewed together in this way, the insights and reflections provided in this book will be invaluable for humanitarian practitioners, students, and researchers alike.

**Diego Fernandez Otegui** has almost 25 years of experience in emergency management and humanitarian affairs, working in East Timor, the Democratic Republic of Congo, India, Mozambique, Trinidad and Tobago, and Spain. He is a board member of the International Humanitarian Studies Association (IHSA) and Representative in the United States of the University Network of the Americas for Disaster Risk Reduction (REDULAC) and has a PhD in Disaster Science and Management from the University of Delaware, USA.

**Daryl Yoder-Bontrager** has worked for over 20 years in humanitarian assistance and community development with Mennonite Central Committee, ultimately becoming Director of its Latin America and Caribbean programs and helping to lead the organization's responses to Hurricane Mitch in Central America and the 2010 Haiti earthquake as well as countless smaller disasters in the region. He holds a PhD in Disaster Science and Management from the University of Delaware, USA.

## Routledge Humanitarian Studies Series

Series editors: Alex de Waal, Dorothea Hilhorst, Annette Jansen and Mihir Bhatt

Editorial Board: Dennis Dijkzeul, Wendy Fenton, Kirsten Johnson, Julia Streets and Peter Walker

The Routledge Humanitarian Studies series in collaboration with the International Humanitarian Studies Association (IHSA) takes a comprehensive approach to the growing field of expertise that is humanitarian studies. This field is concerned with humanitarian crises caused by natural disaster, conflict or political instability and deals with the study of how humanitarian crises evolve, how they affect people and their institutions and societies, and the responses they trigger.

We invite book proposals that address, amongst other topics, questions of aid delivery, institutional aspects of service provision, the dynamics of rebel wars, state building after war, the international architecture of peacekeeping, the ways in which ordinary people continue to make a living throughout crises, and the effect of crises on gender relations.

This interdisciplinary series draws on and is relevant to a range of disciplines, including development studies, international relations, international law, anthropology, peace and conflict studies, public health and migration studies.

### The Humanitarian Fix
Navigating Civilian Protection in Contemporary Wars
*Joe Cropp*

### Citizen Humanitarianism at European Borders
*Edited by Maria Gabrielsen Jumbert and Elisa Pascucci*

### Adolescents in Humanitarian Crisis
Displacement, Gender and Social Inequalities
*Edited by Nicola Jones, Kate Pincock and Bassam Abu Hamad*

### The Humanitarian Machine
Reflections from Practice
*Edited by Diego Fernandez Otegui and Daryl Yoder-Bontrager*

For more information about this series, please visit: www.routledge.com/Routledge-Humanitarian-Studies/book-series/RHS

# The Humanitarian Machine

Reflections from Practice

**Edited by
Diego Fernandez Otegui
and Daryl Yoder-Bontrager**

Routledge
Taylor & Francis Group
LONDON AND NEW YORK

First published 2021
by Routledge
2 Park Square, Milton Park, Abingdon, Oxon OX14 4RN

and by Routledge
605 Third Avenue, New York, NY 10158

*Routledge is an imprint of the Taylor & Francis Group, an informa business*

*British Library Cataloguing-in-Publication Data*
A catalogue record for this book is available from the British Library

*Library of Congress Cataloging-in-Publication Data*
Names: Otegui, Diego Fernandez, editor. | Yoder-Bontrager, Daryl, editor.
Title: The humanitarian machine : reflections from practice /
edited by Diego Fernandez Otegui and Daryl Yoder-Bontrager.
Description: Abingdon, Oxon ; New York, NY : Routledge, 2021. |
Series: Routledge humanitarian studies |
Includes bibliographical references and index.
Identifiers: LCCN 2020057178 (print) | LCCN 2020057179 (ebook)
Subjects: LCSH: Disaster relief. | Humanitarian assistance.
Classification: LCC HV553 .H8555 2021 (print) |
LCC HV553 (ebook) | DDC 363.34/8–dc23
LC record available at https://lccn.loc.gov/2020057178
LC ebook record available at https://lccn.loc.gov/2020057179

ISBN: 978-0-367-68979-7 (hbk)
ISBN: 978-0-367-68975-9 (pbk)
ISBN: 978-1-003-13986-7 (ebk)

Typeset in Baskerville
by Newgen Publishing UK

## Dedication

Plant a tree, have a child, and write a book. I grew up hearing this proverb. Family gatherings, Christmas celebrations, parties, they were all perfect circumstances for aunts and uncles, grandpas and grandmas, and moms and dads to insist to the young about the importance of doing these three things.

I never paid much attention to them to be honest, but now that I have done all three, I feel different. For quite some time, for me at least, the list represented the things that you had to do before being six feet under. They were supposed to be the culmination of a fruitful life. And because of this, I was not in a rush. Something inside of me was telling me that I had to do them all, but I was planning to do them much further into the future, probably even right before leaving this earthly life. Today, I feel complete. And this can mean only one thing: that I was wrong.

This is not a list of things that you are supposed to do at the end of your life, nor are they supposed to be done at the beginning. As I write these lines, it feels like they must be done only when it feels right. They change you, and they change you for the better, but they require a little bit of wisdom and experience. They help you appreciate the beginning of things. If you think about it, planting a tree represents the origin of the places and the circumstances that we all inhabit. Having a child represents the origin of life. And I believe it comes in second place because you need to be capable of understanding, embracing and sustaining those places and circumstances for your child to grow old, surrounded by love and happiness. Once you have the circumstances and life itself, and only then, you can embark on the glorious adventure of writing a book. This comes in third place, because it represents the apogee of your own development. Without the book, without engaging in this troublesome and stressful process of creating knowledge for future generations, everything you created so far is stuck in a timeless bubble, with no option or possibility of evolving into something better.

It took me 45 years to get the three things done. But I do not complain. I am in a good place. I love my life, and I am thankful for what I have, and for what I have done. And if there is one bit of wisdom that I now have, it is that I could not have done any of the three without the support of my family. My dad and my mom made me the happy guy that I am today. I do not know of more loving parents than mine. They did all that is humanely possible to give me and my brother everything they could, and their lifelong effort and their complete and absolute surrender to make me happy will forever be remembered. My brother is not by my side anymore. Life took us along different paths, but he was for many years a brother as much as he was my best friend, and it was by his side that I learned how to go through life in my early years. I will love him till the day I die. My wife is the faithful representation of tenderness and sweetness. She is the one who knows how to bring me down to the level I need to be at when my brain is going a million miles an hour. She has not only been able to cope and endure through my times of stress, sadness and confusion, but she also gave me my sweet little Chopi, a fantastic five-year-old girl who I love beyond comprehension. She is the one who makes me smile every single morning when I wake up, and every single night before I go to bed.

This book is for them.

Diego Fernandez Otegui

# Contents

# About the editors

**Diego Fernandez Otegui** considers himself as a kind, caring, and committed post-disaster humanitarian practitioner and scholar, with abilities in understanding the multiple demands presented to private and public organizations that intervene in post-disaster contexts. His specialization is in the collection and analysis of qualitative and quantitative data for the development of strategic international deployments. He is passionate about post-disaster rapid research using applied, practical, hands-on, people-centered, participatory methodologies; a type of research that requires a complete immersion and access to the minds and hearts of disaster actors.

He received his PhD in Disaster Science and Management from the Biden School of Public Policy at the University of Delaware. The purpose of his doctoral research is to understand the logic behind the decision to deploy personnel in the aftermath of international disasters. With almost 25 years of experience in emergency management and humanitarian affairs, he had the opportunity to participate in missions in various countries among which are worth mentioning East Timor and the Democratic Republic of Congo. He also served in India, Mozambique, Trinidad and Tobago, and Spain. He is a board member of the International Humanitarian Studies Association (IHSA) and Representative in the United States of the University Network of the Americas for Disaster Risk Reduction (REDULAC). He has lectured and presented at numerous international conferences in the Netherlands, South Korea, Japan, Canada, Mozambique, Ethiopia, and the United States, among others.

He currently lives in the United States with his wife and five-year-old daughter. He plays the guitar, enjoys running and swimming, and is also a member of the United Methodist Church.

**Daryl Yoder-Bontrager** holds a PhD in Disaster Science and Management from the University of Delaware. He worked for over 20 years in humanitarian assistance and community development work with Mennonite Central Committee (MCC) in its Latin America programs. He and his family lived for nine years in Bolivia and Honduras before settling in Pennsylvania when he became director of MCC's Latin America and Caribbean programs. He was involved in leading the organization's responses to Hurricane Mitch in Central America and the 2010 Haiti earthquake as well as countless smaller disasters in the region. Since leaving MCC he has pursued graduate studies. His research has consistently explored how non-governmental organizations carry out their disaster-related work.

# Contributors

**Jono Anzalone** serves as the head of Disaster and Crisis, Preparedness, Response, and Recovery for the International Federation of Red Cross and Red Crescent Societies for the Americas and Caribbean region, based in Panama. Jono recently rejoined the Red Cross family after a 16-month engagement as Global Disaster Response and Relief Partnerships lead for Airbnb. Prior to this, he was the Vice President of International Services at the American Red Cross based out of Washington, DC. In this role, Jono oversaw disaster preparedness, response, and recovery programming in more than 34 countries, including the Measles and Rubella Initiative which since 2001 has helped vaccinate more than two billion children and reduce global measles by 84%.

**Helen Barclay-Hollands** is currently the Director for the Eastern Zone for World Vision International, based in Goma, Democratic Republic of Congo (DRC). As the Director for the Eastern Zone, she leads the operations for World Vision across North and South Kivu provinces in DRC. She has previously supported the World Vision response in the Kasai region in DRC as well as the start-up of the Ebola response which started in 2018. She has worked in DRC for over five years, previously as the Programme Manager for Tearfund UK, also based in Goma. Prior to joining World Vision DRC, she worked for other international NGOs such as Tearfund and CORD. She has extensive experience managing 15 responses for complex humanitarian and emergency crises including the Haiti earthquake, the Darfur refugee crisis in Eastern Chad, and the Central African Republic crisis. She holds a master's degree in international development (forced migration) from the School of Oriental and African Studies (SOAS), London, UK.

**Marta Bruno** works on humanitarian and resilience evaluations in the Food and Agriculture Organization of the United Nations (UN-FAO). Before 2012, she worked in the FAO emergency division, focusing on the adoption of sustainable livelihoods, resilience, and disaster risk management in humanitarian work, having moved from a program that focused on mainstreaming sustainable livelihoods approaches. She has always been involved in capacity development, facilitation, and learning. Before joining FAO, she was part of a group that set up and managed a consultancy company called Social and Economic Research Associates, working in development. She focused on sustainable livelihoods analysis and evaluations, participatory rural appraisal, involvement of communities, and local-level institutions in project and program design and management. She studied history and human geography in Cambridge (UK), specializing in the former Soviet Union and gender. She then worked as a researcher and lecturer in two centers for Russian and East European Studies at Birmingham and Wolverhampton Universities in the UK.

**Andrew Cunningham** has 23 years' experience in the humanitarian and development field, beginning with working in Burundi from 1989 to 1991 and then in the Rwandan refugee camps in Tanzania between 1994 and 1996. Following this he spent 14 years with Médecins Sans Frontières (MSF), 10 years of which were in the field in a wide variety of contexts and geographical locations. Later he moved to the Amsterdam MSF headquarters to work in the Humanitarian Affairs Department. Andrew's specialty in his MSF work was in highly insecure contexts, such as Chechnya, Afghanistan/Pakistan, and Somalia. Since leaving MSF Andrew has completed his PhD in War Studies at King's College London, researching the relationship between states and international humanitarian organizations in the context of conflict. Andrew works as a consultant and trainer for various humanitarian organizations. Between 2016 and 2019 he was a member of the Board of MSF International and is currently a member of the board of the International Humanitarian Studies Association. He is also a Research Fellow at the Conflict, Security and Development Research Group at the War Studies Department, King's College London.

**David Eisenbaum**'s humanitarian career began with volunteering at All Hands and Hearts (AHAH) in 2008. He worked for AHAH for two years, in 11 disasters in the US, Haiti, and Indonesia, filling a variety of field-based program and operations roles. Following the 2010 Haiti earthquake and cholera outbreak, David worked for Haiti Communitere leading a program to bring clinicians and health educators to remote communities to treat patients and provide cholera-prevention education. David then served as the organization's Operations Manager. After pursuing a masters in Nonprofit Management from Northeastern University, David rejoined AHAH to help launch and direct programs in the US and Nepal. During the 2014–2015 West Africa Ebola epidemic, David worked with Partners in Health, managing field operations in Liberia. David consulted independently and then for Deloitte's Crisis Management Practice before rejoining AHAH as Director of International Response. David serves as a federal reservist with a Disaster Medical Assistance Team.

**Naomi Enns** has 34 years of insight, experience with community engagement, and humanitarian service. She has a BSc in Nursing, MA in Adult Education, and a graduate certificate in Humanitarian Action Leadership. After a successful Canadian community health nursing and teaching career, she became a full-time volunteer international humanitarian worker with Mennonite Central Committee (MCC). She has worked in community health programs in Chad, directed large humanitarian programs coordinating local partners in Lebanon and Syria, and led trauma resilience workshops for communities of faith and migrants. As West Europe MCC Representative, she interacted daily with Anabaptist communities and organizations in donor relations and conflict prevention and built European networks with an eye towards international assistance and community peacebuilding to meet critical needs. Organizational restructuring ended her 10-year career with MCC. She currently lives in Klaipeda, Lithuania and teaches peacebuilding at LCC International University while helping to design a peace center at the university. When not busy navigating borders, contributing to peacebuilding dialogues, engaging donors, and planting seeds of hope, she enjoys hiking and a good cup of tea.

**Pat Foley** is an applied anthropologist with 24 years of international experience facilitating participatory action research, assessment, evaluation, and learning. Pat is a senior advisor for gender, resilience, and economic security in dynamic operational environments: emergency, recovery, development, adaptation, and risk reduction with the UN, NGOs, the Red Cross, government, academia, and civil society. He is also a musician and theatrical improviser, and has worked with chimpanzees, orangutans, and manta rays.

**Volker Hüls** has 21 years of experience in planning, managing, and improving international assistance, building on a 12-year background in national civil protection in Germany. He has worked extensively in national disaster response, international humanitarian response, recovery, and resilience-building programs. With a wide range of experience working in countries in crisis, developing countries, and middle-income countries, Volker works across the nexus between humanitarian and development programs.

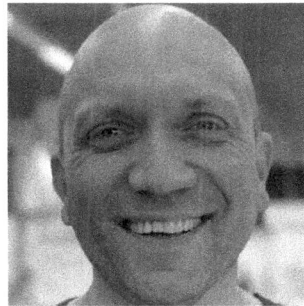

**Matthew Levinger** is Research Professor of International Affairs at the George Washington University. He directs the National Security Studies Program, an executive education program for senior officials from the US government and its international partners, as well as the Master of International Policy and Practice Program at George Washington's Elliott School of International Affairs. He was previously a senior program officer at the United States Institute of Peace, where he trained practitioners in international conflict analysis and prevention. From 2005 to 2007, Matthew was founding director of the Academy for Genocide Prevention at the US Holocaust Memorial Museum. Before moving to Washington, he was associate professor of History at Lewis & Clark College in Portland, Oregon; he has also taught at Stanford University. From 2003–2004, he was a William C. Foster Fellow at the US Department of State. He earned his PhD at the University of Chicago.

**Aninia Nadig** has worked for Sphere in different capacities. In 2017–2018, she was heavily involved in the revision of the *Sphere Handbook 2018*, overseeing the process during much of the second year. Prior to joining Sphere, Aninia was a Country Analyst at the Internal Displacement Monitoring Centre (IDMC), where she was responsible for the Horn of Africa. Before that she worked in the Netherlands, focusing on Dutch and EU refugee and asylum policy issues with Dutch non-profit organizations. Prior to that, she carried out refugee status determination for the Swiss Federal Office for Refugees. Aninia holds a master's degree in international relations from the University of Amsterdam.

**Kendra Pospychalla** is a veteran of the US Marine Corps and holds an MS in Disaster Science and Management from the University of Delaware as well as a BA in International Studies with a specialization in Political Science from the University of California, San Diego. Her experience includes nine years in disaster relief and six years in business development and finance. She began in disaster relief in 2011 and has since served with multiple non-profit disaster relief organizations in volunteer and employee roles. Her experience has primarily focused on emergency planning and program design of relief services, particularly in the areas of situational awareness, mass sheltering, debris removal, home reconstruction, emergency medical services, and water, sanitation, and hygiene. She has deployed in various management and field positions, from smaller, local events to catastrophic, internationally recognized events.

**Rami Shamma** currently works as field operations director for World Vision Lebanon, where he oversees operations through development and relief interventions. He previously worked in a national Lebanese NGO called DPNA (Development for People and Nature Association) for approximately 12 years. He is also a trainer on conflict transformation, active citizenship, communication, negotiation and mediation, needs assessment, municipal work, youth engagement in public life, profound stress, and other skills/topics. Rami has an MSc in Computer and Communication Engineering.

**Gary Shaye** has worked for 45 years with Save the Children. His recent humanitarian experience includes two months in Colombia for the Venezuelan response, three months in Puerto Rico for Hurricane Maria, and three months in Florida for Hurricane Irma. From April 2010 to February 2012, Gary was Country Director in Haiti, following the 2010 earthquake. Prior to Haiti, Gary spent seven years as Director in Bolivia. For 10 years Gary was Vice President for International Programs, with overall responsibility for Humanitarian and Development Programs, and for three years he was Regional Director for Latin America. From 1980 to 1986 he established Save the Children's country operations in Nepal. His first assignment was in the Dominican Republic where he spent four years as the Country Director. Gary received his bachelor's degree from Cornell University, and his master's degree from the School for International Training. He served for two years as a Peace Corps volunteer in Cusco, Peru. Gary is fluent in Spanish and speaks some Nepali.

**Paul Shetler Fast** is the Global Health Coordinator for Mennonite Central Committee, based in Port-au-Prince, Haiti, specializing in participatory evaluation and qualitative methods and the integration of mental health into community health programming. Prior to this, Paul served as MCC's Representative for Haiti, overseeing all relief, development, peace, education, and health programming, including leading all aspects of MCC's humanitarian response to Hurricane Matthew (2016–2019). Paul is a graduate of the University of Pittsburgh, with master's degrees in public health and international development, specializing in evaluation and management of community-based organizations and behavior-change programming.

**Marie Anne Sliwinski** serves as the Program Director for Disaster Response and Sustainable Development at the Evangelical Lutheran Church in America (ELCA). Marie Anne has 18 years of experience working in the non-profit sector, 16 of which were dedicated to international humanitarian and development programs. Currently, Marie Anne oversees the

Lutheran Disaster Response International portfolio, which supports immediate relief and recovery needs of families affected by disasters. Marie Anne
holds a master's degree in international relations from the University of
Chicago, and currently resides in the Chicago suburbs with her husband and
two children.

# Preface

Both of us, Daryl and Diego, met years ago as students in the same doctoral program. We connected almost immediately and since then we have been friends, and have helped and supported one another. Our doctoral dissertations happened to explore similar issues, an excuse we used to travel together to collect data for our research projects. During our trips we spent countless hours talking, sometimes arguing, sometimes even raising our voices at one another, about how to understand what we were observing. What was unique about our conversations is that they took place in a disaster context, in which we engaged both people who had lived through the disaster and humanitarian workers alike. The value of the humanitarian voice, as an idea, was a recurrent theme.

At some point, we came to realize that the body of knowledge about humanitarian action has largely been produced by individual authors or compiled by editors who made decisions about what they believed was important, and decided where and when to publish it. These materials are inevitably imbued with the singular point of view of those that produced it. The themes that are covered, how the issues are framed, and even the writing style, all depend on what each author considers to be of importance for the world to know. When doing research, their background, experience, and even personal traits cannot be entirely separated from the research process. The underlying assumptions and overt viewpoints of the researchers are inevitably woven into the final product. Even the story of how humanitarian actors practice their craft is often the subject of someone else' perception. In the best-case scenarios, humanitarian workers' voices are confined to unique or intimate spaces like conferences or the publication of an article for a newspaper or a magazine. These outlets, though they might be good enough to let us learn about a single individual, are not designed to provide a more complete account of the unique perceptions, feelings, and ideas of the 'humanitarian workforce'.

This is, as we see it, a major vulnerability. In any system, the voices on the inside are critical in working out how to articulate what constitutes it. As a consequence, what the wider world knows about humanitarian action may not represent all that needs to be known about it. Rather, it is what we and our fellow writers think needs to be known, which is to a large extent the product of scholarly imagination, leaving open the possibility of perpetuating an incorrect representation of human life in the midst of suffering. This feeling grounded a somewhat unrestful concern, which is that humanitarian efforts, and the decisions made within the humanitarian infrastructure, could be based on incomplete knowledge, rather than on the reality seen and experienced by expert humanitarians.

And so we decided to produce a book that would help us know more about the humanitarian sector by paying attention to those within it. But this presented a significant challenge. We wondered about how to connect a multitude of dissimilar voices in a way that made sense to the reader. Although from a distance it might not seem like it, humanitarian workers are very different from one another. Their individuality, their humanitarian identity if you will, is unique to each of them.

The humanitarian sector is made up of thousands of individual workers, but it is also a whole, an institution in its own right, with its own way of understanding the world. Early on in our process Diego told Daryl about growing up watching *Mazinger Z*, a Japanese animated superhero story, where a boy named Kouji inherits from his grandfather a giant robot that will battle the evil forces of the world. Kouji and his friends sit in the head of the robot and pilot the huge machine. This became a metaphor for one way that we understand the humanitarian context and led to the name of this book. The humanitarian machine is a giant entity, doing amazing superhero tasks as it works to alleviate suffering all over the world. But like any extraordinarily large creature it also makes missteps, stumbles, causes unintended damage. We wanted to capture how the humanitarians pilot this machine, how they feel about the space in which they work, but we also wanted to collect valuable information about the nature of humanitarianism and how it functions. We concluded that the best way, and probably the only way, to bring their diversity together was by capturing as much as possible their unique individuality. Consequently, we invited humanitarian workers to write their experiences, and gave them the freedom to choose their own topics and the type of information that they would include. We asked them to write about the evolution of their perceptions, their visions, and their desires for the future.

Recognizing that aid workers are very busy and that their lives change from one moment to the other, we told them that we wanted this book to reflect all aspects of what working in the humanitarian field is about. While we stressed that they had freedom to choose their writing style, we encouraged them to write in a way that allows the reader to become immersed in their story. We asked them to tell their story by starting with a short description of who they are, and a very short account of what their life is like. Our hope was that readers would become aware that the humanitarian endeavor was rewarding, yes, but that it also had costs. Humanitarian aid workers are confronted with immense need, are often trying to get more done than is humanly possible, spend lots of time away from families sometimes in isolated and hard environments. We wanted readers to feel the humanitarian reality in their skin. In summary, contributors were given the liberty to provide visceral reflections of how they felt about the numerous issues they face in their daily lives. The purpose was both to communicate the particularities of their lives and to help the reader immerse him or herself in the story and try to feel the things that the writer was feeling at the moment of writing.

We thought it would be useful for our readers to know at least a bit of this process and the questions we asked the writers to respond to. First, we asked them to reflect on the complexities of their work, not as they might do in a discussion with their peers or their bosses, but rather to think in terms of how to communicate a sense of their reality to people uninvolved in humanitarian work. During the individual meetings we had with each writer, we asked them to imagine themselves in a party where they are introduced to a group of people that have no connection to their line of work, but who show eagerness to know about it. But we also asked them to keep in mind that the attention of people in such an environment is probably limited to 10–20 minutes, before it disperses and moves on to other topics.

In summary, the task was a heavy one. Writers had to reflect on the core themes and challenges of their lives and the humanitarian work they carry out, and to determine what these issues might mean to uninvolved people, and then communicate these reflections in an easy, friendly, and interesting manner. We pushed them to think about how they could help non-humanitarian aid workers to very quickly and easily learn about the major issues and complexities that humanitarians face in their daily lives. *The Humanitarian Machine* is the result of these processes. We hope it makes a significant contribution to a better understanding of all humanitarian work.

# Introduction

The world is going through tough times. In 2018 alone, 210 million people needed humanitarian assistance due to multiple ongoing crises. In the same year, 68 million people were affected by disasters around the globe.[1] In response, we have witnessed tremendous growth in humanitarian assistance efforts. Individual citizens who are not particularly related to any organization carry out some of the aid work. They are often well-meaning but inexperienced global citizens who choose to engage with one another around smaller organizations. But there has also been a remarkable increase in more formal and structured humanitarian action over the last two decades. The number of humanitarian workers jumped from 210,800 to 570,000 in the period between 2008 and 2018. This book tells the stories of a few of those workers.

A few days after the 2010 Haiti earthquake, thousands of international humanitarian workers from dozens of countries made their way across rubble-strewn streets to a building on the edge of the Port-au-Prince airport. There, they crowded into an undersized room to attend a United Nations Shelter Cluster meeting. They reported on the challenges of sheltering the masses of Haitians left without homes by the earthquake and listened to accounts of what the UN and various governments were doing. They talked about the activities they were undertaking, heard about innovations, and considered how they could best contribute to the overall work. In what has become a familiar ritual following major disasters, similar meetings were taking place somewhere else to address other needs: food, sanitation, logistics, protection, among others.

This describes well the imagery that many humanitarian workers have in their minds when they think about the work they do. Others, those who are not so heavily invested in the formal process, will probably have a somewhat different image. A person walking through the hastily built camps of temporary shelters after any major disaster will be shocked by the wide assortment of foreign governments, multilateral agencies, and humanitarian organizations that are represented in the insignias on the tents. These logos represent the fueled desire of people around the world to help those in need, but they also symbolize the existence of fierce international competition to be recognized as valuable members of the humanitarian community. View them all together, and one can come up with a good idea of the world's major religions, cultures, and languages.

The perception people have of humanitarian work changes depending on where they stand. In most cases, the images that people have in their heads when they think about it are of concrete actions that take place in the field of operations after a disaster or a humanitarian crisis like thousands of refugees crossing a border. However, take a step back and try to see the entire picture from afar, and you will perceive the space where humanitarians converge as an ambiguous, undefinable, abstract symbolic space, as much as it is made up of the concrete actions of delivering aid.

The humanitarian space is indeed a system with a particular way of understanding the world, as much as it is a massive global machine, increasingly regulated, with a complex political structure, so much so that broad generalizing strokes cannot paint adequate descriptions. Its heart is pure, some would say, but it is big, it is clumsy, and it can easily hurt and inflict pain, most especially when it operates in the developing world, where the destruction and chaos generated by a disaster add to pre-existing conditions of systemic vulnerability. In these complex situations, impulsive, sloppy deployments of the humanitarian machinery and the many peripheral actors that converge on the impacted country can debilitate the environment even more. This machinery is not well oiled. It is unorganized, individualistic, and sometimes explosive. It is porous and amorphous. Sometimes it even serves as a breeding ground for those that are not interested in doing good.

The perviousness of the system facilitated its growth. The hundreds of thousands of humanitarian experts are one piece of it, but there are many others. Some of them have been clearly identified but are only vaguely understood. Others remain hidden in the depths of what is probably one of the most complex social systems in the world. The diversity of the humanitarian machine is also clear in the variety of underlying motivations and objectives of those that converge onto the field of operations. There is also great variation in their sizes, ranging from a few that operate much like multinational corporations with annual budgets over a billion dollars, to NGOs with a few dozen workers. There is also a large variety of different specializations and geographic foci.

These thousands of humanitarians embody a unique sentiment: a desire to be of service to others, to be part of something honorable, bigger than any one individual, to generate the feeling that all of us are equal, in un unfair world that is plagued by suffering. Understandably, humanitarian action has become an idea that is surrounded by an almost mystic and romantic aura of heroism and surrender. It is undeniable that humanitarian work is extremely appealing. As a matter of fact, this idealized conception is what drew Daryl into it. He was born in the United States and felt the attraction of working and living for a few years in a barrio on the outskirts of Santa Cruz, Bolivia. That experience led to another, and then to another. Something similar happened to Diego. He was born in Argentina, where he spent most of his younger years as an active participant in multiple social causes, working side by side with the most disadvantaged populations. Eventually, he was influenced by the idea that being an international aid worker was about crossing borders, travelling the world, feeding the hungry, and saving lives. It took him many years to realize that this was not the complete picture at all, but rather an inaccurate and romanticized idea. He chose to start this project with an honest interest in understanding the humanitarian environment and the weight people involved often feel their shoulders bear, and many times, the loneliness that is part of humanitarian workers' experience.

Humanitarian work is definitely not easy. Aid workers do their jobs in complex situations, are plagued by stress, and often do their tasks for little pay. The moment they learn of a new disaster is unusually difficult to describe. The rush that takes over is made up of a mixture of adrenaline, sadness, and hope. It might be only a matter of minutes before they commit to their new mission. They leave their homes and families behind to travel around the world to unfamiliar places and say, "I am here." They travel without knowing what to expect—depending on where they are going, there could be risk to their lives as they put their trust in a flimsy support network of fellow humanitarian workers. They often travel almost empty handed, with nothing but a 'go bag' and a bit of information. They sometimes do not know who, or even if, somebody is going to be waiting for them. They may not know the geography, the culture, or the dangers they will face. They travel light because they do not know how soon they will have to be relocated and because they hope and wish that shortly after the deployment they will be instructed to return to their loved ones.

Once they get off the plane, anxiety increases. "Where to go?" they will probably wonder. The uncertainty of the 'field of operations', as they call it, is not for everyone. Only a few can really cope with that reality. The field could be as small as a few square acres, or as large as dozens of adjacent towns. Whatever the geographic area, the field is the place where they will exercise their abilities to change the reality of those in pain. It is a unique environment, and an ecosystem that demands that they insert themselves into one of the most difficult realities and maintain their composure while they do it.

Humanitarian actions include all sorts of activities: searching for missing persons, helping disabled people leave their homes and reach a shelter, providing meals for rescue teams, repairing bridges and offering psychological support, accompanying displaced people into temporary houses at the refugee camp. The tasks are diverse, and the range of organizations is indescribable. They differ in size, capacity, amount of available resources, nationality, expertise, and strategic and tactical objectives. The dynamics in these contexts are ever changing. Organizations multiply at a rapid pace. Where there were two organizations yesterday, tomorrow there will be 20 and then the number might shrink back down to five. Only the most courageous (or the craziest) will dare to go beyond the city limits where the need for humanitarian action is concentrated. The rest will remain in the city center where need is also significant, but where the level of comfort and support is higher.

Humanitarian workers are a proud bunch who live by strong ideals. They show great appreciation and honor to be considered humanitarians. Sometimes they can appear to be a unique breed of humans; they operate in physical spaces, yes, but they are also bound by a common understanding of their work, a symbolic space that connects them. Nevertheless, the 'we' that defines them is not concise nor uniform.

To understand the humanitarian machine and the people who work in it, one must understand that, contrary to our assertion that humanitarian workers share a symbolic space, one must also grasp the contrasting idea that they are made up of a dissimilar group of people and organizations who are held together in a common space that defies unambiguous definition. Rather it is an amorphous mix of people. The spectrum of motivations and methods across which humanitarians stretch is as extensive as is the embodiment of their ideals. Even the term 'humanitarian' is ambiguous and ill defined. There is a large discrepancy in the way humanitarians themselves conceive of their craft, and how those that they strive to help think of it. When they meet and interact, their multiple identities collide in extremely complex and intricate networks of action. From the outside, this collision is usually concealed by what appears to be a total and complete surrender to the needs of others. Unfortunately, when humanitarian workers reach the field, they often meet with the despair of the people they want to serve combined with the many obstacles and inefficiencies of the humanitarian machine.

## The goal of this book

All humanitarians are different; they hail from all over the world. This book, however, primarily highlights the perspectives of humanitarian workers based in wealthier countries. In a second volume we hope to be able to listen to those based in other parts of the world. As varied as humanitarians are, they all share important characteristics and traits. They are professionals who believe in what they do and fight for what they believe in. The strength of their commitment to service is paramount. Beyond that, or maybe because of it, no one is ever quite sure what makes an ideal candidate to work inside the humanitarian machine. Yet they possess an innate ability to affect the social world, to alter rules and relational ties and the distribution of resources. Because of the contexts in which they operate, they can also influence recovery efforts, and, eventually, they may even affect the development process of the people they serve.

The original end-product of this project was going to be just a collection of uncensored stories, removed from organizational boundaries. For the two of us, steeped in academic study, stories presented in this manner represent valuable data. Eventually, we felt we needed to pay attention to the potential of the humanitarian workforce to affect the very system that constrains them. To do this, we felt that we had to connect their stories in a creative way, and explore if, in the few accounts of this book, we could find a shared vision. The way that we chose to do so was not by rigorously analyzing the content of their chapters (as we would do in an academic context), but by allowing their stories to spark our own reflexive process. As scholars and editors, we decided to process our reflections through what we know are important ideas within academic dialogues. The outcome of this reflexive process is presented in the final chapter of each part, which we have entitled 'extending the conversation'.

This book is not simply about sharing knowledge and stories, but rather a thoroughly crafted tool to help all of us, academic observers, humanitarian aid workers, and any interested person in the general public, to listen to how humanitarian workers experience their lives within the unique social space dedicated to meeting human need, and learn ways in which we can all improve the humanitarian system and serve better those that live in despair.

We intended the original audience of this book to be those that are not involved in the sector, people who might find themselves removed from the epicenter of humanitarian action. There are many people out there living at the margins of this work. They might have an idea based on information from the media, they might give a donation from time to time, or they might have a friend who had the opportunity to work in the field, but they have had little possibility of understanding what it really means to be a part of it. Our experience is that even our own family members often have only a superficial understanding of what we do or how we do it.

For our non-humanitarian readers, those of you from around the world who are curious about humanitarian work, we present to you a collection of well-written, stimulating, and entertaining stories by top humanitarian workers that are current and important. We hope that you will engage them carefully and thoughtfully, that you will read the individual reflections, and then piece together your own mosaic of the field. By understanding its inside, you will become more knowledgeable about what it means to be a humanitarian worker, to support your favorite causes and be able to relate to politicians and others in the sphere of influence in a more informed way, and maybe even take the step to become one of us.

Our endeavor is also an invitation to humanitarian workers themselves. Our authors both chide the humanitarian sector for not reflecting enough and commend it for constantly engaging in evaluation of what it means to work in the sector. Both are probably correct at different times and places. We believe that in a field that is so disparate and ambiguously defined, a constant process of self-reflection is imperative. We hope that the essays included here will spark further thought about best practices, yes, but also more philosophical reflection about what it means to work in a common social space with others, to engage in a process that makes more explicit the assumptions humanitarian workers hold so that they can be weighed, contrasted, adapted, adopted, and discarded when need be.

We also hope this will be a work that will engage other academics and scholars. For many, the nature of their work is not bounded by the specific reality of individual contexts. They work in a more abstract space where conversations are guided by principles, norms, and values that define how things should be. For them, we want the reflections we present at the end of each part to spark new ideas and suggest a research agenda if necessary. Our reflections are not to be taken as scientific findings, but more like methodologically driven conclusions. What we have tried to do is to present a different way of thinking, but still follow a process that resembles to a large extent the process of knowledge creation that is followed in academia. Our hope for you is that you will find value in connecting the dots in such a different way. We will be more than happy to receive your feedback, questions, and concerns, to engage in ongoing conversation.

We want the content of this book to be applicable to a greater realm, to be of use to other researchers to understand, adhere, and build upon, as well as other humanitarian executives that have the responsibility to lead and shape the humanitarian space. We have even spoken with our contributing authors, and we have all agreed to consider this book, this exercise, as a platform to establish a new type of conversation where humanitarian workers are considered not just as service providers, but as essential elements for academic research.

For all of you in academia, we have the following suggestions and recommendations. First, we hope that undergraduate and graduate students who are hoping themselves to work within the humanitarian sector find inspiration in this book. A second group we hope will take an interest in the reflections of humanitarian aid workers are professors who are teaching classes on humanitarian work. And, last, we hope that these writings will stimulate researchers to use what we present here as evidence for their research.

The bulk of the book is arranged in three parts. While there is much overlap between them, and many of the essays could have been placed in any of the parts, we arranged them to bring emphasis to particular themes that we felt were present in the authors' contributions. Taken together, the contributions present a reflection on the way humanitarian work is managed. All three parts highlight a continuum on which humanitarian actors must place themselves. The first is the spread between standards and flexibility. The second part looks at the continuum itself, discussing the many divides the humanitarian machine navigates. And the third part explores the uncomfortable reality of power and the tensions between how power is present and used. Together the authors help us know better the humanitarian machine and contribute to the humanitarian sector's ongoing process of reflection.

## Structure of the book

Each of the three parts of this book starts with a short introduction that summarizes what we consider to be the main conversation across all the chapters of the section. Of course, there are other themes that can be picked up, and we hope readers will explore those themes as well. The introductions highlight those we focused on.

The parts' conclusions are a bit longer and are meant to extend the conversation that we found among the contributors. We were impressed with how the authors' contributions sparked our own creative and reflexive processes and stimulated discussions between the two of us about what we believe to be the main aspects of the discourse around humanitarian action as it is taking place in academia and the humanitarian arena. The conclusions give the reader a small glimpse into our thoughts as we read the chapters.

Certainly, you can read the entire book from beginning to end; we think that is the best way to read it. If you choose to read it from start to finish, we hope that the introduction to each part gives you a basic idea of what the contributors

talk about and a feeling of wanting more. The chapters are informative, easy to read, and entertaining, but are also, in a way, intimate expressions of the authors themselves and how they interpret their experiences. Their goal was for you, the reader, to get to know the humanitarian space through their eyes. You will end each chapter with increased knowledge about the humanitarian sector, and perhaps more importantly you will get to know the author. By the time you reach the conclusion, you will have encountered the underlying themes that run through the five chapters that we singled out for emphasis, as well as others that are present. The part conclusions will give you a deeper understanding of the conversation through our own eyes.

Of course, an alternative approach to reading the entire book sequentially is to read the three introductions in a row to end up with an idea of some of the major dilemmas of the humanitarian dialogue of our present times. You could also jump straight to the concluding chapters of the three parts. If you do that, you will end up with a bit of extra knowledge and our perspectives about the conversations mentioned in the introductory chapters. We think that if you do so, you will miss the purpose of the book, and the magic of the rich and nuanced stories and reflections these humanitarian leaders shared with us.

## Note

1  CRED, "Natural Disasters 2018: An Opportunity to Prepare," Centre for Research on the Epidemiology of Disasters CRED, 2019, www.cred.be/publications.

# Part 1

# Flexibility and standardization

The mechanics of humanitarian delivery

# Introduction to the conversation

Mary Anderson's 1990 book *Do No Harm: How Aid Can Support Peace–Or War*[1] introduced the troubling idea that humanitarian efforts do not automatically produce good results. Anderson suggested that in the process of helping, humanitarian actors can inadvertently take actions that cause more harm than good to those being served. Today, this is widely recognized, and the 'do no harm' principle has taken root in the humanitarian sector and become a beacon of light for humanitarian practitioners, and a measure against which the work of humanitarian actors is evaluated.

The Rwanda genocide of 1994 added to this conversation and sparked profound humanitarian soul searching. Reports like the 1996 Joint Evaluation of Emergency Assistance to Rwanda triggered major changes and in the years that followed several initiatives were born. The Sphere Project, which builds consensus around the application of standards across international humanitarian efforts, was formed in 1997. The United Nations weighed in a few years later in a Humanitarian Response Review that started by saying, "The perception that humanitarian response does not always meet the basic requirements of affected populations in a timely fashion and that the response provided can vary considerably from crisis to crisis…".[2]

The do no harm principle, however, as simple as it sounds, leaves a lot of room for heated discussion about how to carry out humanitarian work. Some of the divergence of opinion on this matter is the subject of this first part. Some humanitarian actors believe it is important to ensure that all those being helped will get a standard amount of aid. The type and amount of aid that each person receives is supposed to be based on a series of minimum requirements, which are essentially based on the presumption that needs (at least some of them) are universal. At the other end of the conversation, there are those who think there is no such thing as a universal definition of need, that standards are externally imposed and not culturally relevant. They propose more flexibility and freedom to be creative in meeting changing conditions on the ground and aim for a more customized response.

The writers in this first part contribute to this discussion. From those doing direct implementation, to humanitarian workers carrying out administrative tasks inside an office, they reflect on what standards and flexibility mean to the recipients of relief aid. They write about diverse topics including guidelines that need to be carefully adjusted for each context, about measuring humanitarian aid results, and about how local people feel about what they need.

The chapters in this part reflect the dialogue. Volker Hüls tells the story of his experience in Rwanda, the humanitarian crisis that resulted in the creation of organizations like Sphere and ALNAP, a network formed to study and improve humanitarian practices. Both institutions today are respected for their contributions to the humanitarian field. Aninia Nadig then writes about her work in Sphere headquarters, arguing that standards improve humanitarian work. Marta Bruno talks about her experience carrying out evaluations of humanitarian projects. Finally, in a theme that will be repeated by many writers throughout the book, both David Eisenbaum and Helen Barclay-Hollands emphasize that humanitarian workers should be attuned to local needs.

## Notes

1  Anderson, M. B. 1999. *Do No Harm: How Aid Can Support Peace – Or War*. Boulder, Colorado: Lynne Rienner.
2  Adinolfi, C., D. S. Bassiouni, H. F. Lauritzsen, H. R. Williams. 2005. "Humanitarian Response Review". Report, Office for the Coordination of Humanitarian Affairs, New York, United Nations (p.8).

# 1  How standards contribute to the humanitarian sector

*Aninia Nadig*

## The place of rules in my life

I think people generally perceive me as a somewhat atypical Swiss. Slightly chaotic maybe. When it comes to rules, I see them as important, sure. But, in my view, they can be ignored at times, bent at other times. Whenever it feels safe to me, I prefer walking on the street, rather than on the sidewalk – I feel like I have more space. Similarly, I prefer living in a country other than Switzerland. I feel less obliged to understand and follow all the unspoken cultural intricacies that surround me. I understand the reason for these rules but want to be able to adapt them to my situation.

I also raised my kids with that approach. Let me assure you: they do use the sidewalk, and luckily they have turned out just fine. They learned at an early age how to exploit my inclination to allow exceptions. When my younger one was quite little, one of her favourite words was *usnahmswiis* ("just this once" in Swiss German). She said it with a serious face, slightly tilted head and lifted index finger to express how amazingly exceptional this one thing was that she wanted from me, knowing very well that the rule should prompt me to say no. Now, as young adults, they are starting to find their own balance between rules and exceptions. This is what life is all about, isn't it? You think you know how to do things, then life happens, you adapt to circumstances, and your own personality has a lot to do with the solution you choose.

After my studies in political science, my first job was to determine the status of asylum seekers in Switzerland: people from Sri Lanka, Bosnia and Turkey. I received a short special training on how to interview traumatised women, mostly linked to claims of rape. I held that job for one year and then had to give up, as I was as close to burnout as I would ever come in my professional life. Looking back, I see how torn I was between clear rules on what constitutes a valid claim for refugee status and the individual stories people told. I felt like we were playing a game: I set the rules and they would try to adapt their story to fit the rules. My task was to detect the lies – if there were any. This job was not for me. My mind did not work that way, my people skills were probably not developed enough. But I was hooked on the field of forced migration, which became my main focus during my further studies and work.

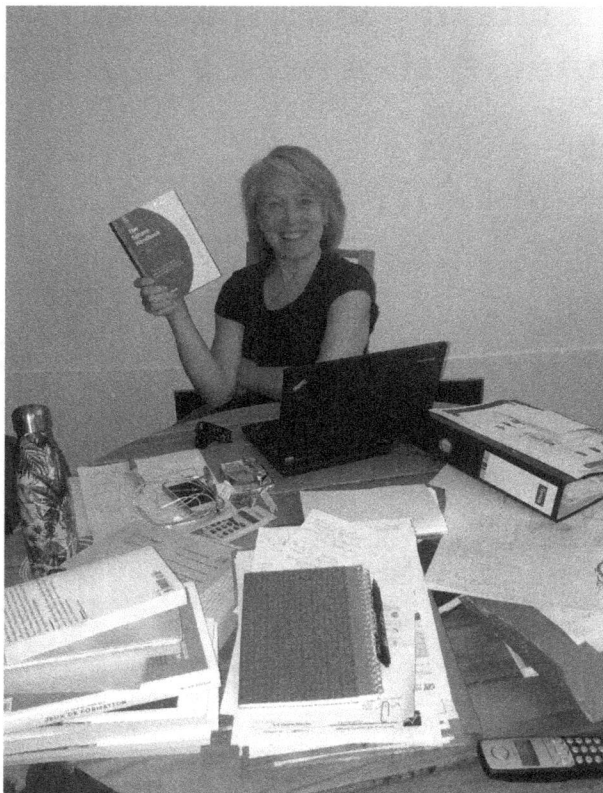

*Figure 1.1* Aninia Nadig with *Sphere Handbook*

After master's studies in Amsterdam and focusing on asylum policy issues in the Netherlands for a few years, I eventually moved into monitoring internal displacement situations and then humanitarian standards. Here you'll pause... standards? More rules? Yes, I ended up working for Sphere, one of the best-known standard-setting initiatives in the humanitarian sector.

I would like to be transparent: I have never been deployed to "the field" for any extended period of time. I'm a headquarters person. I spent years feeling bad about not being able to share stories that start with "When I was in Iraq...", "In Afghanistan, we used to...", "During my first mission in Bosnia...". However, I do hope that I contribute to the sector in other ways: people like me think a lot about how to make standards useful for those who use them. It is our job to make standards accessible so that they can actually make a difference in the quality of affected people's lives.

For the past 20 years, Sphere has developed and updated minimum standards for humanitarian response in a few life-saving sectors. These standards, collected in the *Sphere Handbook*,[1] help you think about the most fundamental things to do in order for a given population to survive and recover with dignity. I've now been with Sphere for many years and sometimes wonder what makes this work so satisfying. Aren't standards dry, limiting options and devoid of all inspiration? I see three reasons for sticking it out at Sphere.

Firstly, many people value Sphere. Over the years, I have received so much spontaneous positive feedback. Each *Handbook* edition has a distinct cover colour, and people remember with which colour *Handbook* they started their career. Sphere guided many of them through their first few difficult years as humanitarian workers. They love the rights-based and people-centred philosophy of the standards. Of course, we receive critical feedback as well, usually with the aspiration of improving the standards and their application.

Another reason is personal. Doing this kind of support work in the background probably fits my personality quite well. I enjoy working with people and organisations in figuring out how the standards can make most sense for them.

And thirdly, working with standards is intellectually quite stimulating. Humanitarian standards are not strict and dry! As I write this chapter, I realise that my tendency to interpret rules quite liberally, my love of international law during my studies, and my work for Sphere all add up. I find the interwovenness of rights, protection, inclusion and very concrete technical standards very satisfying. This is what motivates me. I feel that Sphere provides a relevant contribution to the humanitarian sector – and beyond, since there are no comparable standards for development. I am fascinated by the idea of codifying diverse practices into a globally applicable rule, law or standard, and by its subsequent interpretation translating it back into real life, without losing the set intent. In the case of Sphere, this process seems neither natural nor a given. On the contrary, intense debates have been held in the past around the positive and negative impacts of working with standards and we will get back to that later. But let's start from the beginning.

## Does the humanitarian world need standards?

Legend has it that on a beautiful summer afternoon in the mid-1990s, a couple of aid workers – at that moment stuck in Geneva and sitting on a hill with a six-pack of beer and a beautiful view of Geneva and the lake – came up with the idea of developing humanitarian standards. They were inspired by two different developments, both around the issue of quality of humanitarian work: fundamentally, the humanitarian sector started to realise that it needed some sort of mechanism for becoming accountable for its activities and for donor money. It was no longer enough to presume that humanitarian work was naturally "doing good".[2] Secondly, the one key event that helped propel Sphere into life was the Joint Evaluation of Emergency Assistance to Rwanda following the 1994 Rwanda genocide. That evaluation clearly stated that lives could have been saved if organisations had done their work better, a terribly sobering finding. Some sort of mechanism was needed to guide organisations and the humanitarian sector as a whole. The idea was that sector-wide mutually agreed-upon standards could fulfil that role.

The Sphere Project was thus created based on the need for better account-ability and to support the coordination within those organisations using the standards – at the outset a group of humanitarian international NGOs (INGOs) and the Red Cross/Red Crescent Movement. The Sphere Project developed min-imum standards in the life-saving sectors of water, sanitation and hygiene promo-tion; food security and nutrition; shelter and health.[3] But it did not stop there – it went one important step further and created the Humanitarian Charter. I found the following citation in the first Sphere Project proposal:

> To elaborate technical standards […] without any reference to the rights or aspirations of the assisted beneficiaries and claimants risks becoming a self-serving exercise concerned more with agencies' accountability to donors than the rights of affected people. We therefore believe that any set of "industry" standards must first be prefaced by a set of "consumer rights"; a beneficiaries or claimants charter highlighting a person's rights under existing international law and declarations.
>
> (Extract from the 1997 Sphere project proposal)[4]

These inalienable human rights are put into practice throughout the *Handbook*, in relation to safety and security, water, food, and shelter and health. The Humanitarian Charter – the cornerstone of Sphere – spells out three rights: the right to life with dignity, the right to receive humanitarian assistance and the right to protection and security. I would like to believe that if Sphere did not invent accountability to affected people, it made a huge contribution to bringing the con-cept into the humanitarian way of working. In an interview, Peter Walker, one of the founders of the Sphere Project who sat on that famous hill overlooking Lake Geneva, says:

> The [Humanitarian] Charter shows that the standards don't just come out of thin air. They're not just something that humanitarian agencies have invented. They're actually an expression of people's rights that states have signed up to over the last 50–60 years. That's why pitching Sphere as a rights-based vehicle became very important.[5]

Introducing standards into a highly contextual field like humanitarian response was bound to be tricky. No-one can say this better than – again – Peter Walker:

> The Sphere standards are just a tool. If you use them correctly, they allow you to focus on the victims of crisis – their aspirations, their needs, their rights. That's the language of Sphere standards […]. So in some ways, they're incredibly empowering.
>
> However, you can use the standards in another way, ignoring that aspir-ational aspect and focusing on the technical stuff, this number of calories,

this amount of water… But you may have delivered the water in a way that disempowers people. Sphere is about technical quality and affirming people's rights. That's why you have the Humanitarian Charter up front, and the rest flows from that. [...]

Standards are actually a double-edged sword. If you use standards without much thought, it simply becomes a knee-jerk reaction and you give the same things to everybody. But the essence of any crisis response is context. You have to understand the context and the reality of people on the ground.

For Sphere, this notion of "You have to adapt to the context," means that humanitarian workers have to understand the difference between standards and indicators. The standards are quite generic. For instance, you need to achieve a sufficient and equitable quantity of water – that's the standard. The standard is not 15 liters of water per [person per] day – that's a suggested indicator. I sometimes worry that in developing the standards, we didn't do enough to push this notion that one must understand context.[6]

The challenge of contextualising standards has accompanied Sphere over the past 20 years. In Sphere's early days, a group of French NGOs[7] wrote a letter – the "French Letter" – stating the concern that standards

- would lead to a lowering of the quality of aid because they could not be applied in all situations of need;
- did not guarantee the quality of the aid actually received but rather introduced bureaucratic norms that stifled real professionalism requiring vision, intuition, adaptability, imagination and flexibility, and that less tangible and measurable issues like protection and mental health did not receive sufficient attention; and
- ignored the diversity of the humanitarian community but introduced a way for donors to control northern NGOs and for northern NGOs to control southern NGOs who were excluded from developing the standards and would not be able to abide by them.

These criticisms – also expressed by others – were important incentives for the Sphere Project to improve its standards over time. Each new edition of the *Sphere Handbook* (the fourth was published in 2018) had a stronger focus on cross-cutting themes. Standards common to all chapters, focusing on the people-centred approach and humanitarian processes, were introduced in 2004 and strengthened over time. The 2011 edition included Protection Principles, and the 2018 edition has a specific focus on contextualisation and ensuring the inclusion of at-risk groups. It now includes the Core Humanitarian Standard (CHS) as one of its foundation chapters.

I have been involved in the revision process that led to the 2018 version of the *Sphere Handbook*. I supported the coordination of the content coming together and know how difficult it is to distil all the accumulated knowledge and guidance into concise, universal language that is at the same time applicable in all contexts.

How does Sphere propose to combine these two objectives? Let's take the probably most famous Sphere indicator as an example, starting with the standard it supports:

> **Water supply standard 2.1: Access and water quantity:** People have equitable and affordable access to a sufficient quantity of safe water to meet their drinking and domestic needs.

Before you rush to the indicators of this standard, please stop here for a second and take a look at the standard. It expresses the right of all people to the water they need in a situation of emergency. Now let's note the terms "equitable", "affordable" and "sufficient". These need to be interpreted in context, same as "needs". How would equitable and affordable access to a sufficient quantity of safe water translate into the situation you work in? Once you have thought about this, take a look at the indicators. The first indicator – the famous one – reads:

> **Average volume of water used for drinking and domestic hygiene per household**
> *   Minimum of 15 litres per person per day
> *   Determine quantity based on context and phase of response

Did you note the second bullet point? Even though 15 litres per person per day is a generally agreed minimum, it still depends on the context (see Table 1.1). The relevant guidance note provides the following information:

> **Needs:** The quantity of water needed for drinking, hygiene and domestic use depends upon the context and phase of a response. It will be influenced by factors such as pre-crisis use and habits, excreta containment design and cultural habits. A minimum of 15 litres per person per day is established practice. It is never a "maximum" and may not suit all contexts or phases of a response. For example, it is not appropriate where people may be displaced for many years. In the acute phase of a drought, 7.5 litres per person per day may be appropriate for a short time. In an urban middle-income context,

*Table 1.1* Minimum basic survival water needs, *Sphere Handbook* 2018 edition, p.107

| Needs | Quantity (litres/person/day) | Adapt to context based on |
|---|---|---|
| Survival: water intake (drinking and food) | 2.5–3 | Climate and individual physiology |
| Hygiene practices | 2–6 | Social and cultural norms |
| Basic cooking | 3–6 | Food type and social and cultural norms |
| Total basic water | 7.5–15 | |

50 litres per person per day may be the minimum acceptable amount to maintain health and dignity.

There are also all the other parts of the *Handbook* that help you contextualise the indicators: key elements of the CHS are reflected in Sphere's technical indicators; chapter introductions, appendices and guidance notes all provide useful further information and elements to consider. If all parts of the *Handbook* were used equally, it would be really difficult not to focus on, and be accountable to, affected people. It would be difficult to overlook children, persons with disabilities, older people and other at-risk groups. The problem comes from considering a single part of the *Handbook* (usually an indicator) in isolation.

Standards – and all the information that supports them – provide a reliable space for innovative work within a defined field of key desired outcomes. These outcomes – or standards – are concrete expressions of the right to life with dignity, through water, food, shelter, health and many other response lenses. They were determined to help a given population survive and recover with dignity, without people's health deteriorating further because of their living conditions.

## The contextualisation challenge

We human beings tend to make decisions based either on what worked before or on what others do. Our brains are not always conditioned to move into uncharted territory. Thinking outside of the box, approaching a new situation with an open mind – particularly in an emergency – is generally difficult. Minimum standards such as the Sphere standards provide something reassuring. In situations of urgency, suffering, insecurity and many unknowns, they tell us what to think about, where to start. They help make sense out of chaos, which aspects to consider and what direction to follow.

It is tempting to use the standards and their indicators as some sort of tick-box exercise. But they are not meant to be used that way. Working with standards demands a lot of creative thinking and careful contextual interpretation. Humanitarian standards provide guidance to ask the right questions at the right time. As illustrated above, working with standards means asking what "sufficient quantities of water" or "sufficient covered living space" mean in each situation; what is feasible at the moment; what is the Sphere minimum, and how can I achieve that over time, or find alternative ways to work towards a particular standard.

Therefore, to use standards effectively, much of that thinking should be done in advance. Training on standards and working with them for disaster preparedness is important. Otherwise you will indeed be thrown in at the deep end, and you'll likely revert to the most assuring elements of the *Handbook*, the indicators. This is where contextual and local understanding becomes so important. Affected people and communities know best what they need.

I imagine the role of standards reflected in the image of an hourglass: developing and revising standards are processes that allow each sub-sector (such as health or shelter) to determine what global legal frameworks and conventions mean to them, and to translate conventions and rights into practice. At the same time, each of these sectors determines the state of best practice, based on current knowledge, evidence and common sense. Over the years, *Sphere Handbook* revision processes have become key moments of consulting and re-defining each sector and improving coherence within and between sectors. All this knowledge then needs to be distilled, codified into humanitarian standards through the lens of people's right to survive and thrive with dignity. The standards are the narrowest part of the hourglass. They need to be broad enough to be applicable to every humanitarian situation, and yet concrete enough to avoid complete arbitrariness of their interpretation. Applying them in all possible contexts means broadening the hourglass back into the diversity of real life.

Sometimes it is not possible to implement all humanitarian activities. There are so many factors that may make it impossible to reach people in need or to deliver goods or services. Without wanting to shy away from our humanitarian responsibilities, we should not forget the primary responsibility of the state for the people in its territory. It is therefore also important to keep in mind the limitations of what humanitarian actors can do and where they may need to revert to other means, such as advocating (if possible) for access and for people's right to receive minimum levels of aid. Standards are a great advocacy tool, and one of the organisations that uses them very effectively to point out response gaps is Médecins sans Frontières, one of the most outspoken contributors to the French letter some 20 years ago.

We do need to talk about donors. In the past, many of them may have requested that organisations fulfil Sphere indicators without sufficient understanding of context. Today, in my experience, most donors are ready to work with organisations to adapt their proposals (including, for example, logframe indicators) in order to address an evolving context. In fact, the importance of organisational and project-related learning, also expressed in CHS Commitments 2 and 7, has been gaining traction and I believe that most donors understand and welcome this development.

It has always been difficult for organisations to talk openly about things that go wrong. And sometimes this goes way beyond a single project not getting the results it promised. Incidents of sexual exploitation and abuse, perpetrated by humanitarian workers, are expressions of a sector having become too complacent, too certain of its own exceptionality. But I'd like to believe that the sector as a whole can learn from such experiences and improve. Affected populations and communities have an absolute right to be treated with respect and dignity – in the same way humanitarian actors would want to be treated.

Sphere and other humanitarian standards offer a way to support rights through hands-on technical guidance. I find this really powerful. Latin and Central American aid organisations in particular seem to have embraced Sphere's approach, almost intuitively understanding the standards' rights-based foundation and the philosophy behind it. A number of countries, for example Guatemala and Ecuador, have integrated the Sphere standards into their disaster preparedness and management guidelines. Sphere welcomes this context-specific uptake of the standards. Its small Geneva secretariat is there to support practitioners and organisations working with Sphere standards, but Sphere does not supervise them, nor does it check how they use the standards.

Sometimes people express frustration about "not reaching the standards". For example, after the 2011 Haiti earthquake, the minimum spaces between shelters (Shelter standard 2) and the covered living space of 3.5 m² per person (Shelter standard 3) were not possible to achieve in many places. A shelter specialist asked me at the time what would be the absolute minimum distance between shelters... my answer was that Sphere is meant to be aspirational in many situations, and that if it was not possible to increase the distances between shelters, they may need to find other ways to avoid disease outbreaks, fires and other dangers. This may be easy for me to say, I understand. But it does not mean that Sphere is not applicable in challenging contexts.

Sometimes I wonder why many find it so difficult to contextualise the Sphere indicators, even though Sphere gives them the full freedom to do so, as long as they understand they are below the suggested minimum. I wonder why the standards may be seen as Western-based, although we keep saying that they are outcome statements based on universal rights. Why it is not completely obvious that Sphere applies everywhere? I get a glimpse of possible answers when I start talking with people whose daily realities are very different from mine, and whose world map reflects a different political order and economic reality than mine, often determined by a colonial past. Then I understand that people can perceive the Sphere standards differently. But I also know how quickly those moments of understanding other realities and universes can pass, how easy it is to go "back" to my "normal" work.

I think that people like me, who work for an organisation that aspires to be relevant to all humanitarian actors, should ideally always feel like they are out on a limb. Always just a little bit beyond their comfort zone, alert to power issues, herds of elephants in the room, perceptions and too often very real limitations and barriers to humanitarian response. It may be easy for me to say: "don't worry if you can't reach the indicators that are relevant to you – just understand why that is and how you might get there over time". It may be a very different reality when the fact that standards cannot be met is a constant reminder of difficulties and political realities that are mostly out of the hands of humanitarian workers.

Standards are being contextualised, as stated above with the example of Latin and Central America; and they should be contextualised more often. The process of making them your own, with your own words, your own examples, your own adaptation of certain indicators, is key to keeping Sphere alive globally and to making it work locally. Standards could be seen as the glue that holds the humanitarian system together. They are underpinned by international law and conventions and are themselves the basis for implementation guidelines. As such, standards fulfill a specific role in the humanitarian landscape.

Standards also contribute to professionalising the humanitarian sector – whereby this concept can again seem like a double-edged sword: the complexity of humanitarian crises and of the sector's ways of working have increased. Coordination has improved – the UN Cluster System and coordinated humanitarian response plans are a case in point. The concept of working together towards collectively stated outcomes is well established. This ought to be a positive development. At the same time, this trend towards professional-isation has prompted an enormous increase in guidance documents for a wide range of topics. At times, it feels as if new silos, new sub-sectors, have been created.

It is difficult to strike a balance: new evidence and knowledge must be recognised. But equally, it is important not to lose sight of the people we ought to work for when focusing more on compliance instead of people's realities. Take inclusion of at-risk groups, for example. At headquarters level in particular, there is now strong focus on various at-risk groups such as persons with disabilities, older people, children and gender. This focus is very important. But I sometimes wonder if the intent to make at-risk groups visible might get lost in the struggle to adhere to new guidance. After having talked about breaking down silos for so many years, it seems as if new silos are being created, built on the mountains of collected guidance. Fortunately, these themes are well-anchored and mainstreamed in various sets of humanitarian standards.

Standards can make essential issues tangible. In a specific field of work, there may at some point be sufficient collective knowledge for people to say: let's organise all this knowledge and evidence and give it shape, so that everyone can easily understand and use this knowledge. To illustrate this, there is, similar to Sphere, the example of the Child Protection Minimum Standards, first published in 2012.[8] At the time, some of the areas covered may not have been completely solid yet; some indicators may have been built on somewhat shaky ground. But by developing these standards, child protection received visibility, a platform. This has not turned child protection guidance into a rigid, soulless manual; rather, it helped position child protection as a central and important element of humani-tarian response. It also helped solidify the knowledge base for the first *Handbook* revision. A similar story could be told about many standards.[9]

Another example where standards can help keep the focus on essentials is the humanitarian response to COVID-19. The pandemic prompted a surge in new guidance, much of it very detailed and technical. Eventually, the learning from all this will be reflected in the next *Sphere Handbook* edition. At the same time, we need to revert to existing, "basic" minimum guidance, for example in contexts with little or no special medical equipment. This is where Sphere can already provide the relevant, uncomplicated starting and end points for affected individuals and com-munities and healthcare workers. In early 2020, the Sphere secretariat developed a brief note describing how Sphere's holistic approach combining rights and tech-nical guidance supports any COVID-19 response.[10]

The note highlights three central factors: firstly, people should be seen as human beings, not just cases. Human dignity is referenced heavily in the Humanitarian Charter and woven throughout the *Handbook*. People living with conditions associated with stigma or indeed those who fear they may be stigmatised for having the Coronavirus can be driven to hide the illness to avoid discrimination. It is important therefore to provide supportive messaging and care, so that all people can be screened, tested and – if found ill – treated.

The second point is that community engagement is crucial if hygiene promotion with a focus on handwashing and other messages is to be successful. This involves building trust and mutual understanding by engaging communities in communications and decision making, through which rumours and misinformation can be addressed. With regard to physical distancing, existing community perceptions and beliefs can support or hinder a response, so it is important to understand and address them. Some social norms, such as shaking hands, may need to be changed to prevent disease transmission.

And thirdly, we should not forget affected people's other needs, nor the long-term medical needs of the wider population. Therefore, all other health standards of the *Sphere Handbook* continue to be relevant as well. These cover maternal and reproductive health, non-communicable diseases, injury, child health, mental health and palliative care. During the 2014 Ebola outbreak in West Africa, the number of deaths from abandoned health centres and regions was significant. We may be seeing a very similar picture now.

Especially with regard to palliative care – a difficult subject in the COVID-19 response, with many people having to die alone – Sphere's contribution can be what a health colleague called "intentional thinking", with strong focus on the dignity and on the psychosocial and emotional wellbeing of the dying person and family members. Dying with dignity and surrounded by loved ones can make a huge contribution to emotional healing of entire communities. Especially when the process of dying and mourning and burial rituals need to be adjusted, ways must be found to ensure dignity is maintained as much as possible. Sphere's palliative care standard can provide guidance.

I do think standards have their place in the humanitarian machine. But what has been the real impact of humanitarian standards on the lives of disaster- and crisis-affected people? And what could be that impact in the future?

## Shaping the future role of standards

Over the past 20+ years, a lot of things have gone well for Sphere. At the global launch of the 2011 edition of the *Handbook*, Valerie Amos, the then UN Under-Secretary-General for Humanitarian Affairs, referred to the Sphere standards as the gold standard for humanitarian assistance. On another occasion, Nan Buzard, then Executive Director of the International Council of Voluntary Agencies (ICVA), referred to Sphere as the most successful NGO initiative ever.

Sphere was probably the right idea at the right time, and its success continues. But how do we know it is making a difference? It is notoriously difficult to measure the impact of the standards. And yet, as one aid worker once said to me: "Just imagine what the humanitarian sector would look like without Sphere". This always brings me back to the values and beliefs and principles without which technical standards would be just that: technical standards. It is the human aspect that makes these standards truly valuable and that sees their true strength and application evolve over time, as mentioned above.

At the 2017 World Humanitarian Summit, localisation became one of the Grand Bargain workstreams. And while "localisation" at a global level appears to remain somewhat stuck at the collaboration between INGOs and their local partners, there seems to be a groundswell of a different kind of localisation: affected governments are becoming more assertive in their intent to lead response activities where they have the ability to do so. Local response activities receive more attention and support, for example through organisations such as the Alliance for Empowering Partnership (A4EP), which strive to go beyond merely consulting affected people and move towards true empowerment of local response structures and affected people themselves. The Network for Empowered Aid Response, (NEAR), has a similar aim, advocating for more financial independence of local actors. There are efforts at various levels that strive towards making local and national organisations less financially dependent on INGOs and UN agencies.

I believe that standards have a huge potential in empowering national governments, local aid organisations and affected people themselves – again, because they build on rights and are universally applicable. We can continue to argue that they were developed in the global north, based on Western values, and I'm certain there is some truth to that. But I'm not sure what universal mechanism could replace humanitarian standards at this stage. So maybe the way forward is to continue to make them better. One way of doing this could be to ensure that the basic inalienable right to life with dignity is expressed in a way that makes the standards meaningful everywhere. Over the past 20 years, the *Sphere Handbook* has been translated into well over 40 languages, a very direct sign of its importance everywhere. Further adapting its content to specific realities is a great way of strengthening jointly identified needs and desired outcomes.

In some situations, Sphere has become the common language it claims to be, based on broadly recognised minimum survival needs. It is referred to in coordination meetings, bringing diverse actors to the table. This is not perfect yet. Often, the "common language" of standards is muted by meetings held in a dominant language prohibiting meaningful participation of organisations speaking the local language. Dominant terminologies may be utterly meaningless in certain places. The word "accountability" is a good example of this. Rights are not perceived the same way everywhere. Yet I think that, currently, the humanitarian sector does not have anything better than these standards upon which we can build a meaningful conversation, beyond information exchange.

Often, conversations are not as inclusive as they should be. In particular during *Handbook* revision processes – roughly every 6–8 years – Sphere becomes the platform for the humanitarian sector to codify into standards the commonly agreed-upon good practice and knowledge at that particular point in time. This crucial task is effective as long as Sphere continues to enjoy the reputation of a neutral, credible convenor for the sector. Sphere therefore always puts considerable effort into involving local actors in its revision processes. It is working well, but challenges remain, maybe to some extent because we do indeed not yet always speak the same "language". Sphere will continue to strive to involve as many humanitarian actors as possible. This can only make the *Handbook* content richer.

It may be that the one big challenge for Sphere in the future is to not succumb to the temptation to becoming everything to everybody. The very first *Handbook* was beautifully short and clear. Subsequent editions have become increasingly complex. What if we dared to make the next *Handbook* simpler again, allowing it to once again become the entry point into humanitarian work, focusing on *what* needs to be done and leaving the *how to* to guidelines and tools? Sphere could then focus on what I think could be its true contribution: taking on a bridge function between the global and the local levels. There will – and should – always be a connection between these levels. The question is who leads and who follows, and how the real needs can be determined and addressed as objectively as possible. Standards can be a big contributing factor to levelling the playing field. We're not there yet, but I think it should be the ultimate goal to create a system in which the control of funds and agency is much closer to those whose lives are affected.

Maybe it would be desirable to create one single structure that could be the home of all humanitarian standards. Maybe this could be done in an unbureaucratic, participatory way. Then again, maybe not. Maybe the reality will be a continuous global dance around consolidation of knowledge followed by decentralisation, followed by a new cluster of knowledge and so forth, maybe all in parallel and at the same time. Yet, if the humanitarian sector wants to keep being reckoned with, we may want to take standards more seriously. Our sector faces the threat of becoming irrelevant in the face of other actors less bothered by humanitarian principles. Private sector firms are gaining importance, not least because of the increasing role of cash transfers as an aid modality. In many countries, the military plays a key role in disaster response. Governments may have their own approaches to delivering aid, based on political realities. Principled humanitarian standards can be our way of reaching out to these actors and saying: here, this is what we are all about. This is how we translate our humanitarian principles into practice. Let's consider these standards as the basis for working together.

Standards – bureaucratic? Limiting? What if we saw them as a foundation for our sector's present and future?

## Notes

1 Sphere Association. 2018. *The Sphere Handbook: Humanitarian Charter and Minimum Standards in Disaster Response*. Geneva: Sphere Association.
2 One other key outcome of this realisation was the Code of Conduct for the International Red Cross and Red Crescent Movement and NGOs in Disaster Relief, which will be at the core of Sphere's Humanitarian Charter.
3 The sections evolved slightly over the years.
4 Walker, P. and Purdin, S. 2004. Birthing Sphere. *Disasters* 28(2): 100–111.
5 Sphere standards: radical but inevitable. An interview with Peter Walker: www.spherestandards.org.
6 Ibid.

7   Gasman, J. 2020. *Humanitarianism and the Quantification of Human Needs: Minimal Humanity*. Abingdon: Routledge.
8   Alliance for Child Protection in Humanitarian Action. 2019. *Minimum Standards for Child Protection in Humanitarian Action*. Geneva: The Alliance for Child Protection in Humanitarian Action.
9   The Child Protection Minimum Standards are part of the Humanitarian Standards Partnership. The Partnership further includes standards for education in emergencies (INEE), humanitarian inclusion of older people and people with disabilities, livestock and livelihoods (LEGS), economic recovery (MERS), market analysis (MISMA) and the Sphere standards. For more information on the HSP, see www.spherestandards.org/humanitarian-standards/standards-partnership/.
10  Sphere Association. n.d. COVID-19 guidance based on humanitarian standards. www.spherestandards.org/coronavirus/.

# 2 FAO goats don't die

## Can evaluations make aid more inclusive?

*Marta Bruno*

### How did I become an evaluator?

I'm a historian turned human geographer by university and academic training and my passion has always been stories with multiple narratives and plots where reality and facts could be viewed from different and sometimes opposing perspectives. So, when initially considering my contributions to this book, I liked the notion put forward by the main authors on how they wanted 'this book to be the voice of humanitarian practitioners, without too much academic or organizational jargon'. Contributors have been asked to write from a place of feeling and emotions and this will make a great change from the aseptic, jargon-filled reports that I regularly produce as part of my work.

One of my favorite novelists, the Nigerian writer Chimamanda Ngozi Adichie, once gave a brilliant TED talk entitled 'The Danger of a Single Story'. In the talk, she describes how

> a single story creates stereotypes, and the problem with stereotypes is not that they are untrue, but that they are incomplete. They make one story become the only story. [...] The consequence of the single story is this: it robs people of dignity. It makes the recognition of our equal humanity difficult.[1]

For the past ten years, I have been working in humanitarian evaluations, and if I were asked to select one single piece of advice for people starting in this area of work, it would coincide with the reflections shared by Chimamanda, applied to evaluations.

I have spent most of my working life listening to and collecting multiple stories. First, as an academic and researcher collecting stories from Russian women in the years of the disaggregation of the Soviet Union, trying to understand the multiple narratives that shaped their working and private lives during one of the most radical shifts in political and cultural systems in recent history. Here, I first understood how differences in gender, age, geographical location, education and socio-economic contexts of origin play a primary role in shaping narratives and in determining which story becomes the main description of reality that shapes and dominates values and political dynamics.

After my years in Russia, I worked for a number of years and in various capacities doing participatory rural appraisals at the community level in places like Central Asia and the Caucasus. My biggest challenge was to tell the stories of local communities, groups and institutions in such a way that they would be listened to and considered in the design of a range of sectoral and regional investment and development projects. I learned that ethnicity, race and language also play an important role in shaping narratives. Central Asia and the Caucasus had been *de facto* Russian colonial areas, and their relative proximity and absorption capacity of the dominant Russian culture played a very important role.

In this period, I was often the youngest as well as the only woman on teams of 'experts', sent by international organizations and donors to 'resolve' the problems of former Soviet societies and help them modernize their systems, become more democratic and develop capitalist economies. Of course, the projects did not state these objectives in such basic language but it wasn't difficult to understand that this was their aim. To put it simply, the western, democratic and capitalist part of the world had prevailed after the demise of the Soviet Union and now wanted to 'mold' the former Soviet countries.

I worked with many international experts (economists, engineers and portfolio managers), who knew (or thought they knew) what would work on the basis of their technical expertise. The ones whom I had no patience for were the ones who would refuse to travel outside of the capital city, did all their analytical work based on two or three conversations with the relevant minister and his deputies and then focused on Excel spreadsheets and formulas; the ones from whom I learned the most were the ones who would come with me to community after community and listen to local associations, local officials and farmers and would be curious to find out how things had been done until then. I also experienced what professional marginalization felt like: I was young and a woman – therefore my knowledge and skills had less value than those of other older males with technical profiles. The irony was that I had spent years living in, studying and becoming passionate about the post-Soviet contexts and their common language and very often I was the only one in a position to communicate directly with people in communities and ask them what they needed but also what were their aspirations and how they wanted to manage their lives and livelihoods.

Over the years, I became a livelihoods and disaster risk management 'expert' (I prefer facilitator – but in order to get contracts I had to portray myself as an expert). I shifted gradually from development programs to the humanitarian arena in an early bid to reconcile emergency response and distribution activities with longer-term support to the basic needs and coping strategies of families and communities in crisis situations. I saw the essence of my work as an attempt to secure the space for multiple perspectives and narratives, trying to question and influence the power balance of donors and implementers of emergency response towards a greater inclusion of the voices, preferences and solutions found among the people at the receiving end of the humanitarian chain.

Eventually, my role as broker of narratives, information and knowledge between the different actors both inside my organization and with others outside prompted me to shift to the field of evaluations. I started working on evaluations as a knowledge management expert, processing and organizing learnings and knowledge from evaluations carried out by others. After spending some time observing from the sidelines, I decided to start getting into the thick of things and get involved in the management and conduct of evaluations. Thanks to my knowledge and experience of the humanitarian space, I started working on resilience and emergency evaluations of the Food and Agriculture Organization (FAO) and this is what I have been doing until the time of writing.

My motivation to get involved in evaluations derived from the observation of the many elements and drivers that determine inclusion and exclusion of stakeholders and how these elements determine how and for whom the evaluative narratives are told. I thought that more could be done to make evaluations participatory and inclusive and the story I want to tell you in this chapter is about my journey into some of the institutional and cultural obstacles that prevent this from happening, as well as some of my personal endeavors, experiences and learning on how to make evaluation narratives better capture the multiple voices and aspirations of people in crises.

In theory, evaluations collect information from, and then share the results of the analysis process and the learning with, all stakeholders: senior managers and staff of the organization, members of the governance of the organization, donors, partner organizations, national governments and institutions and, last but not least, people at the receiving end of aid programs and interventions, both

*Figure 2.1* Work with Food and Agriculture Organization in Jordan

as individuals and through their representative organizations, leaders and associations. This is the theory. The reality is that, most of the time, evaluations collect information from all but fail to give it back to all. And the ones usually left out are people and organizations on the ground as well as national staff of the organization and local-level government institutions.

## What defines humanitarian evaluations?

Before I get into the thick of my story, I have to explain that the narrative has changed from when I first submitted the initial abstract. The reason is simple: the emergence of the Covid-19 global crisis has thrown most of the work evaluators had been doing until now off-course, and by doing so, it has challenged most humanitarian practitioners to re-think and re-shape much of their 'business as usual' work. More recently, the social movements triggered by the Black Lives Matter marches and campaigns around the world have further contributed to accelerate change. In the last section, I will reflect on how some of these events are likely to bring positive change in terms of generating more inclusive evaluation narratives.

As not all readers will be familiar with evaluations, the next paragraphs provide some background on the place of evaluations in the aid and humanitarian sectors and the main drivers and principles underpinning their conduct and their utilization. I will touch upon the main challenges and characteristics of humanitarian evaluations linked to inclusion and exclusion of stakeholders, as well as elements which I consider important, such as evaluative language and profiles of practitioners that play a role in the inclusion and exclusion dynamics.

Evaluations are an oversight function; they are usually established as independent offices and are tasked with providing accountability to senior managers and member countries (in the case of the United Nations) and other constituencies (from donors to the general public) in the case of other organizations. Learning is the other objective accompanying the accountability focus. It is generally understood and agreed that learning from evaluations is firmly anchored in the principles of independence and evidence-based analysis so it ends up being more an invitation to learn from evaluations (once the report is finalized) rather than learning through or with evaluations (during the design and conduct of the evaluation).

### Drivers and principles of humanitarian evaluations

The aid sector is artificially divided into two separate parts: development and humanitarian. This divide has been created over the years by separating many organizations into different arms: the offices, teams and staff dealing with long-term development interventions and focusing on progressive improvements and change through longer-term interventions; and those focusing on the response to crisis events such as the tsunami, earthquakes, cyclones, droughts and epidemics or working on short-term remedial activities in contexts of protracted crises, such as conflicts, often compounded by natural hazards or other crisis events. This separation of the long term from the short term which is present across governance, financing, programs and operations is known as the humanitarian–development divide.

Following the same pattern as the rest of the aid industry, evaluations are also divided into development and humanitarian classifications. The latter, while following the same modalities as development evaluations, frequently face issues of access to people on the ground (usually described with the term 'humanitarian space') divided by conflict lines who have been displaced or are facing extreme challenges in access to food and basic human rights. This makes evaluations more complex to design and manage as well as making it harder to ensure balanced and comprehensive coverage and direct interaction with all concerned.

Evaluations in general are governed by a set of broadly accepted international criteria and norms[2,3] that have been developed to ensure they provide credible evidence-based analysis. When evaluations are used for changing a program's course of action or for introducing new policy and programmatic directions they must have recognized quality standards backing them up to give them widely accepted legitimacy. A bit like medical or scientific protocols, the decisions taken as a result of evaluations may significantly affect people and organizations and change the operating environment and conditions. They have to be 'solid'.

### Inclusion and exclusion of stakeholders

Evaluations, both in their accountability and learning dimensions, are underpinned by the certainty of their own veracity, their conviction of having a narrative that adheres to reality thanks to the rigorous application of a proven set of methods as well as telling a story from a place of independence, and therefore with low bias. The gaps and weaknesses in the narrative are usually acknowledged in a section addressing limitations – but these sections present factors ascribed to insufficient time or resources, or weaknesses in the utilization of certain methods (low response numbers in surveys, for example), rather than in recognition of how hard it is to reflect the multiplicity of stories and viewpoints collected. The fact that people and communities in contexts like Somalia or Yemen can only be interviewed remotely or indirectly by national service providers who specialize in providing data and information to international organizations is generally accepted as the status quo. Information can usually only be collected from village chiefs or community leaders, leaving out minorities along gender, age, ethnicity or socio-economic fault lines. Evaluation reports do not acknowledge that their coverage and narratives may be partial, biased or incomplete as a result. This would admit the intrinsic partiality of the evidence and undermine the basic imperatives of providing evidence-based comprehensive analysis and fulfilling accountability and learning.

Most organizations need to carry out large numbers of evaluations, resulting in what I call an 'industrial approach' to assessments. Many evaluation offices have sought to standardize evaluation frameworks and guidelines to ensure comparability and reliable quality assurance across evaluations. The imperatives of accountability mean that these evaluation functions have to cover large portions of their organization's program. Unfortunately, the evaluations that prefer quantity and standardized lines of enquiry are usually shallow and predictable.

### Language and practitioners

The language evaluations use is also an issue worthy of note: good evaluation reports have to be de-linked from their writers. Informal guidance to evaluation teams is to stay away from expression of feelings and emotions. Thus we write: 'the evaluation found that…' or 'the evidence analyzed indicates that…' rather than 'the evaluation team believes…' or 'the evaluation team feels that…'. The majority of evaluators have long and solid professional experience, and thus the messages they choose to report in their findings are an attempt to summarize a balanced and fair view of a dynamic reality. Their (or our – as I too am an evaluator) account of the reality of a humanitarian process, its usefulness and relevance to the context and people it was intended for and of the results it produced, has to be coherent, and thus they have to make judgement calls. If there are contradicting narratives these have to take sides even if they are well-informed and based on different versions and accounts. Evaluators, most of the time, have to choose the most convincing viewpoint from which to tell the story and go for a single story to be coherent and credible.

Another semantic trait of evaluation narratives is that messages, even when critical, have to be presented as constructive feedback so as not to demotivate the stakeholders, especially internal staff. Thus, if some activity was badly performed, it is not recorded as such but in terms of what should be improved… the assumption must always be one of trust in the good faith and intentions of the implementers of humanitarian action. If you suspect, or discover, malpractice, then the evaluation should stop and the enquiry process be passed on to audit or investigations, depending on the severity of the situation. While both the assumption of trust and the constant constructive wording are a positive and commendable trait, they do sometimes make it virtually impossible to hit the nail on the head. Problems and issues can rarely be stated in a clear and direct way.

Let me give you an example from a recent evaluation: most of the evaluations of the Syria crisis have had to be conducted in a way similar to herding elephants in the proverbial crystal shop. In such a highly politicized crisis, even getting a visa for the evaluation team members is an issue, let alone trying to collect data and evidence and write it up in a moderately honest and direct way.

Once in the part of the country controlled by the government, as there was no access to the rest, you could not call the war a war… so you had to prepare and comply with a very intricate and vague terminology to ask questions about the on-going… well, war. As the report would no doubt be scrutinized by government authorities, you could only address certain contextual issues in a very roundabout way. We unexpectedly obtained permission to conduct a survey of households who had received support from projects but the government vetted the version of the survey form we could use and this did not allow us to collect any personal information such as names, gender or age, household size, whether a household was displaced or not, what they were doing previously, or anything about their current livelihood strategies or their future intentions. Analyzing the results and trying to interpret them was a very creative intellectual endeavor and made it difficult to understand people's needs, choices and aspirations.

The situation was made worse by the so-called donors' red lines. Most western donors, whose governments were opposed to the Syrian government, were willing to fund humanitarian activities but no capacity development or more permanent investments in infrastructure as this may have benefitted the régime. So they funded education but not the reconstruction of school buildings, they paid for vaccines for livestock but were not ready to fund any training or capacity development of local institutions that should have managed and coordinated the vaccination campaigns… The examples are many and across all sectors. Except that, even if they were officially not funding these activities, many of them realized that providing textbooks and school meals if you don't have school buildings was a bit pointless. Many organizations were encouraged to go ahead with the institutional and infrastructural minimum activities to enable the functioning of the rest of the response but somehow keep it quiet or hidden. Humanitarian workers got so frustrated by this that the topic ended up being one of the most frequently discussed with evaluation teams, as a way to vent frustration at being asked by the very ones setting the red lines to subvert them on the sly. Writing the final evaluation report was an exercise in extreme creative writing. It meant trying to discuss the context, the nature of the evidence collected at the community level and the constraints (bordering on the breach of human rights) from donors' red lines. The sub-text and hinted narratives of the final report were way more relevant and significant than what was explicitly written up.

A major issue that characterizes evaluation conduct is the cultural dominance of western thinking and approaches. Evaluations have their roots in the accountability and measurement cultural tradition of the global north and its institutions. They are still dominated by experts and professionals from OECD countries and their institutions (donors as well as academic centers and companies).[4] Despite a sustained and concerted effort to build national evaluation capacities in the global south and developing countries, evaluators with recognized international professional profiles that come from non-OECD countries are still a minority. It is increasingly standard practice to include evaluators from developing countries in evaluation teams but usually they are recruited as 'regional' or 'national' members.

This cultural dominance is inevitably reflected in the way that evaluations are designed and conducted. Most of the attention tends to be on the internal institutional and organizational aspects that shape and determine the quality (good or bad) of the delivery on the ground. The milestones are set by the standards of the humanitarian architecture and evaluations measure and weigh using these same metrics. Donors and managers want certainties and clear-cut evidence trails on the effectiveness and results from delivery of aid. Evaluations cater to these needs.

I would now like to offer some personal reflections on what I have learnt and how I try to manage and mitigate the negative aspects or limitations of evaluations, while at the same time trying to sustain and promote a more inclusive and equitable approach that is based on multiple and diverse narratives and viewpoints.

## Is it possible to have evaluations with diversity of narratives?

My first reflection is that evaluations are a useful way to get groups and teams of humanitarian practitioners to take the time to reflect on and learn from what they are doing. The final evaluation product and learning is as good (or as bad) as what goes in. I have learned that the main function of evaluators is to help others collect and re-organize the information, stories and feelings that contribute to shaping humanitarian activities. While it is useful to adopt standards in methods and conduct, these should be used in an aspirational way rather than a straitjacket textbook practice. When rendering evaluation narratives, it is useful to try and push oneself out of the box, to constantly test the meaning of what is written and also to find creative ways of letting personal experiences of aid come through the text, while maintaining an impartial narrative. Using quotes and stories from people to illustrate a finding, using visuals and pictures to transmit a context, having complementary evaluation videos with footage and testimonials from field-work are all ways to make a dry evaluative narrative come alive, stimulate the limbic system and trigger emotional perceptions.

I find it useful to design each evaluation as a writer would approach a new novel, making use of past experience but fully aware that each evaluation is a new journey, with new stories to be collected and told. Compared to standardized evaluation formats, I prefer and promote an artisanal approach to evaluations that favors the emergence of nuanced and deeper narratives. A more artisanal approach to evaluation design means that, while the quality may vary more, there is a chance to maximize the learning and involvement of all stakeholders. Rather than pretending that the evaluators are neutral and have no bias and no preferences when evaluating, it is more useful and constructive to acknowledge and manage the emotional intelligence that we carry.

Evaluation interviews and data collection are loaded with compassion, aha moments of insight and emotional negative reactions to certain parts of the story telling. Evaluation methods comprise both quantitative and qualitative data collection methods: the first bring the solidity of numbers and describe the size and the extension of a phenomenon, the second bring the nuance and the understanding of complex dynamics. We evaluators bring with us our prior experience, knowledge, beliefs and preferences and we are guided by these in the way we select, approach and seek information. Then, during the process, we inevitably develop instinctive likings or dislikes to key informants. In my case, I know that if I happen to interview a particularly dynamic and innovative woman farmer or refugee who has found positive strategies or has a strong capacity for leadership, I will most likely give more weight to that narrative than I would give to an interview with a respondent who waits for others to solve his or her problems. Initiative and inventiveness have a stronger hold on me than helplessness and a complaining attitude. I have an optimistic and positive outlook on life and I am emotionally more drawn to these characteristics in others. But I have also worked with colleagues who tend to see the glass half empty; they see gaps and shortcomings more than successes. This latter attitude can be useful to complement learning from positive practices and include suggestions for corrective change in project implementation.

The reality is that both attitudes are important to facilitate learning and both can enrich the analysis and understanding of humanitarian action. What is fundamental is to be conscious and address these biases (whether positive or negative) explicitly and ask oneself and one's evaluation team whether we have done a fair job in capturing all the important elements of the stories we have heard or if we have filtered something out or dismissed it because of our personal emotional or cultural perspectives.

At this point, it is important to apply the formal evaluation practice of triangulation: if a story or information has emerged from three or more different sources, then it becomes evidence. At the same time, some insights that emerge from a single source can bring unexpected insights into a specific issue. This kind of sifting through information and stories and turning it into evidence and findings is best done through a group discussion. In this respect, it is very useful to work with a team, especially if there is a high degree of diversity among its members. I will add to this later in this section.

The second element of reflection is an attempt to answer the question: who owns the story? Evaluators must choose who should tell their story or provide their account; of listening to the stakeholders and recording their story; of comparing the messages and narratives with those of others and bringing them together in a unitary and coherent overarching narrative. Finally, we are also responsible for finding the words and turns of phrases to present it as a neutral and impartial account. Formally, evaluation findings and conclusions are ultimately owned by the evaluation teams and/or the evaluation office – depending on each organization's set-up. They, and only they, decide what the final narrative is. From an ethical perspective, this is a delicate and complex issue, with many implications, but it is also one that is seldom explicitly addressed

Good evaluations, of course, open up many of the findings and analysis to reviews, correction and validation by the evaluand (the evaluand being the staff in the organization whose work is under scrutiny) as well as to other stakeholders. They will be revised and adjusted but the final authority over the narrative is never relinquished. This is because evaluations need to be portrayed and also perceived by users as independent and free of bias.

I have learned over the years that building consensus around the evaluation narratives requires careful and constant inclusion and dialogue with those whose work and activities are covered in the evaluation scope. People need to recognize themselves and read their own words in the evaluation. They also need to recognize that others' viewpoints and explanations should also find space in the analysis. With some patience and a good degree of trial and error, it is possible to engage staff and partners into a substantive exchange and dialogue to reach consensus on evaluation narratives. This is much harder to do it when it comes to people, communities and local organizations and institutions who have been affected by the crisis events and, as a result, included in the response activities. Walking the last mile on this aspect is, as far as I'm concerned, a fundamental issue to be addressed. Below are some stories from my experience on how I tried to cover this and what I have learned from it, even though I know I still have a long way to go.

The underpinning logic of evaluations is to provide an independent and impartial account of humanitarian action that should examine the role of all actors concerned. But in essence, evaluations are written for donors and staff that have the ability to read complex and technical language and are familiar with the institutional set-up of humanitarian architecture and all its complex dynamics and features. They are not written with or for the recipients of aid, even though they try to encompass their feedback or viewpoints. As described in the example from Syria, extreme attention to government and donor sensitivities and internal red lines prevented evaluations from putting forward some of the more groundbreaking findings, for fear of subverting the status quo. Evidence has to be neutralized and white-washed so as not to upset delicate balances and dynamics in and around the humanitarian machine. Evaluations can sometimes make implicit inferences to aspects that cannot be spelled out and sometimes they just have to refrain.

It is extremely hard to reach out to communities and people affected by crises in a way that is not skewed towards getting answers to questions that may be formulated from a very different perspective than their own. The need to expedite the answers is difficult to counterbalance. Let me illustrate this point through an example: I am now taking you to South Sudan at the time when there were many evaluations of the 2014 level three emergency response.

The Inter-Agency Humanitarian Evaluations Steering Group (IAHE) commissioned an evaluation of the system-wide response. Because of the nature of the crisis, which saw different ethnic groups dominate the different sides of the conflict, it was decided not to engage any national evaluators on the team, as they may have carried with them too strong a bias. Even if the national evaluator was not biased, the danger was that he or she would have been perceived as being biased by the range of external stakeholders that needed to be engaged in the evaluation process. The final evaluation report, while useful in informing the successes and failures of the system-wide response in terms of coordination and other performance issues, had little information on the results on the ground. In other words, it failed to answer the crucial question of whether and to what extent the system-wide response had managed to save lives and protect or restore the livelihoods of the people in South Sudan.

My office was carrying out an evaluation of the response at the same time as the inter-agency assessment. Contrary to the decisions made in the IAHE, we decided to go in the opposite direction. To me, the crux of the exercise was to what extent and how the response activities had been useful and relevant to households and communities that were using the aid. I managed to recruit a team of national consultants who came from different regions and groups, from both government and opposition-controlled areas. They told me where it would be safe or unsafe for them to go and they brought with them deep knowledge of the locations and their dynamics.

We spent time training ourselves in participatory methods which built a strong team cohesion and allowed us to address issues of bias, independence and conflict. We developed tools and evaluation questions. The national evaluators spent over a month in the field. Every evening another colleague and I would talk to them and discuss the findings and experiences of the day. At the end of field-work, we held an analysis workshop which brought together the stories and evidence and made sense of them through a team discussion. As many of the consultants were not strong in written English, we captured their contributions in writing and emerged with a rough draft of the report. We involved many of the colleagues working in the country office in the analysis, so that by the time we had the first draft, most of the learning from the evaluation had already been internalized and was being put to good use by the main evaluation stakeholders. The report managed to capture and express the views, voices, preferences and demands of a range of diverse communities across South Sudan.

The extended field-work carried out by national consultants who came from the areas covered, spoke the language and understood the context and issues was a way to partially redress the representativeness of the narrative and find a way to give a voice to the marginalized. We learned much about local power dynamics and about the unintended benefits of some of the activities, as well as how to better combine external support with self-reliance strategies. It was an intense experience that took us well away from the acceptable standards of independence and objectiveness usually required in evaluations, but was all the more valuable in terms of learning because of our proximity and involvement, including the emotional domain. We underwent criticisms and scrutiny, but in the end, the power of our narrative and its closer adherence to local realities ensured that our story rang true and triggered reflection, learning and change.

Ever since this extremely intensive and fulfilling experience in terms of impact and learning, I have been trying to push all evaluations I have managed in the same direction. I have sought to make them as participatory as possible in terms of using implicit and local knowledge from communities, local partners and national consultants and to take more responsibility for the weaker capacities in terms of writing the reports in a format that would meet international standards. I learned an important lesson on the power of capturing oral narratives and knowledge through verbal accounts and joint analysis and how to render it into a language that was acceptable and useable in a written report.

With time, I have also become more daring about including external partners in the evaluation design process from the very beginning. In a recent evaluation of the El Nino response in Southern Africa, we organized a workshop with internal staff and external partners from government counterparts, implementing partners, the Southern African Development Community (SADC) and other UN agencies to design the evaluation. With the support of a strong facilitator from one of the countries, we managed to trigger the empathy of the participants with the local communities in their region. The quality and richness of the insights and questions proposed for the evaluation was astounding. One colleague from one of the implementing partners' organizations told us about how he had managed to achieve a high rate of success in a goat pass-on scheme. Poor households received does and billy goats and, once they had kid goats, they had to give some to another family to start their own herd. The NGO was worried that, due to the high levels of poverty and scarceness of resources, families would eat the goats or sell them immediately. He decided to start a campaign to convince families receiving goats that FAO goats were of a special breed so they did not die, get ill or stolen. On successive monitoring visits, he found all the goats were still in place. This story was the trigger for an in-depth analysis of the motivational aspects and coping strategies of households and, through collective reflection, enabled us to ask very tailored and pertinent questions during the field-work. It enabled us to speak the same language as the recipients of the aid assistance and made us go a long way in understanding the dynamics of livelihood strategies, choices and fears, as well as understanding what may have been household-level resilience. For the first time, we decided to make a video of the evaluation results and learning for the communities we had talked to in the course of the evaluation so that we could report back to them and not just to the donors and the staff of the organization.[5]

## Can we re-imagine humanitarian evaluations?

The main learning from my work as a humanitarian evaluator is that compassion, empathy and attempts to get as close as possible to the perspective of people at the receiving end of humanitarian aid are fundamental elements in evaluations. It is critical to design and manage evaluations with full awareness of the power imbalances inherent in the delivery of aid and also to find ways to extract, capture and use oral and implicit knowledge from people on the ground or from those that are closer to them, such as national staff, extension workers or other actors who work close to the community level. I also believe we can push evaluations further, so they become an exercise in co-design and co-ownership of results with people and communities at the grass-roots. The first step to do this requires changing the mind-set, institutional habits and ways of working of evaluation commissioners and evaluation offices. We will need to relinquish control and take risks in terms of standardization and possibly end-quality of the evaluation products.

The first thing to do is walk the extra mile in order to include local communities for face-to-face knowledge generation. If you manage to do it systematically, you soon realize that the second issue is that you may not be asking the right questions. More precisely, you are probably asking questions that are of interest and relevance only to donors or humanitarian industry professionals, but not to local NGOs or people in the communities. Your questions are designed to extract information about whether what was done generated the intended benefits, rather than asking them if it was what they wanted. You ask them about short-term gains rather than about agency and long-term choices. You record gratitude or short-term satisfaction rather than seeking ways to support equity and empowerment in the long term. You select the proxy indicators for resilience and impact and go looking for them in a narrow range of options rather than allowing people to define and tell you what they are. You look for answers and not for questions.

Evaluations reflect the humanitarian industry and both are still a long way away from redressing imbalances in power and control over processes and choices. We, humanitarian workers at large, retain the power to decide through design and through expertise who gets what, where, when and for how long. We are convinced we know best. And to a certain extent or in a partial way we do, because we are experts, we have experience and we have capacity. At the same time, we must be more open and ready to share our accountability and our authority with people at the local level. We should seek to work in partnership and relinquish at least some of our decision-making power.

In his stimulating model of Re-imagined Aid, which pushes for a more equitable, decolonial, self-determined and holistic aid system, the humanitarian practitioner Arbie Baguios identifies some of the main attributes that are needed to make better aid happen: the aid process should be robustly analyzed, relational and adaptive, and radically accountable.[6]

Evaluations could be a useful tool to pave the way to re-imagined aid, as they are not tasked to deliver goods and services but only knowledge and understanding through narratives. We could be the ones to trigger change by telling a different story from a different perspective. Or at least to tell a story with more parts to it, some of which could serve the learning for collective and individual needs of local communities as well as those of the more traditional stakeholders. If evaluations found ways of more openly addressing the power dynamics and drivers that determine the design and processes of aid, and they could do this for a broader and more inclusive or diverse range of audiences and users, they could provide that radical accountability and robust analysis.

The final reflections I have to offer are on why Covid-19 restrictions and the post-Covid world may offer a good opportunity to shift the balance of evaluative work towards one of inclusion and empowerment of actors at the local level. The initial impact on evaluation conduct has been to suspend, cancel or postpone most evaluations. I have, with difficulty, managed to re-organize some evaluations through remote consultations, even managing, thanks to the support of a Syrian colleague, to reach Syrian refugees in a camp in Jordan, through phone interviews. It has been a very interesting experience and it has definitely forced us to think outside the box, especially in terms of the reachability, but also in terms of the trust and connection of people in communities in remote areas. If, like in my case, you believe and promote the conduct of extensive and in-depth field-work as one of the cornerstones of good humanitarian evaluation practice, then it becomes apparent how easy and straightforward this was before Covid-19. By being there in person, it was more possible to get people's trust. But if you are operating remotely, the challenges become enormous. I spent a lot of time trying to draft a one-page leaflet, to be translated into Arabic and distributed to potential respondents in the refugee camp in Jordan, trying to explain why we were carrying out the evaluation and why we wanted to talk to them on the phone.

In the end it worked. People were willing to be interviewed and were extremely collaborative and honest in their answers. But the effort really made me question again, and with more strength than before, whether the whole evaluation process and the questions we wanted to ask had any relevance whatsoever for the people involved in the project activities, receiving the support. What aspect, if any, of the evaluation, would resonate with them? And why should they care?

This line of musings soon became interconnected with the revived discourse and Zoom reflections that have led to humanitarian organizations acknowledging that the paradigm needs changing to one that values local agency and shifts the balance of decision-making and authority to the local level. Or putting the policies about the importance and role of local actors – what we call localization – usually found on paper in humanitarian organizations' offices, to use in real life.

The few agencies that had managed to implement various degrees of localization, such as the International Federation of the Red Cross (IFRC) in the Ebola response in the Democratic Republic of Congo (DRC) – when internationals lost access to certain areas – have become the how-to example to follow. Most country offices and related headquarters have been trying to find ways of keeping activities going. Given the near impossibility to move around in most countries because of Covid-19 restrictions, local-level NGOs, associations and groups are increasingly being looked at as the only possible solution. Many organizations are looking to modify some of their long-held and, until now, unchangeable operational procedures and rules, to be able to partner better with those inside or close to the communities.

It remains to be seen to what extent these partnerships will be equitable, shifting the authority and decision-making power along with the responsibility to keep the humanitarian action going. The recent events linked to Black Lives Matter seem to have opened the flood-gates of debate in the humanitarian sector. Hopefully, the flooding will also reach and rock the domain of evaluations.

What would a localization drive look like in evaluations? Tying this to the question of the relevance and usefulness of evaluations for local actors, I would ask: would it be possible to co-design an evaluation with local stakeholders so that their participation is not only in terms of being involved in answering questions but actually in determining which questions to ask? Most likely, many of the questions they would ask would not match or resonate with the questions that donors or organizational senior management would expect to find in evaluations. Would they be ready to let go of the process and open it up for a broader and more equitable constituency? And more: what would happen to the founding principles of evaluations, such as independence and impartiality? Could you tell a multiplicity of stories, derived from personal and, by default, biased perspectives, based on many voices and points of view, rather than a single dry, tidy and professional narrative? And would the rest of the humanitarian machine be on board and ready to learn through and with evaluations, rather than from them? I plan to test these hypotheses as soon as possible by piloting evaluation activities that are co-designed and co-conducted under the leadership of local actors and associations. I am hoping to do this with organizations of self-representing refugees and community organizations.

To finish off where I began, I would like to use another part of Chimamanda's reflection:

> We need what the Nigerian writer Chinua Achebe calls 'a balance of stories'. Stories matter, many stories matter. Stories have been used to dispossess and to malign, but stories can also be used to empower and humanize. Stories can break the dignity of a people, but stories can also repair that broken dignity. When we reject the single story, when we realize there is never a single story about any place, we regain a kind of paradise.[7]

## Notes

1 Ngozi Adichie C. (2009) The danger of a single story. TEDGlobal www.ted.com/talks/chimamanda_ngozi_adichie_the_danger_of_a_single_story?language=en.
2 OECD-DAC (2019) Better Criteria for Better Evaluations: revised evaluation criteria definitions and principles of use www.oecd.org/dac/evaluation/daccriteriaforevaluatingdevelopmentassistance.htm.
3 United Nations Evaluation Group (2016) Norms and Standards for Evaluations www.unevaluation.org/document/detail/1914.
4 The same imbalance is present also in the humanitarian sector at large, as has been evidenced by studies and research. For a summary, see: https://medium.com/an-injustice/how-white-people-conquered-the-non-profit-industry-c1221cd93a83 and https://odihpn.org/blog/is-racism-part-of-our-reluctance-to-localise-humanitarian-action/.
5 FAO (2020) Evaluation of the El Nino Response in Zimbabwe: the farmers' perspective www.fao.org/evaluation/resources/videos/multimedia-detail/en/c/1314664/.
6 Baguios A. (2020) Re-imagined Aid https://drive.google.com/file/d/1TcYFl64fluXIWiplrLztp7EkCO3ssRsz/view.
7 Ngozi Adichie C. (2009) The danger of a single story. TEDGlobal www.ted.com/talks/chimamanda_ngozi_adichie_the_danger_of_a_single_story?language=en.

# 3   COVID-19 and cholera

## Reflections on humanitarian principles and their impact on public health emergencies

*David Eisenbaum*

## Introduction

If you're reading this, chances are you are connected to the humanitarian field in some way. Perhaps as a professional, a donor, a board member, an academic, a survivor, or a volunteer. Most likely you're a combination of several, and if you've lived through the COVID-19 pandemic, then you have experienced at least one humanitarian crisis as a survivor. I believe that the humanitarian space is shaped by all of our collective perspectives. The experience of a survivor is far different from a donor's experience, yet they are inextricably linked. My goal is to share my experiences to help shape your perspective, regardless of how you are connected to the humanitarian world, by convincing you that everyone has a shared responsibility to practice, discuss, advocate for, and insist upon several key humanitarian principles, regardless of how they fit into the humanitarian world.

Perspective matters, and the best way to understand how I arrived at my perspective is to understand my past. I have worked in the humanitarian space since 2008, often directly for non-governmental organizations (NGOs), and also as a consultant, and as a federal reservist with a United States Health and Human Services Disaster Medical Assistance Team (DMAT). In that time, I have responded to hurricanes, tornados, floods, earthquakes, wildfires, and epidemics in the United States, Navajo Nation, Marianas Islands, Haiti, Liberia, Nepal, Mozambique, Indonesia, Australia, and the Bahamas. Much of my experience is in the field, managing programs and operations ranging from days to years after an event. I've been fortunate to have the opportunity to work in several humanitarian sectors, including Health, Shelter, WASH (water, sanitation, and hygiene), Education, Logistics, and Early Recovery.

I first entered the humanitarian field as a survivor. Like many survivors, I did not expect to experience what I did, but was profoundly impacted by the experience. In August 2007, I was backpacking in Peru and experienced firsthand the 8.0 magnitude earthquake that struck the central coast region. The quake itself was a harrowing experience, and I recall standing in the middle of a narrow street, arms locked with a group of strangers, all trying to stay on our feet as the ground shook violently and telephone poles swayed overhead. In the hours and days after,

I experienced the challenges, uncertainty, and confusion that come with many rapid-onset disasters: being cut off from the outside world (communications and transport), scarcity of food and potable water, and a lack of safe shelter and sanitation. I also experienced the kinship and kindness of other survivors who shared their homes, food, and companionship. After three days I found a group of US military personnel who were being evacuated, and 12 hours later I was back in the US. That was the day I decided I wanted to be a professional humanitarian and specialize in emergency response.

It's critical to note that I entered the humanitarian field with a high degree of naiveté and ignorance. In the simplest terms, I wanted to help people who were experiencing calamity. At first, I viewed the profession as fairly "black and white" – those who have the means to help others are obliged to do so, to whatever degree they can. If there is a need for food, bring food. If there is a need for doctors, bring doctors. It was only by experiencing the complexity of humanitarian work, and later engaging the field from an academic perspective, that I gained awareness of how truly complex humanitarian work is. I learned that humanitarian work is not as simple as bringing resources where they are needed after a disaster. Issues around sustainability, vulnerability, and global socioeconomic imbalances are at the root of the field, and an academic understanding of these issues widened my awareness and motivation to improve my professional practice. Moreover, I came to understand the critical need to create greater awareness around standards and best practices to help translate the collective good intentions of people in the humanitarian field into effective action.

Now, more than a decade into a career in the humanitarian field, my perspective has changed much from the idealism and oversimplification of my early years. I am inspired by those who are challenging the status quo and striving to move the humanitarian field past emergency resource management, and into a more holistic discipline, rooted in critical reflection, continual improvement, and an emphasis on resilience and sustainability. By critiquing shortcomings in the way that aid has often been provided, in addition to the success stories, we can hope to avoid the sometimes all too predictable additional human suffering which follows humanitarian crises.

It is my goal to share my reflections in the hope that some of the lessons I've learned can serve other humanitarians, whether they are survivors, aid workers, donors, volunteers, or leaders in NGOs, government, and business. Only by holding ourselves to a higher degree of accountability to those we aim to serve through humanitarian work can we hope to improve the field.

Throughout this chapter I will reference and reflect on certain important humanitarian principles and best practices. That said, this is not intended to be an overview of humanitarian principles and standards. A great deal of literature exists on the topic of humanitarian principles, and these reflections are informed by my own understanding of those principles and how I have seen them applied (or not applied) during humanitarian crises.

My initial concept for this chapter was to reflect on my time living and working in Haiti and the important lessons I learned as a novice humanitarian professional.

Then COVID-19 happened, and every person on earth suddenly became part of an unprecedented humanitarian crisis. I realized that many of the key humanitarian principles I wanted to share with readers were no longer purely theoretical for those unfamiliar with the humanitarian field, but could be related to their own experiences during the pandemic. The consequences of a decentralized response, resource scarcity, unknown timelines for recovery, the realities of a "new normal", and countless other realities that historically were only known to the humanitarian world and those it serves became commonplace and nearly universal. This presents an opportunity to make the challenges and realities of the humanitarian world relatable to those for whom it was once a completely foreign and alien world. This relatability, paired with an understanding of the key issues within the field, could perhaps have a beneficial impact on tackling future humanitarian crises more effectively, by empowering people at all levels of influence with an understanding and sense of responsibility about net positive humanitarian action.

I have seen many of the same themes repeat themselves across humanitarian emergencies in vastly different countries and disaster types: inadequate coordination leading to a fractured and inefficient response, good intentions failing as a substitute for a true understanding of the local context, and humanitarian actors unintentionally doing more harm than good. These themes are well understood by humanitarian professionals and have informed a growing discourse about principles and standards that reflect hard lessons learned and an ongoing debate about the nature of aid itself. While this is a highly complex and evolving area of

*Figure 3.1* Humanitarian intervention

academic and cross-disciplinary discourse, I intend to highlight some of the most important principles, as I see them, and illustrate their significance through the things I've seen and experienced.

## The golden rule: do no harm

The principle of "Do No Harm" is at the center of ethical, effective humanitarian work. Indeed, all those involved in humanitarian aid strive to have a net positive impact on the wellbeing of those they serve. Yet there are countless case studies of aid programs and interventions doing more harm than good. While it was never anyone's intention for aid to create more problems than it solved, it happens often, and frequently despite the best intentions of those responsible.

Post-earthquake Haiti is full of these cases. We saw a flood of donated food dilute the local market so severely that Haitian rice farmers saw the demand for their crops disappear, and their livelihoods along with it. We saw hundreds of foreign NGOs fill gaps in social services for so long, and to such a high degree, that the country became dependent upon them, hampering the development of a self-sufficient social service sector. We saw NGOs laden with funds from sympathetic donors build schools and clinics that never opened because there was never a sustainable long-term plan for their operation and funding, and no accountability for the effectiveness of donor dollars. Local leaders were not engaged adequately, if at all, and consequently local communities lacked commitment to the very projects intended to serve them. Perhaps the worst harm we saw was the introduction of cholera from abroad to Haiti, an island nation which had been cholera free, and a cholera epidemic started accidentally by the improper disposal of human waste from a camp used by members of the international humanitarian response effort.

Aid inevitably becomes part of the local context. If the context is not considered and well understood before aid is delivered, or if aid programs are not rigorously monitored for impact (and those delivering aid are not held accountable by donors, impacted communities, and other stakeholders), there is no way of knowing whether the net impact is positive or negative. History has shown it is often the latter. Humanitarian crises are inherently complex, and the natural desire to help often means an urgency to "do *something* now", but urgency, complexity, and good intentions cannot be excuses for humanitarian interventions that do more harm than good. Fortunately, humanitarian principles and standards provide all stakeholders involved with humanitarian work with the means to work towards achieving accountable, effective, net beneficial aid.

The principles and standards I explore below are all rooted in the concept of Do No Harm, and are intended to improve how aid is delivered, and, by promoting a resilient global community, to reduce the need for it in general. In my own work, I strive to practice adherence to Do No Harm in all aspects of the role. This means a granular approach to planning, monitoring, and evaluation, and continually asking if our impact is net positive. This could be as specific as ensuring our waste is properly disposed of, or as broad as providing humanitarian standards training to better prepare field staff. I also champion and practice the principles of participating in and facilitating a coordinated effort, knowing the context, and seeking sustainable solutions that reduce vulnerabilities to hazards while increasing community resilience and self-sufficiency. I will reflect on more of these principles and how they have shaped my changing views over the last decade.

## Why coordination matters

I've learned that coordination during humanitarian crises is critical. I've also learned that it needs to include a broad spectrum of stakeholders, from the largest NGOs and wealthiest governments, down to the grassroots community organizations and leaders. The challenge and necessary time and resources to engage grassroots organizations and leaders cannot be overstated. Language and cultural barriers must be overcome. Trust must be established, and all of this in the context of the trauma of the emergency, when hierarchies and communication channels are likely diminished. Yet, to maximize effectiveness, we must do much more than throw resources at a disaster or public health emergency. It is crucial that the response includes, to a high degree, the perspective and existing capacity of the affected community.

During the 2010 cholera outbreak in Haiti, only months after the earthquake, many different actors responded with medical supplies and personnel. When coordination was done effectively, these resources helped stem further spread of the outbreak by targeting hotspots before they could spread. As is often the case, not all actors took part in the coordination effort, and many responded in a vacuum, deploying critical resources to areas that had already received assistance, or where the number of cases was fewer than had been reported weeks earlier.

I was fortunate to work with a network of smaller grassroots NGOs and local community groups. While larger aid groups and the government were focusing on urban centers, community members from remote mountain villages used our coordination network to call attention to smaller outbreaks that weren't being addressed. We worked with several partner NGOs and the local community, to mobilize medicine, sanitation and hygiene supplies, clinicians, and health educators as part of a coordinated response effort to provide care and stem outbreaks in hot spots, before they impacted whole communities. This effort was successful because it was done collaboratively, and harnessed the resources, knowledge, and experience of various parties, including the impacted community. In fact, the clinicians and supplies were only able to get to the remote villages on the backs of pack animals provided by the community. This effort was then reported to the wider health coordination group (one sector of the United Nations (UN) Cluster System) to provide public health data that in turn informed the nationwide response. Resources were better able to be deployed where needed, and all response partners were made aware of the situation in our region.

It is easy to see parallels in the current COVID-19 response in the United States. The lack of effective centralized coordination early on meant inconsistencies in travel restrictions and lockdowns in various U.S. states, and led to unintended movement of people across jurisdictions, potentially furthering the virus's spread, rather than slowing it. Eventually state and federal governments did begin coordinating their efforts and sharing information more aggressively, but future research will likely show that too little was done in the early stages to restrict movement and track and share public health data. This led to more lives being lost and a higher toll on the economy.

If we look closer to the ground, we can see how a decentralized approach to resource management created challenges around personal protective equipment (PPE) costs and availability in healthcare facilities. Without coordination, the world's hospitals, governments, and NGOs were all competing for scarce resources. When coordination is effective, resources are connected with needs, based on a shared understanding of what resources are available, and where they can do the most good now. For example, in the early days of the COVID pandemic, we saw some field hospitals receive tens of thousands of units of critical PPE, while others were forced to manufacture their own from supplies purchased at hardware stores. There was no rhyme or reason to it – in most cases it was a matter of which support network the hospital was part of. Those affiliated with government or large health networks were able to receive PPE when it became available, and after weeks of waiting, often received it in unnecessarily large quantities as each of the channels through which they'd requested it came through independently. There would have been a broad benefit to a centralized mechanism to coordinate getting the appropriate amounts and types of PPE to the right places, at the right time.

Clearly the need for coordination is key following a disaster, public health emergency, or any humanitarian crisis. These events draw in a broad range of actors who fill a spectrum of roles. Governments at all levels, from a village council to a federal government, are charged with the responsibility of representing their constituents, and can bring critical resources where they are needed. Government also can implement and enforce laws and regulations that can help or hinder a crisis. This could be the military or emergency medical teams helping build and staff field hospitals, or a regional government enforcing rules that prevent the spread of a disease (for example closing local markets, or reducing the number of people who can congregate).

NGOs, from local grassroots organizations to international NGOs (INGOs), also bring resources, and often have insight into needs and demographics of impacted communities that might not receive the assistance they need. These can be small community groups that are best positioned to identify vulnerable people in their own communities and connect them with resources, or multibillion-dollar foundations that fund research on disease eradication, or provide critical materials and personnel during a crisis. The private sector too, from trade associations to multinational corporations, has a role to play in the provision of resources and the ability to mobilize large groups of people for the common good. Businesses of all sizes will be motivated to restore normalcy. They can provide donated resources (people and materials), coordinate activities through existing networks and partnerships, and use innovation to help find solutions to challenges quickly.

Diversely represented coordination is elusive, even when those involved know it is critical. Often the rapid onset and severity of a humanitarian emergency brings together an ecosystem of varied players, each with their own priorities, networks, stakeholders, bureaucracy, and governance, and this invariably introduces formidable challenges. Simply harmonizing communication can be difficult. Different players use different terminology, and systems for managing emergencies vary widely globally. Challenges communicating across different languages inevitably impact coordination.

Unfortunately, not all humanitarian actors participate in centralized coordination. I often see organizations respond to a crisis in their own vacuum. I believe the most common rationale behind this behavior is a belief that participating in coordination is bureaucratic and counterproductive. Humanitarians who act on this belief are not entirely wrong; it can be time consuming and frustrating to participate in a large-scale coordination, especially during the often chaotic and sometimes inefficient early stages of a response. However, putting in the work and resources to improve coordinated information sharing and action pays dividends in the future. Unfortunately, actors who fail to coordinate can do more harm than good. If a medical team treats cholera patients in a remote village, but doesn't report their action to the ministry of health and other would-be partners, think of the awareness that is lost. What resources could have been brought to reduce the likelihood of a future outbreak in that village? Too often, humanitarian actors that prefer to "fly under the radar" or "do their own thing" perpetuate vulnerabilities by only addressing an immediate need without addressing a root cause. By failing to share their awareness with partners who could provide continuity of assistance to an impacted community, they are ultimately making things worse.

Tragically, competition between NGOs vying for funding can lead to poor coordination. NGOs may seek to "claim" an impacted geography or sector, believing that they can address all the unmet needs. While geographic or sectoral divisions can be an effective strategy, sometimes it happens because an organization wants to claim a large volume of "work" against which to fundraise. While NGOs need funding, this should never be the driving force behind decisions on where resources should go, or what information should be shared. Donors have substantial influence in this space, as they can hold organizations accountable for practicing, or not practicing, effective coordination.

In my work I have seen a number of strategies improve coordination. Developing and maintaining partnerships has become a best practice for me and much of the sector. By establishing and growing partnerships with peer organizations, donors, and regional and sectoral networks (e.g. education, WASH) before and in between emergencies, all parties benefit from improved coordination during a crisis. For example, while trying to prepare for the dual challenges of COVID and hurricanes, these types of proactive steps have been invaluable in helping us to develop real plans for likely future events.

Additionally, I have found that arriving early and quickly engaging with existing coordination has led to a more effective and efficient response. It takes days or even weeks to gain situational awareness during a major emergency, and a lack of reliable information often means expending precious time to develop a common operating picture among response partners. This underscores the need to quickly plug in and align with the overall response effort. In some instances, I have seen no apparent coordination mechanism prioritized or put in place. This is often due to a commonly accepted practice that the government is ultimately responsible for leading a response, rather than foreign INGOs or NGOs. If the government lacks the will, resources, or knowledge to take up that leadership role, a vacuum can result. In my experience, a local stakeholder often fills the vacuum in this early stage, sometimes a mayor, local business leader, or grassroots community group. I have found supporting this initial coordination effort, and encouraging other partners to do so, can be effective to lay the groundwork for a more formal coordination mechanism that eventually develops.

I generally encourage others to come into the coordination mechanism to improve sharing of critical information, and to reduce redundancy while maximizing the impact of available resources. This often means seeking out local grassroots groups who can represent the local context, particularly marginalized and vulnerable groups which may otherwise be excluded from coordination due to implicit or explicit power structures. During the cholera epidemic in Haiti, it was through a network of grassroots NGOs that we learned of hotspots, and it was through those partnerships that we were able to deliver services and care.

Another method I use to support effective coordination is maintaining a working knowledge of emergency management systems and ecosystems. I think of this similarly to speaking different languages. For example, by understanding the UN Cluster System, and the structure used when the UN is coordinating a humanitarian emergency, usually through the Office for Coordination of Humanitarian Affairs (OCHA), I can more efficiently plug into a response effort. I know which agencies are leading various sectors, I understand how information sharing works, and I am generally able to focus on doing the work without a learning curve. Humanitarian emergencies are exceedingly complex and fluid, so removing this added challenge can save time and improve effectiveness. In the US, we use a very technical emergency management system that is designed to support effective coordination by incorporating the whole ecosystem of potential stakeholders. When working in this system I must operate under a totally different model, and with specialized terminology and methodology. During COVID, the ability to operate in various emergency management systems has meant being able to translate lessons learned from one context to another.

## Knowing the context is key

A related and equally critical principal to coordination is knowing the context. Knowing the context allows those involved to act effectively, efficiently, and without doing harm, whereas acting without knowing the context often leads to unanticipated, avoidable harmful impacts on an already stricken community. So, what does this mean?

Knowing the context means striving to understand a situation holistically before engaging. Good intentions are not enough; you also need a plan based on the realities on the ground. If, for example, you bring doctors, nurses, and health educators to a remote village to treat cholera patients and educate the community on how to prevent cholera, you need to understand the socioeconomic context, not just the medical one. Let's say you treat all the patients and educate them on hand hygiene – you should have solved the problem, right? This played out often in Haiti, and despite the lifesaving care and hygiene education, the problem was not solved. Locals might say,

> I understand that I need to wash my hands to protect myself and my family, and purify my water to make it safe to drink, but it's not that simple. I have no running water – we must walk 20 minutes to the nearest source and carry by hand. I have no soap, and cannot afford to buy it. I have no water purification tablets, and we have already used all the local trees to boil water, cook our meals, and heat our home.

A medical solution is not enough for this community – they need an economic opportunity to become resilient and self-sufficient enough to buy soap, water purification tablets, and/or fuel. They remain vulnerable to cholera and other infectious diseases because of their socioeconomic context, and this must be understood and considered when planning and executing an initiative to address the problem. Unfortunately, issues like this are often addressed with shortsighted solutions, such as the provision of materials for a defined period of time, but this means the community will either remain reliant on aid, which is unsustainable and counter to the idea of a life with dignity, or will eventually return to the same state of vulnerability they were in before outsiders temporarily came to their aid. The people most impacted by humanitarian emergencies are best positioned to articulate what they need, but too often they are not asked. By including the impacted community in coordination and decision-making, the whole response benefits, as response actors gain firsthand awareness of the local context, explicit needs, and root causes of vulnerability that may have led to the emergency in the first place. This underscores the importance of involving grassroots stakeholders and seeking sustainable solutions with a focus on increasing a community's resilience rather than just addressing an immediate problem.

During the COVID pandemic the Navajo Nation has been a hotspot of infections, and seen some of the highest per capita infection rates in the US. Without understanding the local context, it would be impossible to effectively address the pandemic. For example, the early approach adopted by public health officials and government was the same as adopted elsewhere in the US: promote widespread messaging encouraging people to stay at home, practice good hand hygiene, and practice social distancing, including family. However, Navajo families often live three or more generations in a home, so social distancing guidance needed to consider this unique context. It didn't, so people inevitably continued living as they did. This meant elderly members of the family were often inadvertently exposed.

Public health officials considered addressing this by establishing sites where low-acuity COVID patients could stay while recovering, without returning home. Unfortunately, since stay at home orders were in effect every weekend, people were often staying at home infecting their family before coming into the hospital. It's worth noting here that part of the local context is that many people on the reservation live in remote areas, many hours' drive on unpaved roads to the nearest hospital.

Similarly, public health messaging encouraged good hand hygiene. Unfortunately, up to a third or more households in the Navajo Nation lack running water. Given shortages of hand sanitizer everywhere, this meant a sizable portion of the population was simply unable to adopt the guidelines put forth to protect them. Had the local context been thoroughly considered and incorporated into an effective coordination mechanism, an alternative and more contextually appropriate guideline could have been adopted and promoted.

I believe knowing the context is very challenging. The rapid onset of humanitarian emergencies means actors rarely have adequate time to develop a deep understanding of the local context. Large-scale emergencies inherently draw humanitarians from outside the impacted area, as local capacity is unable to address needs without support. It would be unrealistic for every humanitarian to be familiar with every possible context they may work in. Moreover, context is subjective, and it can be challenging to access all the perspectives that make a local context. Additionally, the context is fluid in the aftermath of a humanitarian emergency, and when preexisting social dynamics intersect with the disruption caused by the event, it creates an evolving context that everyone struggles to understand.

Unfortunately, I have also encountered humanitarian actors who simply do not think the local context is important. They apply the same thinking they've used before, and homogenize events, for example, suggesting that an epidemic in one impoverished country is the same as another. This leads to "rinse and repeat" programs that perpetuate ineffective aid and community vulnerability.

In my own work I use several best practices to understand the context as much as possible. Prior to an event, I research possible locations of future emergencies. This may sound grim, but unfortunately vulnerability is a fairly good predictor, and this means it is possible to predict where future humanitarian emergencies may occur. By studying vulnerability, its causes, and the wider context behind it, it is possible to develop some context prior to an event. As mentioned previously, engaging with potential partners in an area prior to an event is an excellent way to build awareness around the local context.

Advance preparation of course isn't always possible, nor can we predict all future emergencies, as recent events have shown us. Sometimes you just need to deploy and figure it out on the ground. In these instances, I find it critical to proactively seek out a multitude of perspectives with which to inform my own understanding of the local context. It is not enough to speak with high-level emergency managers or local leaders; one must always engage directly with impacted people, and the most vulnerable and marginalized demographics, as they are so often the ones whose needs are least effectively met (often because no one asked them). This type of interaction is a major focus for me during the assessment phase, and I think of it as performing diagnostics prior to an actual procedure. In instances where lives are on the line, this process must be balanced against the need for immediate assistance, but the intervention should be part of a broader process that incorporates ongoing awareness around the local context.

## Creating a more resilient world

There is a natural tendency to view humanitarian crises as the result of a natural hazard, like a hurricane, drought, or as the result of conflict. This oversimplification allows us to fool ourselves into thinking that the solution is often simple: if there has been a storm, fix everything like it was before the storm. If there is a drought and famine, provide food until the drought passes. If there is a conflict, send peacekeepers to stop the fighting. Yet we can look around the world and see that humanitarian crises are never simple.

The tendency to oversimplify humanitarian issues is perhaps human nature. I believe that most people faced with the suffering of others, even strangers, feel compelled to take action. At its simplest, this plays out as charity, the provision of resources to others who are in need. When I was new to humanitarian work I viewed the field in similar terms. As a program manager in the field I delivered results in my narrow slice of the humanitarian response effort. However, it did not take long for me to understand that the enemy was not hazardous events, like a hurricane or earthquake, but systemic vulnerability, rooted in socioeconomics. The rural cholera-impacted communities we partnered with needed medical care, supplies, and training on how to avoid future outbreaks. We brought doctors who treated patients, and educators to provide training, as well as medical and hygiene and sanitation supplies. I remember a local leader asking me what would happen when the supplies ran out, and all I could say was that we would work with them and partners to bring more supplies in the future. Yet these communities lacked running water, road access, and electricity. It felt like all we were doing was providing a stop-gap solution, but what was needed was a much larger plan to improve conditions in these communities such that they could be more self-sufficient and better prepared for future hazardous events. This dramatically changed my perception about my work. I no longer thought of myself as responsible for a narrow part of the response effort. Instead, I began to see the positive influence I could have more broadly, by viewing my projects and programs within a larger context, and working to partner with those who would help transition the immediate response work into longer-term solutions to local challenges. This meant bringing more local voices into partnerships, advocating for wider coordination and information sharing, and seeking out partnerships that could produce tangible, permanent solutions encompassing the emergency response, local capacity building, and disaster risk reduction.

In my mind this is all about increasing resilience and reducing vulnerability. In the humanitarian context, vulnerability is a state of exposure to potential hazards. Wealthier communities and countries invest in reducing vulnerability through robust emergency planning, and by making resources available to prepare for, mitigate, and respond quickly to hazards, reducing their negative impact. In places like Haiti, the context that exists before a hazard strikes makes communities vulnerable. Resilience, on the other hand, is a community or country's ability to weather hazardous events with minimal negative impact. These terms have become mainstays in the humanitarian field, with a growing emphasis on sustainable development that reduces vulnerability and increases resilience.

I know I said humanitarian issues are not simple, but perhaps they are in this way. Communities built physically and socioeconomically resilient are less vulnerable to hazards, whether it's a storm, a pandemic, or a conflict. Reducing vulnerability while increasing resilience is increasingly the mantra of sustainable development, and has begun to positively shape humanitarian work more broadly. Yet, when faced with human suffering, there remains a tendency to oversimplify. The next time there is a massive earthquake or hurricane that grabs global media for several days, there will be a flurry of support from the global community. We all know what this looks like, and can probably recall how we've been personally involved at this stage during past humanitarian crises.

But while the world is prepared to spend billions on immediate aid in the form of aid materials and personnel, what will the outcome be? Yes, lives will be saved by emergency medical teams. Yes, displaced people will be provided with temporary shelter and food aid. But if the global humanitarian community, particularly those with influence on policy and funding, does not invest billions in reducing vulnerability and increasing resilience, the whole terrible drama will play out again.

In writing this I've reflected on why people outside the humanitarian space (and many within it) generally tend to oversimplify humanitarian crises and opt for short-term fixes that don't address underlying causes of vulnerability. I know for me personally, it felt good to feel like I was helping address a problem I didn't create. I didn't make the cholera epidemic happen, I'm just here to help stop it and prevent another one. Donors could feel the same way about the medical supplies they provided, and NGO leaders could feel accomplished for the lives their group had a part in saving. Basically, it feels good to help people in emergent, urgent need. But we must hold ourselves, our organizations, and our governments to a higher standard than just addressing the obvious need to *some* degree. Humanitarian principles and standards, and the discourse around their evolution and adoption, are critical in addressing the systemic causes of vulnerability that perpetuate and indeed often create or exacerbate humanitarian crises.

So why should you care about any of this? I started with an assumption that if you're reading this you are somehow involved with humanitarian work. This means you have influence, whether you use it actively or passively, and chances are the decisions you make impact the humanitarian field. My hope is that you will do so thoughtfully, and as a champion to reduce vulnerability and increase resiliency, even if that means challenging the status quo.

If you're on a board of directors, or a long-time donor to a disaster NGO, do you see your organization investing in addressing the underlying causes of the suffering it seeks to address? In other words, is it actively trying to eliminate the need that created it, or is it simply "handing out band aids"? Is the organization you support doing more harm than good? And has it done enough to understand the local context to say one way or the other? Does your organization actively coordinate with other stakeholders, especially the communities it serves? Good intentions are not enough. Even with good intentions humanitarian actors can harm already stricken communities.

In summary, I believe there are several ways we can hold ourselves accountable in the humanitarian field. Adhere to the Do No Harm principle as the foundation of our work, and never stop assessing if and how we may be unintentionally doing more harm than good. Know the context, and insist that decisions are made based upon a thorough understanding of the immediate and long-term context, inclusive of the disaster event, but not solely around the event. This applies not only to those working in the field as professionals or volunteers, but also to decision-makers on boards and in leadership roles, and especially to donors and those with influence on funding decisions.

Practice, and insist that other humanitarian actors practice, effective coordination that includes a variety of perspectives and stakeholder groups, including the impacted community and marginalized people within it. If you are operating alone, you are likely doing harm. If you see others operating alone, bring them into the coordination effort, at least to share awareness around the situation. Advocate for and implement durable programs that apply resources to increasing resiliency and reducing vulnerability, rather than just providing quick fixes or "getting things back to normal". NGOs exist to fill gaps in social services that are not addressed by governments. The goal should be to create a global resilient society that is able to avoid hazards, and address them with local, rather than foreign, resources when they cannot be prevented.

In reflecting on my own journey as a professional humanitarian, I realize how my thinking has evolved in the time between cholera and COVID. I'm increasingly aware of the larger global factors that influence the field, in my opinion, largely rooted in socioeconomics and politics, rather than weather, medicine, or the other traditional roots of "acts of God". I have strived to reflect on and improve my own practice through dialogue with other humanitarians, academics, and survivors. While I feel my work is grounded in the Do No Harm principle, and all that it encompasses, I believe this will continue to be part of a continuous evolution within the humanitarian field. For me, this means questioning the status quo, and asking others to join me in continually asking how we can improve the field, and work towards reducing the need for emergent humanitarian work by strengthening global communities.

# 4 How to be relevant

## A personal journey in the aid system

*Volker Hüls*

## A personal journey

I came to be a humanitarian worker by chance. Growing up in a small town in Germany, I pursued a career in science, graduating in biology and working in a research laboratory. Having joined the German civil protection system as a volunteer at the age of 16, for many years I saw it just as a rewarding hobby, serving my local community in my free time. Little did I know then that it would make me leave my country and my previous existence in pursuit of a very different life.

Despite my keen interest in science, as a young person in the late eighties and the early nineties I could not help getting fascinated by global events. The fall of the Berlin wall, the collapse of the Soviet Union, and the subsequent crisis in the Balkans right on our doorsteps were world events that I got to witness from a very short distance. These events ultimately would also trigger a personal journey for me that was very different from what I had envisaged as a young adult, abandoning science and embarking on a career in aid.

Making the decision at the time was somewhat easy. I had no family of my own, I was disillusioned by my work in research, and to be honest I was also looking for adventures. As much as I had had some exposure to humanitarian aid as a volunteer, I had only little training, counting on learning by doing. In many ways I was privileged to be able to do this, picking up assignments without much formal qualification, and progressing on the strength of my accumulating experience.

I have now been in this work for a quarter of a century. Since I left Germany I have not returned to live there. After living in Kenya, then Zimbabwe, and later Tanzania, I am now in Denmark where I work as a global advisor for a large international NGO. Living abroad for such a long time has certainly changed me. I have learned to feel at home in different places and cultures and to find commonalities while not pretending that I am not different. At the same time, increasingly, I have become very conscious of my ethnic and cultural origins. At 50, as a white European male I am mindful of how people look at me in my role as a humanitarian. Do they trust that I understand what they really need? Do they believe that I can add value to their lives?

Questioning my role and people's perspectives on me also lead me to reflect on how the humanitarian system is perceived. Like me, it is a creation of high-income countries and is still partly driven by this group as they are the most affluent donors to the system. Like me, it also did not start with all its knowledge, but went through critical experiences, took time to question itself, and the process made it what it is today. Arguably a lot better than when I joined it, more critical of its achievements and failures, and certainly not yet perfect. Therefore, as much as I am telling a story of my personal experience, this is a story of how the aid system got to where it is now.

## A directive and supply-driven system?

Humanitarian work is sometimes glorified as altruistic, where people selflessly assist other people. Like in many comparable professions, such as care or the emergency services, this is not necessarily the only driver of people's motivation. Like in any other job we also look for job satisfaction beyond feeling good about ourselves, and at least for me I am also very much motivated by factors that are found in any profession, such as interesting challenges and opportunities, interesting people to work with, and variety and change. I also take immense satisfaction in producing quality work that has the intended effect.

In humanitarian aid, the intended effect of our work ultimately is to improve the situation of people that have been affected by a crisis. Aid workers therefore regularly question whether we truly make a difference, and this question has certainly always been on my mind throughout the years. In our profession we have created some terminology around this, also because we have become a lot better at measuring our impact. When we measure the effect of aid, we increasingly talk about how relevant it is. This basically asks the question whether we are doing the right things to have the intended effect. For me being relevant is therefore quite fundamental, because if we do not do the right things, what is the point of doing them? In the following paragraphs, I want to reflect on my learning, and that of the humanitarian system, about how to be relevant.

I don't have any personal items on my desk at work bar one photo. It is of me surrounded by a bunch of kids. They watch me while I test water samples. It was taken in the town of Goma in what was then Zaire in early 1995, where I was a young volunteer in the response to the refugee crisis that followed the genocide in Rwanda.

The genocide in Rwanda was effectively halted in June 1994 by the incursion into the country by the exiled Rwanda Patriotic Front. Fearing retaliation, an unprecedented number of Rwandans crossed into neighbouring Zaire; within a few days, an estimated 850,000 arrived into the Goma area alone. Many had settled in makeshift camps on impenetrable volcanic rock near Lake Kivu, the only source of water. Without sanitation facilities the lake water quickly became contaminated. People started dying from cholera. Estimates go as high as 80,000 dead within a few weeks. Under intense media attention donor countries and international NGOs scrambled to respond in what was then the largest aid operation globally. They faced many factors not in their favour. The ground in the area is too hard to break and drill for water or to dig latrines. Building simple roads required skilled experts and heavy machinery. Relief goods had to arrive by air and the airport struggled to cope.

As a civil protection volunteer, I had come as part of the German government's response. When I arrived in March 1995, the humanitarian system had settled into a working balance. There were still numerous aid organizations at work, to the extent that we talked about locations in camps by using the name of the NGO that set them up. I was in charge of water quality testing and went to the camps every day. I would park on the side of the main road, where water storage tanks were located, and with no roads inside the settlements continue on foot, guided by the bare pipes that were impossible to bury into the hard ground. The latrines I encountered were often shallow and close to overflowing. This daily journey gave me a glimpse of how many different organizations were involved, but also how hard it was to provide quality assistance, even eight months into the response.

As short as the mission was, it made me question whether my work there was having any impact on people, and whether it was the right thing to do – was it relevant? Surely, everyone needed the water and food the system supplied. I remember schools and safe spaces for children, and there were health centres, and all those made sense. The underlying issues were a different ball game altogether. Essentially, we maintained a base for many of the perpetrators of the genocide, who effectively held the other refugees hostage. I often encountered men in fatigues with firearms in the camps. Sometimes I saw children with guns. The security issues in the camps were well known, but member states could not agree on a UN military mission to secure the camps.

With hindsight the operation in Goma exposed a lot of what was not working at the time in the humanitarian system. Many organizations were involved but often just worked alongside each other, each with their own individual solution. The aid operation covered the basic needs and kept everyone alive at the time but didn't solve the bigger problem. We effectively perpetuated a situation where a large number of people were held hostage by a group of perpetrators who had no interest in reconciliation back in Rwanda. And by doing that, we effectively supported their interests. As often happens in humanitarian emergencies, a multitude of issues came together, and we only patched up the worst without addressing the underlying problems.

A joint evaluation of the response[1] brought its shortfalls to the world's attention. The report became a seminal work that triggered major improvements in the aid system. Directly inspired by the evaluation's findings that many organizations worked in many different ways, with a multitude of standards, the Sphere Project was conceived in 1996, producing the set of universally accepted standards that we now apply consistently in our humanitarian work. The Active Learning Network for Accountability and Performance in Humanitarian Action (ALNAP) was borne out of the experience of the evaluation to create a platform to collectively learn from such experiences, as was the process that ultimately gave us the Core Humanitarian Standard (CHS). Today this standard is the benchmark for many aid organizations to be measured against. In a very short time, the learning from this particular humanitarian response had left a permanent mark on the humanitarian system in a very good way.

The response in Goma was therefore pivotal for the system. It was also pivotal for me. It was the moment when I realized that science was not for me. Three years later I packed up my life and moved to Nairobi as an aid worker. Running a relief base for the German government there, I learned the ropes as I went along, and over the next five years truly became a professional aid worker.

In 2002, Goma gave me a second opportunity to observe the humanitarian system in action in very different circumstances. The volcano towering over the town had erupted. Having fled in advance of the eruption, virtually the whole population of the town was across the border in Rwanda, seeking higher ground. Again, aid agencies responded quickly. Within a day or so the first supplies started coming in by air. Anticipating the need to set up camps for the displaced people, the response was geared towards supporting many people in one location. But while the humanitarian machine was still gearing up, the displaced people returned to Goma, where most buildings were still intact. Those who had lost their homes took shelter with family and friends. Camps were not an option anymore.

For about a week I witnessed the dynamics of a machine scrambling to change direction while in motion: Camp supplies like tents and material to build shelters had to be largely mothballed. Coordination meetings discussed intensely how to identify people in need in the city and how to reach them, and whether the water in the lake was safe for drinking or not. While these discussions took place, each organization did what they felt was relevant, such as drawing up lists of people in need in the area they operated in. These lists became a coveted commodity. I remember hearing the story of such a list being stolen just as the organization wanted to start distribution of food. Meanwhile people just continued to go to the lake to fetch water, and when the international aid operation finally declared that the water was safe it was almost not newsworthy.

It was again a very formative experience for me, if less so for the humanitarian system – to my knowledge there was no wider learning from the response in Goma in 2002, although agency-specific lessons learned documents can be found. This second experience in the same place certainly made me realize that we were a long way still from really understanding how to do the right thing in a humanitarian crisis.

When I decided to become a full-time aid worker, I was partly looking for adventure. The experience in Goma in 1995 was formative also in this regard, with its size, its large number of players, and the very common personality type of the 'emergency cowboy', the type of aid worker who would go to places and get things done because they knew what to do and how best to respond to an emergency. It seemed at the time that these were the qualities to have to succeed in this profession. But it was not just a personality type – when I look back, I feel it was also how agencies operated at the time. Aid agencies had their specializations, they had their pre-positioned stocks, and they had their experts on call to respond to a new emergency. This is what I saw in Goma in 1995 and in 2002, and it did the job to save lives. But increasingly I and the aid system realized that there was a lot more to aid than just saving lives.

On reflection it was not an easy realization. Someone like me who grew into the system through experience saw this very experience as the ultimate goal, which came with the desire to demonstrate that I knew what to do in any situation I would encounter. Many times, I was on assessments where I looked at a place, talked to a few people, and then kind of 'knew' what needed to be done. This was a narrow mindset, but I would dare say that in those earlier years of my aid career it was pretty common in my fellow aid workers. And I would dare say that it was pretty common in the system. Over the last decades the humanitarian system has been quite directive, often supply-driven, and very much stuck in a habit where humanitarian professionals decided what assistance was best for people.

## The power and the challenges of 'just' asking

At a conference last year someone said something very simple yet remarkable. When you think of how to do the right thing in an emergency response, pause to think what you would want if this was your own village, your own community, and you would yourself need assistance. This is a very powerful thought. It makes us think of what the right things would be for people directly affected by the crisis – how what we do is most relevant for them.

Of course, the easiest approach is to ask them. Strangely, this simple step has consistently been missing in aid responses, with various reasons why. To me the

*Figure 4.1* Volcano eruption in Goma, 2002

power of this small but crucial step is reflected in my experience after the volcano eruption in Goma in 2002. Had we asked the people who fled the lava, had we just spent a few minutes with a few of them, especially the older people, they would have told us that this was not the first time. I was told that in fact what happened after the last eruption 25 years previously was that people had also returned to their homes as soon as it was safe. Interestingly, the humanitarian operation missed that scenario at the time, and was stuck with preparations to support displacement camps when there were no displaced people left.

Asking people in crisis about what their needs are is not without risks. The way international aid works is that we are organized in 'sectors' that attract specialists in certain fields such as health, nutrition, or water and sanitation. While some agencies cover many sectors, others only specialize in a few or even just one. Ideally, in a large emergency where many aid agencies respond this should result in any kind of assistance being available. In reality, it is not, or it is complicated to organize. Therefore, when for example, an aid worker sits down with people in an emergency and asks them what they actually need there is a real risk that this aid worker or the aid agency cannot provide that. This could lead to a lot of problems for the agency, for example when people get frustrated that they cannot be assisted with what they believe they need. It is therefore often easier to come in right away with stating what the agency can do – and what it can't – and then providing what from their portfolio appears most relevant.

Letting people participate in decision-making about assistance is important. The humanitarian system has declared that it will get better at it. Nine years after the 2002 debacle in Goma the multi-agency body that governs the humanitarian system, the Inter-Agency Standing Committee (IASC), defined 'Accountability to Affected Populations' as a common principle. The IASC is quite influential, as it consists of the executive heads of 18 UN and non-UN organizations. The decisions it makes and the principles it defines are normally expected to be followed at least by its members but also by the humanitarian system as a whole, with the expectation that the major donors will only fund organizations that follow these principles. A few years later, as part of the World Humanitarian Summit in 2016, a specific agreement named the 'Grand Bargain'[2] was reached between donors to humanitarian aid and implementing organizations that included what was called the 'Participation Revolution'. Signatories to the Grand Bargain undertook to 'include people receiving aid in making the decisions which affect their lives' to make aid better and more relevant.

Sadly, the evidence shows that while it is clear that we understand how important it is to ask and listen to people affected by crises, the practice has not yet become the norm. In 2018 an NGO called Ground Truth Solutions in a study of the practices of humanitarian organizations found that 'despite commitments in the Grand Bargain and elsewhere to include people who receive aid in making decisions that affect their lives ... people affected by humanitarian crises generally do not feel included in such decisions'.[3]

Personally, I understand that it is not always easy to ask, and at times risky. For example, as I mentioned earlier, what if we cannot offer what people need? Will they get angry at us? Or what if we have to provide assistance in the midst of conflict, where we often have very little time to ask questions and have a meaningful dialogue because it may not be safe to stay in a place for longer than absolutely necessary? These are valid and often very real and practical obstacles. However, they can also be overcome. If everybody, every aid organization and aid worker, is committed to asking as much as is possible and safe, and collectively all organisations are committed to then provide the assistance that is needed, there is a lot less risk for individual aid workers and single agencies. We may not be able to always do it, but we can certainly do it a lot more often.

So why don't we? I believe there are more fundamental issues at stake, and I think the evidence points to the business model of the humanitarian system. For our work we rely on public funds and those funds rely on the public to pay attention to a particular crisis. Very prominent crises are likely to get more attention and more funding than the others. The attention span for any crisis is usually quite short, and we are often under pressure to demonstrate results quickly and visibly. This is not the best environment to spend time on consulting people affected by these crises, nor is it a good environment for being open-minded to what type of intervention is needed. Unfortunately, the general mindset of the system in these situations is still to rely on proven interventions and making assumptions rapidly on what is needed, to catch the momentum of global attention and consequent funds for our work. This does not always lead to people feeling their highest-priority needs are met.

This is what I saw in Goma in 1995 and in 2002. The failure to intervene in the genocide in Rwanda was such a blemish on the conscience of donor countries that the refugee crisis in neighbouring Zaire became an opportunity for redemption, to be seen to be acting decisively. It is clear from the evaluation report I mentioned that the response in Goma in the first months was driven by donor countries who felt the need to act, especially as the international media were reporting from Goma from the very first days and throughout the deadly wave of cholera in the camps. Years later, in 2002, the volcano caught everyone by surprise and agencies resident in Goma were themselves displaced and affected by the emergency, while additional money for the response was made available quickly. With a lot of international attention on a fast response there was no incentive to engage people in meaningful participation in this situation either.

What would have happened if we had asked the people in these two scenarios what they really wanted? I can only speculate, but I am certain that it would not have quite been what we gave them at the time. In the situation in Goma after the genocide in Rwanda they may have asked for a safe way of returning home, which would have entailed the international community providing a large and well-organized security force together with political mediation to address the issues that kept people in camps. We may not have needed so many organizations to sustain these camps for several years. In the situation in Goma after the earthquake people may have asked for money and materials to re-build their homes and the water system of the town. This would have entailed a very different type of assistance with little need for aid workers but actual cash for families and small businesses.

Over the last decade I was lucky to work as an evaluator, and evaluators have the privilege of asking many questions to many people. And they have the benefit of hindsight. For me, doing evaluations was an eye opener. Observing ongoing humanitarian responses or their results I realized how much discrepancy remains between what people really need and what they get from aid agencies. A more recent example comes to mind from an evaluation in South Sudan only a few years ago. An agency had installed water taps in a small town for people to come and fetch water in canisters to carry back to their houses. When we visited them, we noted a small group of women repeatedly filling many canisters at these water points and carrying them away. We asked the women what it was about, and it turned out they did not take all this water to their families but to the houses of wealthier people who were willing to pay for this service. It turns out that providing free water was not sufficient, and these women were looking for a way to generate income for their other priority needs. Had they been asked beforehand the organizations working there may have realized that family income was as much a need as clean water, which was not met by just providing these public taps.

As far as my personal experience goes, this last decade has convinced me that asking people before assisting them is the key to doing the right things, to being relevant. Of course, it will not always be possible, but we must do it a lot more often. Of course, cultural differences may be barriers to overcome, as will be interpreting what is said correctly. But taking the step of asking is important, and we can learn along the way of how to make sure that we not only listen, but that we also hear what people are telling us. The Grand Bargain means that increasingly donors are supporting and expecting more meaningful participation, giving us the space and capacity to do it. There still have to be a lot more incentives for meaningful participation, for example by recognizing that it often entails different approaches to identifying needs (we can only decide what the priority needs are after we have spoken to people) and more flexible funding (we can only plan our activities once we have found out what the priority needs are).

Despite the challenges we are going in the right direction. As I write this, the COVID-19 crisis is still unfolding in the poorest of countries. Being relevant in a global crisis is a different challenge altogether. When the pandemic hit Europe and North America, we were all wondering how it would affect countries already experiencing a humanitarian crisis, and in the beginning, we extrapolated from the experience in our countries. We were concerned about hospital capacities, about respirators, and about personal protective equipment, all of which were severely short in poorer countries. They are, and these shortages cost a lot of lives, and in some ways the pandemic played out in a similar fashion as elsewhere. It certainly needs as robust a health response as possible. However, the pandemic is also a time to ask people about their concerns in the face of it, and what they think they would need. Many of us in the humanitarian system did just that. And the results are instructive in their own right. Beyond the health response, the economic effect of shutdowns, the inability to go to work, the inability to earn a living and feed a family often dominates people's concerns in countries where there are few economic opportunities to start with. If your family is at risk of starving if you don't work, the risk of catching an illness becomes relative. By asking people in advance of being affected, we saw very quickly that we needed to plan for responding to a lot more than just a health crisis. If we now look at the topics dominating the headlines around international aid for COVID-19-affected poorer countries, we are very much addressing these other dimensions. We as a system have learned, and it is so good to see that it has given us so much more relevance in how we support people affected by the pandemic.

## Much more than just 'ticking the box'

On my journey in the aid system I have learned that asking people in crisis what is best for them makes it more likely to be relevant, more likely to result in doing the right things. I also believe that, at least in principle, and increasingly in practice, the humanitarian system has learned this too. I believe there is a strong argument that asking those affected and giving people what they think is best for them is the most effective way of providing meaningful assistance. We still have a long way to go and I sometimes worry when I see how much we continue to struggle with the basics and often barely make a simple complaints system work in a meaningful way. A lot is left to be done.

But I also feel that my story is important beyond this practical argument for strengthening participation in aid. There is a risk that participation becomes a 'box-ticking' exercise that we do because we have to, but we don't change the way we work. That we work in this way, directive and supply-driven, because these are the power structures of the aid system and they won't change – not even if we know that people in crises need something other than what we have to offer.

It is important that we see participation, talking to people in crises as equals, including them in our planning and decision-making, and making them part of the solution rather than passive recipients, as a fundamental right. When I look back, it is intriguing how dominant the aid system is, and how little consideration over time it has given to the people it aims to assist. The language that we still widely use is indicative of this – we speak of 'aid recipients', or 'beneficiaries', or, even in the very topic I am writing about, 'affected populations'. All these are passive terms for people who are usually capable and empowered individuals that happen to have been exposed to a severe challenge and lost some of their means and resources as a consequence. Like everyone else they have the right to be seen as competent partners and not just passive recipients of assistance. Many organizations recognize the need to shift this perspective, and more of us now talk about 'clients' when we speak of people in need. Appreciating that they are our real clients, not the donors that provide our funding, is a fundamental step to changing the culture of the system.

The dominance of the humanitarian system is largely driven by the substantial money that we bring into countries. In the mind of people who may have lost everything they had this gives us immense power. This power divide is hard to overcome, and it takes this big cultural shift. When we ask, we need to be serious about addressing concerns or we will just be paying lip service to a process.

There are a lot of ingrained habits in the aid system, and I feel that the underlying confidence of knowing better, and knowing what to do, continues to afflict our collective mindset. Together with the power we wield this can be harmful. The real challenge for us, for the system, is therefore a lot more fundamental. We have to change a mindset, a business model, a culture where we are the experts and those in crisis are the victims who we assist. And this will be a lot harder than just spending some time talking to people and setting up feedback hotlines. It will require a cultural change in our industry and may change the way we work altogether.

I believe we can do it. Having had the privilege of living through the evolution of the aid system for a quarter of a century and seeing how much it has changed for the better gives me hope. The system does not always shine, and sometimes we get it badly wrong. But we often get it right, and we get it right a lot more often than we did 25 years ago. The institutions and structures that we have now give us core standards, allow us to be more principled, and make us more accountable to people in crisis than we have ever been. To me this shows that we can change, and even change our culture to be even better and even more relevant. And I intend to stick around to see it happen.

## Notes

1 Eriksson, J., Adelman, H., Borton, J., Christensen, H., Kumar, K., Suhrke, A., … Wohlgemuth, L. (1996). *The International Response to Conflict and Genocide: Lessons from the Rwanda Experience edited by David Millwood* (Vol. 9). https://doi.org/10.1093/jrs/9.3.334.
2 Interagency Standing Committee The Grand Bargain (official website), accessed 9 August 2020, https://interagencystandingcommittee.org/grand-bargain.
3 Humanitarian Voice Index – Participation Revolution?, accessed 9 August 2020, https://humanitarianvoiceindex.org/policy-briefs/2018/12/04/participant-revolution.

# 5 Flexibility in fragility

*Helen Barclay-Hollands*

## Who are you?

When it rains here near the equator it pours. Not just heavy rain but spectacular storms with lightning shooting across the sky and strong winds forcing everything in their wake to bend and submit to their force. Blossoms and branches are wrenched from their source and flung far from their roots. After the storm, perfect petals are found strewn on the ground and branches litter pathways, reminiscent of the brutality wrought by the wind and rain. However, as I look across my garden, I notice that, despite the pressure, all these plants have an ability to bend and flex, to resist and bounce back. Not only this, but powerful root systems connect plants and trees to one another, providing a network that underpins their flexibility and contributes to their strength. Mother Nature has developed a powerful resilience to the most violent of shocks.

In the midst of the COVID-19 pandemic we are all feeling pushed and pummeled by the storm raging on around us. We are having to bend and flex in ways we were never asked to before. As I look at the natural world and the beauty in its resilience, I also see that reflected in the region where I live: bearing crisis upon crisis, the people here show a remarkable ability to weather the fiercest storms. They are used to the unpredictability of the context and the fragility they face on a regular basis. Having lived in the East Africa region for over six years I have learnt a lot from the people here, who have taught me just as much about myself as about their context.

The Democratic Republic of Congo (DRC) is often thought of as a "fragile context". The Organisation for Economic Co-operation and Development (OECD) gives the following definition:

> [A] fragile region or state has weak capacities to carry out basic governance functions, and lacks the ability to develop mutually constructive relations with society. Fragile regions or states are also more vulnerable to internal or external shocks such as economic crisis or natural disaster. Fragility refers to a wide array of situation: countries in crisis, countries at war, reconstruction context, humanitarian and natural crises, situations of extreme poverty.[1]

In DRC, this is evident in poor infrastructure, inadequate health services, limited access to water and visible poverty. The reality of working in these contexts is complex, with gaps in access to basic services for the population resulting in a variety of negative consequences. Living and working in these environments requires flexibility as no day is ever the same and planning or predicting a day or a week ahead often feels futile when so many external factors can come and disrupt our best-laid plans.[2]

However, it is possible to work and be effective in fragile contexts by maintaining a flexible approach as well as keeping one eye on the horizon for the next change about to come your way. We are all having to learn a similar lesson in flexibility during this global pandemic as our "normal" ways of working have been severely disrupted. In the midst of this crisis we are all feeling the frustration of having plans changed, and when we look ahead all we see is uncertainty leading to fear, panic and a sense of hopelessness.

My friends will tell you I am brave, courageous even, to work and travel in conflict zones and be committed to such a challenging and demanding career. The reality is challenging indeed, with humanitarian work focused on reaching the most vulnerable in some of the world's most dangerous places. I would say that I am driven by the challenge and the desire to support others in finding a way out of the crisis. I am also fueled by curiosity, eager to learn from others and find out more about their reality and their world. I am motivated by a desire to find solutions to these challenging and complex issues, and have understood along the way that the answers must come from the communities themselves. I have learned, and re-learned, many valuable lessons along the way.

As the palm trees in my garden flex and bend to the elements, I too have learnt that flexibility and understanding of the context is key to having an effective impact in fragile contexts. Nature here has an ability to survive the storms or scorching heat. It appears that despite this hardship nature is able to flourish.

My career started with an internship in a non-profit organization based just outside London. Someone on the disaster management team heard me speaking French to a colleague in passing and made a recommendation for me to pursue an upcoming opportunity. A few months later I found myself on a plane to Haiti, my first real deployment to a disaster zone. I arrived in the aftermath of the 2010 earthquake, a context still bearing the scars of destruction, exacerbated by years of poor infrastructure, weak governance and inadequate service provision, and not yet starting to rebuild. The mantra then across the humanitarian sector was "build back better" but arriving in a country with a historically fragile infrastructure I was often uncertain if the buildings were being torn down or built up.

My career then followed a francophone route to Chad, Central African Republic (CAR) and most recently DRC, where I have worked for the past six years. Throughout this trajectory the phrase "build back better" haunted me as I worked in increasingly complex and fragile settings that seemed locked in a constant state of crisis. What did it mean to be sustainable when the context was so volatile? Was it even possible? Here are some musings on what has kept me working in these settings for almost a decade.

I write this from the shores of Lake Kivu, where I currently live with my husband, toddler, dog, cats, chickens, and a goat named Carlos. All thoughts and reflections are my own and not representative of any organization that I work for or have worked for previously.

## What is the story?

My journey as a humanitarian started with theoretical learning. I studied and researched deeply during my master's degree studies, delving into international development theory, learning about humanitarian law and international frameworks. I graduated with a greater understanding of the mechanics of the humanitarian "machine" and the aid system as a whole, how it functions as well as some areas of obvious dysfunction, but was not fully prepared for the reality I would face in the field.

A master's thesis in international development, focusing on community empowerment, understanding conflict, and political economy had informed my expectations of what humanitarian work would look like at the field level. As a "newbie" first arriving in Haiti and the chaos that ensued following the 2010 earthquake I soon grasped that, whilst this theoretical knowledge was important, it was not as useful as the local knowledge I soon gleaned from my Haitian colleagues.

The first and most important lesson I learnt was that local solutions to local problems are the most effective. Project design and the reality of implementing humanitarian programs in a complex context such as Haiti could only work if adapted to the local context. Trying to make sense of the history, politics and present reality of a new place was a steep learning curve, yet essential to ensure that any intervention would align with community needs. For the communities the complexity came from bearing repeated crises (both political and natural with the 2010 earthquake followed by hurricane season and a cholera outbreak in quick succession), and their daily struggle to survive as their means to respond and "build back better" had been eroded by the repeated shocks they had weathered.

When visiting a shelter project the local Haitian construction engineer explained to me why some houses were accepted by families and others rejected. The design needed to align with the local needs and houses had to be built with two doors (to let the spirits in and out) and if not, the community would refuse to live in them. Setting up water system rehabilitation projects took me on hikes for hours in the blazing heat to find spring sites with the local team, who were the only ones with the knowledge to find the solutions and identify the sites of local water sources. This was even more important after the earthquake as natural spring sites had shifted with the movement of the earth. I quickly understood that these efforts were essential to the success of any project.

In fragile contexts, implementation is also often beset by political upheaval and conflict. These places have weakened government support, with few functioning systems in place to support the population. In both CAR and DRC, the best-laid plans for humanitarian project implementation had to be put on hold because of resurgent outbreaks of violence. One visit to an internally displaced persons camp in Bangui, CAR, required security clearance from the UN just to reach the site, only to find after a short visit that the return route was now unsafe due to fighting on the road between two opposing groups, and we would have to wait or find an alternative route home. Delivering projects in such an environment required a huge amount of personal and organizational flexibility. At the same time the communities expressed their desperate need for assistance, as they tried to survive in camp conditions and often having to flee or move again when violence broke out again. We had the privilege to return to (relatively) safe accommodation each evening whilst the communities we were trying to reach were left uncertain of what the night would bring.

The reality of working in these fragile contexts presents additional stresses and strains on the working environment and on your own personal resilience to such pressures. Travel to project sites, hosting visitors, even managing staff in such contexts can all be sources of stress and uncertainty, as the situation can be unpredictable and change at any moment. Working in these contexts means working at the pace of an unrelenting emergency response over the course of several months and even years. This takes its toll, both on those deployed and on the communities living in these areas over the long term.

In order to survive and even thrive in such settings as a humanitarian you need to build your own personal and professional resilience to respond adequately and quickly when the need arises. Burnout, depression and post-traumatic stress are common in this profession, being exposed to stress on the frontlines of conflict. Building in coping strategies to find ways to manage this stress is essential. I've often wondered how communities in these settings keep going despite the relentless challenges they face, and from my observations it often comes down to deep-rooted links within their own community, or their own personal faith, or simply family being close by to support. As international staff moving to new contexts and often for the short term, it is often hard to give up the networks of family and friends back at home to take on a role in a challenging situation. I wonder if this is why as humanitarians there is a unique camaraderie, recognizing the need for a network, support, a community to keep going. Many of my closest friends are those with whom I have shared challenging experiences in humanitarian settings, a bond that is forged under stress, but that has built a strong foundation for a long-lasting friendship. A natural human need to feel connected and understood in these challenging circumstances brings us together, both as humanitarians but also in sharing powerfully some of the common challenges of living and working in the local context.

Ultimately, however, as international staff, we are only committing to these tough places for the short term. We have the choice and the ability to leave, whether for a "break" or at the end of a contract, or simply when we feel it is time to move on. This privilege is not something to be taken lightly, as those we work with, staff, communities, local leaders, do not have the same opportunities. On one hand this gives humanitarians the ability to bring a breadth of experience from multiple places where they have lived and worked, but on the other hand does not allow for us to engage to a depth and level of understanding that is often needed to truly understand the context. I have lived and worked in eastern DRC for over six years, and yet I still feel that I fail to fully capture the nuances of the local culture and norms.

This is why as humanitarians we need to adapt how we operate in these settings, recognizing the value-add that local staff and expertise bring to addressing some of the issues at play in complex crises. Adapting to work and life in fragile contexts requires flexibility and understanding of what needs to change and when. It is also a process of recognizing that our preconceptions as visitors or foreigners in a new context need to be reevaluated. It is ultimately a process of un-learning and re-learning to ensure that as humanitarians we have the flexibility to function well in these settings.

Taking on a leadership role within the humanitarian sector I learned the hard way to manage my perfectionist expectations and to listen and learn most of the time, coaching or guiding rather than teaching along the way. I worked hard to maintain the principle of learning from local solutions, and found this can also be applied to local capacities. In doing so I discovered many new (and better ways) of doing things from my local colleagues. This challenged my own preconceptions and was often an uncomfortable process as I understood my role to be more of a facilitator, maximizing the local capacity that existed already to ensure success in each specific context.

Adapting to the context is a daily challenge. The more I learnt about the reality for staff and communities, the better my understanding of what needed to be adapted in our own approaches as humanitarians. I learnt much from my colleagues, those who had lived through previous crises, been displaced, lived in camps and fled on foot from violent conflict themselves. Their motivation to continue to respond to other vulnerable communities is inspiring, particularly as they face daily struggles and frustrations for themselves and their families as they work in these fragile contexts.

## What are your reflections?

Flexibility and the willingness to adapt to a new way of working is essential in the light of the COVID-19 pandemic. The "usual" approaches in programming and operations are being challenged as they cannot be delivered or implemented in the same way, and in turn, perceptions and assumptions must be held in question. It is an uncomfortable reality and yet a necessary one as the world changes rapidly before our very eyes. This is especially important for humanitarians who are adapting to a crisis that is transforming our usual ways of working.

In my experience, responding to crisis often means coming with preconceived ideas and models of what works, either taken from theory or from previous experiences. It is hard to separate experience from bringing the solution to the issue ahead, and yet it is necessary to take a humbling journey and question those assumptions at the outset. My own educational background equipped me with theories and case studies of what has worked (or not worked) in many different contexts around the world. Yet I often came up against significant challenges during implementation if I did not stop first to listen to those whom we were trying to assist and learn from their own perspective what needed to be done. I learnt quickly that my own ideas were insufficient unless I focused on fostering a dialogue and finding local solutions to local problems. My educational background provided theory, but it was the communities who provided their reality.

Creativity and innovation often emerged through dialogue and I found myself learning so much more about what needed to be done through asking a few questions and really listening to what was happening. The feedback from the community often required us to adapt and change the ways we were doing things, in order to become more effective. At a community water point installed in south DRC, the local engineer told me how the choice of tap needed to be changed to ensure replacements could be found on the local market in order that they could repair it easily and cheaply. Communities were empowered to find their own solutions and these were the most sustainable.

To help me avoid the danger of my own assumptions leading me in unhelpful directions I ask "why?". I often inadvertently make my own assumptions as to why things are a certain way, but unless I ask why, I can never learn the real reason behind it. I might feel like a toddler asking "why" repetitively but this persistent question has helped me get to the core of an issue and understand the root causes of certain situations or events. On the long, slow bumpy road out to a project site in eastern DRC I discovered from our local staff that our proposed nutrition project also needed to find a way to address issues of land access for the local population. They explained to me that tensions surrounding the protected national park boundary and the active armed groups in the area trying to seize land had left the local community with nowhere to farm. Moreover, the only land available was hilly, rocky and had poor soil quality, contributing to low crop yields and thus high rates of malnutrition in the community. Being able to identify and start to address the root causes of issues is important in ensuring that project interventions are both responding to the needs and also addressing the longer-term dynamics.

Adapting to the context around me is one of the hardest things to do. I recognize that I come to any new setting or situation with my own preconceived notions and expectations of how things "should" be. I might feel I have an expertise to help things improve and be done "better", and it can be very difficult to accept when these ideas are not immediately accepted or adopted. We need to remove our own preconceptions before we can move ahead and enter into a space where there is a possibility to adapt and learn from others. I was told on one occasion by a colleague that I was "just a white girl who would never understand", which was tough to take at the time but held a certain truth to it that forced me to question again my own culture and assumptions that needed to be addressed. I learnt that true adaptability requires humility and an ability to challenge and even remove one's own preconceptions to be able to move forward. It must then be a co-creation effort, and if as humanitarians we fail to acknowledge and include the communities at the heart of what we do, the impact will not last long.

Since independence, DRC (formerly Zaire) has been beset by political upheaval and civil war and the Congolese people have borne the brunt of the fallout. Two

Congo wars (1996–1997 and 1998–2003) followed in quick succession, leaving a country broken and in turmoil, at the cost of millions of lives. An estimated 5 million people died, not as a direct result of the violence, but often from easily treatable diseases such as malaria, typhoid fever and diarrhea. Where conflict took place, people fled and were displaced, moving to makeshift camps or poorly resourced areas where they had no shelter, water or access to health care. In eastern DRC, where factions of over 100 militia groups are still active, the same trend continues, with women and children often suffering most as a result. It is a context often described as a complex humanitarian emergency, beset by repeated acute crises, layered one on top of the other, exacerbating the fragile situation further.

In this context that has suffered multiple crises over decades, I saw how communities came together and adapted by capitalizing on their interconnectedness. During the Congo wars and even currently, a vicious form of attack by armed groups has been to systematically pillage and rape, destroying communities and families. This infamous practice ripped apart the social fabric of communities, with repercussions that continue still today. I have heard countless stories from women and children that have broken me deeply, and yet at the same time seen communities finding ways to rebuild and come together to tackle the issue. I visited a 14-year-old girl who had been raped, and then given birth to the child, tell me in tears how she wanted so much to be a teacher one day, but now felt unable to return to school. Her mother, struggling with another mouth to feed, had set up her own business with the help of the local women's association, selling homemade peanut butter and bread in order to find a way to get her daughter back in school. Groups of women formed cooperatives to generate income, faith groups rallied together to tackle stigma and advocate for provision of medical treatment for women and girls who suffered from this abuse.

In addition, the depth of the impact of this program came from facilitating open conversations about the gender inequalities present in the community, and together common objectives were discussed and put into place to address the root causes of these unequal power dynamics between men and women. Deep-seated imbalances in perceptions between genders were discussed and the community themselves began to understand and challenge their own cultural norms that had long been accepted. It was strange to realize that this was the same process I had myself been through in tackling my own preconceptions about the culture and context. I observed the changes taking place slowly, led by the community members themselves and united around a common cause to protect children and women from any future abuse. The true sustainability of this program came in us partnering with key leaders and the women to adapt and build a better future that was led themselves, not just by responding to the immediate needs we had first identified.

I saw how changes in the climate are having a devastating impact on crops and harvests for a primarily pastoralist population. Communities formed cooperatives to enable farmer training schools and discuss innovations along with humanitarian actors to protect crops from extreme heat or unexpected rainfall during the planting season. At the request of the farmer cooperatives, the humanitarian actors bought additional resources, in the form of improved seed varieties and plants to prevent erosion. The interconnectedness of these initiatives boosted crop yields and allowed the community to store the harvest and seeds for later sale and planting, which boosted the income of the farmers and the community as a whole. The leader of the cooperative proudly showed me rows upon rows of onions and garlic they were storing as seed for later seasons, or to sell when the market prices were higher. I was impressed with how quickly the cooperatives put to use the simple techniques that had been demonstrated and multiplied their own productivity as a result. Together they were able to take their learning forward and expand it further. In this case they had the ability to adapt but needed us to support with tools and resources to boost their capacity to adapt and weather the changes in the climate to support their own livelihoods.

In the midst of an Ebola epidemic I saw again how interconnectedness of communities helped to tackle stigma around the virus by ensuring that local leaders were equipped with the correct public health information to tackle rumors. This was the tenth Ebola outbreak in DRC's history, but the first time it took place in an area troubled by years of conflict, and during a sensitive presidential election period. Misinformation was spreading fast and contributing to the spread of the virus, but trusted role models became the catalyst for change. At one community event, trusted local leaders asked us why humanitarians had brought Ebola to their community, accusing external actors of inventing the virus simply to make money. Despite the tough questions and evident misinformation, it allowed the space for questions to be answered and public health messaging to be shared. Bringing together humanitarian partners and the communities broke down barriers of mistrust and led to powerful behavior change within the community itself, eventually changing the health outcomes of communities over time. It took time and was challenging to overcome some of the preconceptions held by the community of humanitarian actors and even the local health providers. As the outbreak continued and more and more were affected, the "fake news" and rumors were challenged and gradually communities began to trust in the prevention measures and tackle the spread of the virus themselves. It is an ongoing challenge for humanitarians in the current COVID-19 outbreak who face similar challenges and rejections of the public health messages that are being shared. As with Ebola, many preconceptions are that humanitarians themselves have brought the disease in order to make money out of the situation.

In all of these contexts, humanitarians have to face the deep-seated mistrust communities have towards external actors. You only have to walk a few meters down the street here to hear the word "muzungu" shouted ("foreigner"), often accompanied by a request for money, or "biscuit" or "chupa" (bottle). The perception is that foreigners are here to give, and leave again. A legacy of financial contribution but little long-term impact only serves to reinforce this. External support may bring some benefits but can also contribute to perceptions that outside actors are responsible for causing the problem if not managed and anticipated well. It is tough as an individual to recognize that my role is also deeply intertwined in this broken aid system, and therefore as a humanitarian I have a responsibility to use my experience, and my learning, to contribute where I can to make a positive difference. We ourselves as humanitarians need to reflect internally on how we can "build back better", not just in the communities we serve, but in improving how we function as a system and a sector.

I share these examples to show how crucial it is to build on the interconnectedness between humanitarian agencies and the communities they serve. Often in the midst of a crisis there is an impetus to act fast and see immediate results. In the short term this is necessary and possible when life-saving work is required. However, for this life-saving work to be sustainable, particularly in complex settings such as DRC, energy and resources need to be channeled into building and sustaining trust relationships with communities. This requires sensitivity, flexibility and humility. Moreover, as the stories above show, it is when the communities themselves come together and take the lead that change takes place, and often remains for the longer term. This in turn helps to foster adaptability and focus on local solutions.

Yet, adapting is difficult. It takes time and resources. Constraints on funding often prioritize short-term solutions and focus on the immediate life-saving activities. Funding streams are ear-marked for certain activities, often with different sources funding emergency response and other sources funding longer-term development. Short-term projects end abruptly, leaving communities struggling to address some longer-term needs in the hope that another source of support will come in to address the gap. It has often been frustrating trying to mobilize funding for programs that provide the much-needed flexibility for communities; scaling up in emergencies and scaling back in calmer times, when donor funding does not follow the same dynamics. In fragile contexts when crisis upon crisis continues to hit communities, the humanitarian sector must think more deeply about the impact of the cyclical funding that fails to address the root causes of the problem.

Part of the challenge also lies in our own ability to adapt and learn as humanitarians. I have seen many aid projects and program interventions focus only on learning at the end of a project, with an evaluation conducted long after the activities are completed. Too often these lessons learnt are archived and forgotten about or rely simply on the institutional memory of certain staff and are rarely considered for the next new project. I have found well-documented recommendations after a project has started that were never integrated into the design to make improvements. This is often also due to short-term contracts of staff, who leave before the next project starts, taking with them their valuable insights.

This slows decision making and often results in "top-down" processes being reinforced as the authority for decisions is ascribed to a donor or perhaps an external actor not familiar with or present within the context. Therefore, the ability to adapt, or retain flexibility, is severely limited and can lead to a sense of dissatisfaction on the part of the communities who are expecting to benefit. Projects and interventions cannot adapt easily when the context changes and therefore their impact can be limited. Delays and frustrations arise, and often communities feel disempowered, particularly when their decisions are seemingly not considered. For example, an initial assessment reveals that there is a need for school classrooms to be built, dilapidated by seasons of heavy rain and limited maintenance. However, funding is only available for water and sanitation projects and not school classrooms, leaving the community feeling that their needs are not being addressed. For both communities and humanitarian actors it can be frustrating, feeling unable to adapt as quickly as the situation requires.

Moreover, within the humanitarian sector, there is a lack of a systematic way of integrating community feedback, and adapting accordingly can perversely do more harm than good. Projects then fail to meet their desired results or have sustainable impact, and a new design or approach is then attempted to respond to new needs that were identified when the original project failed to respond or adapt to arising needs. A cycle of implementation rather than learning and adaptation continues and, despite the mantra "build back better", a repeated cycle of projects and programs is proposed. In my first deployment to Haiti, shelter projects multiplied quickly, but even a year after the earthquake I saw the same construction malpractice (watering down of cement) taking place for some local constructions, one of the root causes of much of the destruction caused in 2010 when buildings collapsed so quickly because of poor construction techniques. It seemed to me that, despite the best efforts of the humanitarian sector, limited access to resources and training meant that many previous practices would simply return once the response had finished.

The short-term nature of the response in Haiti and in many other contexts limits the potential for a longer-term impact and change to take place in some of these settings. It is out of this frustration with some of the limitations in the current system that I believe fostering a mindset of adaptive management and community-centered engagement, along with community feedback, could lead to many errors and mistakes in project design and implementation being avoided. If the humanitarian sector became more agile and adaptable, taking stock regularly of the situation and learning from others, this in turn could transform the impact taking place in many fragile contexts. If as humanitarians we can look beyond short-term response and how to support projects that can adapt to shifts and changes in these places, this might be key to greater success. It is this adaptability and learning that is needed as we respond to the rapidly changing situation as a result of the spread of COVID-19.

However, meaningfully maintaining a mindset of adaptability and flexibility requires building trust with a community, meaning a longer-term relationship is required. Responses are short term and often in a crisis there is little time to listen and learn from others. In almost all projects I have worked on, good practice is to conduct assessments with the communities beforehand, as well as during the project, yet many of these consultations are brief and lack the depth of engagement required to fully understand the nuances of the context. Urgent needs distract from taking the time to look deeper and engage more meaningfully, and with external pressures to deliver, the result is that projects are limited in the positive impact that they can bring. In Haiti, the short-term nature of many of the responses over several years has led to an ingrained dependency on aid, and has undermined both the trust in external actors (that they will bring something meaningful) and in their own communities (that they can survive without external aid). As a result, communities are often left feeling neglected when a project finishes and humanitarian actors leave to address more pressing needs elsewhere. This fuels distrust of humanitarian actors, particularly in areas where communities have experienced multiple acute crises.

Tackling this distrust means relying on those who know the context the best: local staff and communities. This means allowing them to lead and make decisions alongside the community. This sounds logical, but in practice, when the culture around humanitarian funding is based on transparency and strict contracting agreements, creating space for this trust-building is severely restricted. In a fragile context, where needs are high, incidences of fraud and corruption further compound this compliance and in turn create a risk-averse culture. I have seen local staff overlooked for a leadership role as it is deemed that international staff will manage risk more objectively and effectively. This may be the case in some contexts, but it also discourages professional development and trust-building within a local context. This dynamic within the humanitarian system where both agility and adaptability are deemed as essential capabilities, yet risk management is rigidly enforced, often means operating in these contexts can be immensely frustrating. I feel that there is scope to review the balance between these seemingly opposing priorities to ensure that humanitarian response can be improved.

We are now facing the reality of operating in a COVID-19 environment with travel restrictions and limited ability for international staff to reach some of these contexts for a more localized response. This will require reflection on how we operate and who takes the lead. The reality is that now, more than ever, there is a need to promote local solutions to local problems (equipping local partners, NGOs or communities to take the lead in the response and drive their own development). Working closely alongside communities in DRC allowed me to see how they could influence change in a way that international actors would fail to do so, simply because of their in-depth local knowledge. Moreover, allowing for community members and leaders to direct their own development through active community participation and ownership only serves to strengthen the response. This will allow for more flexibility and agility in responses, as local staff and communities will be able to quickly identify their particular needs and respond. Local communities are always the first responders in a crisis. Yet for this to happen there also needs to be much greater understanding and review of the risks inherent in this, and much more willingness on the part of international humanitarian actors to allow for this shift of power and decision making to be locally led.

Trusting in local staff and in the communities to be able to bring solid solutions to a crisis or to tackle the root causes means listening to their voices. Meaningful open channels for feedback are essential, yet often are failing in many programs. Often limited to complaint management, these channels do not provide for open conversation and dialogue. I think sometimes we are uncomfortable as humanitarians in having our interventions challenged. It takes additional time and effort, and if a project is already designed and approved there is little incentive to have that challenged and face a re-design. When many projects are donor-funded with specific objectives, it can be complicated to gain approval for changes to be made and risk not delivering on the agreed objectives. An open acknowledgment that an approach has failed takes incredible humility, ability and willingness to change. Coupled with the fear that failed programs might result in reduced funding, the incentive to open up to constructive criticism is severely hampered.

I feel that honoring the dignity of the community is essential, and lifts up their voices to inform a humanitarian response. In the humanitarian sector, our underlying belief is that we are coming to "help". We are reminded that the communities are our "clients" and without them there would be no humanitarian response, that we are deeply and intricately interconnected. This requires an openness to be challenged, to foster a meaningful dialogue and discussion. This means dedicated time in the community, taking time to hear all voices, regardless of gender and age, and even ethnicity in some contexts. It can be tiring, but very rewarding to sit and listen to community perspectives. I often found myself sitting in the heat of the day for several hours to gather valuable feedback that would support project development. This time and effort put in to discussing and listening helps to strengthen local capacity, leadership and ownership. Coming together from different perspectives brings new ideas and innovation, a melting pot of potential solutions. The humanitarian sector will not solve these complex problems, communities will. We cannot be adaptive alone.

For true adaptation to happen I believe there is a need for a mindset and behavior shift. Thinking beyond what we think we already know to find adaptability. If as humanitarians we only focus on fixing our own internal shortcomings we fail to see the huge value-add that comes from working together with others to find collective outcomes that can bring powerful results. When adapting a project recently in eastern DRC, the main focus was to listen and learn from the community about their needs. It took time, but surely enough, the resulting integration of water facilities into schools and the improved seed varieties for farmers transformed the project and it continues to have positive results in the communities today. This shows how important it is to support local communities to lead local response and recovery efforts. Working together with communities who bring to the table incredible strength and depth of character enables their voices to be heard in a meaningful way, and opens up the scope for learning and transformation of humanitarian approaches into a more collaborative space.

This mindset and behavior shift cannot happen if there is not already a culture of flexibility and resilience. I am continually inspired and challenged by the depth of character expressed by my DRC colleagues and the communities I meet. Here in the midst of COVID-19 there is not despair, but their ability to shoulder another crisis is wearing thin. Over years of working alongside remarkable local staff I am continually inspired by their resilience despite the challenges they face, persevering despite not always being given the space to have their voices heard. For example, many meetings at the UN I attended did not feature nearly enough representation from local staff or locally led organizations. They are experts in the context and often have the equivalent if not more years of experience than many international staff. They bring a powerful inner strength and resilience to the table, and I believe that it is our role as humanitarians to listen, build up their capacity to respond, and support them in finding a way forward.

Flexibility is essential for working in a fragile context or to a crisis such as the COVID-19 pandemic. Flexibility allows us to change rapidly and respond to evolving needs. In addition, resilience is required in these settings to weather the shocks and ride out the storm. The ability to bend and bounce back quickly despite external pressures is key to survival and even to thriving in these environments. Moreover, finding new solutions and innovation comes from working together with local communities to find creative ways to solve existing challenges. Each have their part to play, and by bringing together flexibility and resilience we can find innovative ways of adapting together.

## Why are your reflections important for the overall humanitarian practice?

Fragility is complex and complicated. Every setting is influenced by a myriad of factors that impact how the situation evolves. This means we need to have a new way of thinking and learning in order to respond adequately. In the light of COVID-19, there is even more uncertainty globally and tried and tested project designs or approaches may not fit when the situation is fast moving and unpredictable. We must learn to be agile and responsive where there is fragility. This requires a humility to learn and to listen, and to challenge our own expectations.

Over the past ten years working in the humanitarian sector, my expectations and perceptions have been repeatedly challenged. This has taught me a lot about myself, but also about the nature of the work. There is a need to pilot new approaches and test ideas, yet in order to simply adapt our approaches greater flexibility from donors is required, in terms of both funding and compliance measures. Despite reservations to the contrary, it is indeed possible to maintain transparency and accountability without limiting agility. If as humanitarians we fail to foster this space for innovation, and allow for co-creation with communities, they will continue to feel disempowered, and it perpetuates the idea that their voice and dignity are not valued.

Within the humanitarian sector the interconnectedness of international actors and communities we serve cannot be ignored. As the world changes and shifts, with potentially huge implications for humanitarian aid globally, now is the time to ensure an open dialogue with communities to share ownership and start to foster a culture of collaboration and trust. This requires a concerted effort to invest the time in co-creation of initiatives and further empower communities. Coming to the table with preconceived notions and ideas fails to recognize the strength and resilience communities bring, and so there is a further un-learning and re-learning process that must take place.

Meaningful dialogue with communities and a culture of learning and improvement based on changed mindsets and behaviors is what is required to build adaptability into humanitarian responses. Continuous learning should be embedded into organizational culture, ensuring that challenges are overcome, systems and processes are sufficiently flexible yet accountable and priority is given to focusing on having a long-lasting positive impact on communities. When we fail to learn and change as the humanitarian sector, we are failing to adapt to the changing context and risk the potential that old ideas, interventions and even institutions quickly become obsolete.

As humanitarians we recognize that living in a fragile context requires constant flexibility. Resilience pathways are built up over time and often through a number of different experiences. These strengths, particularly of those staff and communities present in the context, should be the basis for discussions on adaptability to ensure that these can be adequately resourced for the future. The co-creation discussions can bring in innovation and partnering to ensure a depth of impact for the longer term. Failing to acknowledge these strengths and ignoring the root causes of the crisis will just lead to cyclical short-term programming that has little long-term impact.

As I watch the COVID-19 pandemic sweep the globe, forcing the world to change ways of working and perceptions, there appears to be a greater openness for change. Preconceptions and well-established processes are being reviewed and there is an urgent need to adapt. There is a need to act fast, but also to act locally. The humanitarian sector must adapt to ensure that responses are appropriate to specific settings to protect the most vulnerable. There is the need to have a flexible approach in fragile context settings to ensure that responses will do no harm.

The pandemic represents a strange crisis as all those that are responding are affected personally, as in many disasters when the first responders come from the affected communities themselves. Humanitarian organizations globally are reeling from the impact on their staff, revenue and operations. This response is already like no other. Much like the nature surrounding us, we too will have to become resilient, developing networks and interconnectivity in order to learn from those who have weathered the storms before and adapt.

## Notes

1 OECD definition: https://stats.oecd.org/glossary/detail.asp?ID=7235#:~:text=OECD%20Statistics,%2Doperation%2C%20OECD%2C%20Paris.
2 The best-laid plans of mice and men often go wrong or often go awry: this saying is adapted from the poem "To a Mouse, on Turning Her Up in Her Nest With a Plough, November, 1785", by Robert Burns (1785).

# Extending the conversation

Universal standards are a relatively new thing. In the early 1990s the humanitarian sector had lost some of its sheen; there was a growing recognition that its actions sometimes did not turn out as well as was intended and started to be questioned. The Rwanda genocide in 1994 prompted the largest international humanitarian response up to that point, involving multiple countries, many UN agencies and around 250 NGOs.[1] The crisis, which several writers reference as a watershed moment for the humanitarian sector, uncovered the danger of having large numbers of NGOs working with little regulation to guide them, and sped up the drive to a new dialogue. The result was seen in efforts like the Sphere Project, in which several humanitarian organizations collaborated to find ways to improve the quality of their work. Sphere, as it is known today, has since published four editions of minimum standards, each produced after broad consultation with the humanitarian community.

An important portion of the discussion floats around the need for accountability. And here is where the dialogue in this first part comes to life. Accountability is often thought to be owed to those who are paying for the services. In the marketplace, for example, many businesses offer easy exchanges of merchandise to the customer who provides the money in the transaction. The same is true with humanitarian aid, where the donor expects to be satisfied with the way their money is used. This is critical because the bulk of humanitarian funding comes from the Northern world, with the combined contributions of the United States, Germany and the United Kingdom providing over half of all aid.[2] If humanitarian organizations are accountable to their funders, then Northern societies will have considerable influence over how aid is used.

But humanitarian action is more than a simple business transaction. It arises from the very best of human impulses – to give a hand to people who need help and do it in a way that builds dignity in both the helper and the one being helped. It means recognizing that every person receiving aid is not just an empty basket into which aid can be poured, but a human being who should be able to act independently within their own environment. That part of humanitarian action recognizes and defends human agency, wants to build human dignity, and strives to be accountable not just to donors, but also to the users of its aid.

It is not easy to be accountable to both the donor and the recipients of relief. Common standards in humanitarian aid provide a kind of accountability structure to help deal with some of the tension. With standards in place, an aid agency's work can be measured against agreed-upon criteria. Before Sphere, this was not possible. Standards also make it easier to provide aid at the massive scale needed in today's crisis-filled world. As one of our writers puts it, standards provide reassurance to workers by giving them a starting point in chaotic situations. However, they run into challenges when agreed-upon guidelines are perceived by the local community as differing from their own needs and lifestyles. That is when aid workers on the ground start arguing for more flexibility. Often the tensions around accountability can be observed in the perspectives of humanitarian workers who are in different places. Headquarter workers relate more closely to donors; workers on the ground relate daily to the communities they serve. They both pursue the same goal but may have differing ideas as a result of seeing their work from their own particular vantage point.

The two perspectives can be looked at in a different way. Underlying humanitarian action's methods are two compelling instincts on opposite ends of a continuum. The first is a drive toward professionalism and technocratic management which strives for efficient use of the resources the sector is distributing in the world. At the risk of oversimplifying, we can say that its strategy assumes that plans will follow a logical direction which can be targeted, followed and measured to determine if the goals have been accomplished. The second is a philosophy that assumes that the relationship between aid workers and the people they serve is the core of humanitarian work. Its underlying approach considers aid users to be equal players in the complex world of humanitarian assistance. The 'equal actors' stance opens the door for new kinds of expectations, which may or may not follow a logical sequence and may or may not be what donors and humanitarian workers were expecting. Often, this view is concerned not just with achieving goals, but with the methods used to reach those goals as well.[3]

Considering aid users as equal humanitarian partners fits the values of the sector that we described above, values that hold that every human being should be able to act of their own volition in ways that fit their own culture and world view. However, since most humanitarian aid originates in the wealthy world, and most users of that aid are in poorer contexts, the differences among the two collectives inevitably lead to tensions with that posture. Most humanitarian organizations are designed on a Western-oriented bureaucratic organizational model, which may not be a natural fit in the contexts in which they are working. Also, most of the individual workers and the people using the aid come from widely diverging backgrounds with distinct world views, values and ways of life. The developed part of the world is generally more highly regulated and stable. The developing world is often not so settled; if a good legal system is in place, many people follow the regulations only superficially. The result is that the rules of the game can change often, to the point that "no day is ever the same", as Helen Barclay-Hollands expressed it. Ex-patriot humanitarian workers often find that these contexts produce feelings of stress. They can feel that their working location is uncertain and more complex than their native environments. For the local population, the ever-changing environment is simply the reality in which they live.

Carrying out humanitarian work requires a good sense of flexibility, not just to navigate an unpredictable environment, but to move among different cultures; flexibility is often named as the most sought-after personality trait in humanitarian workers. But a sense of flexibility also needs to be applied at a broader level. Institutions within the humanitarian sector also need to have a flexibility trait, especially if they hold the value that aid users are equals. Humanitarian organizations and the entire 'machine' within which they are working should be able to adapt their well-intentioned interventions to the contexts they find themselves in.

It has often been said that disasters are always local.[4] The local character of humanitarian crises brings special urgency to the standard/flexibility continuum. To operate efficiently while still upholding their values, humanitarian organizations will need to be as self-conscious as possible about the influences that shape their ways of working. They need to be able to navigate and resolve the tensions between upholding standards as closely as possible and a possibility that local communities' expectations may differ, as well as the tensions between the norms of Western-style management customs and the looser practices of aid users.

While none of the contributors in this part is on one extreme or other of the spectrum, we can see them nudging each other in one direction or another. We hope their conversation will contribute to the ongoing dialogue within the humanitarian community. Their essays also show how the parts of this book are interconnected. One cannot discuss the relationship between standards and flexibility without also thinking about how an aid worker might bridge the gap between them. They remind us that however standards are applied, they were not meant to be check boxes, just as more flexibility does not mean less arbitrary decisions. Rather, they each represent one end of yet another gap that humanitarian workers need to bridge, the subject of the next part.

## Notes

1  Margie Buchanan-Smith, "How the Sphere Project Came into Being: A Case Study of Policy-Making in the Humanitarian Aid Sector and the Relative Influence of Research" (London: Overseas Development Institute, 2003), www.files.ethz.ch/isn/96043/ODI%20wp215.pdf.
2  The Global Humanitarian Assistance Report 2019 (Development Initiatives, 2020), https://devinit.org/resources/global-humanitarian-assistance-report-2019/international-humanitarian-assistance/.
3  David Lewis, *Non-Governmental Organizations, Management and Development*, 3rd edition (Abingdon, Oxon; New York, NY: Routledge, 2014).
4  Steven T. Ganyard, "Opinion. All Disasters Are Local," *The New York Times*, May 17, 2009, sec. Opinion, www.nytimes.com/2009/05/18/opinion/18ganyard.html.

# Part 2
# **Bridging the divide**

Neither here nor there

# Introduction to the conversation

In 1971 a group of young doctors and journalists in France formed Médecins Sans Frontières or Doctors without Borders, as the organization is known in English. With this simple name, the organization's founders encompassed the ideals of a whole generation of humanitarian workers: neutral, oblivious to political boundaries, willing and able to help people in need across the world.

Such ideals immediately bring into focus the breach between those with resources and those who need them. At the global scale, this often means that some portion of the wealth found in the global north gets channeled across some invisible poverty line to places where need is more prevalent or where crises have hit. Aid workers act as the bridge across which resources flow to provide the assistance.

But there are many other ways in which humanitarian action connects and bridges gaps. Many of them are hidden from view like a gully in a forest, covered by tangles of vines and trees, and can only be seen by digging down underneath the surface. At this level, humanitarian action is about connecting spaces that are cognitive, as much as they are concrete. The services they provide must be appropriate, but also feel relevant to those they seek to help. In their attempt to provide support, humanitarian workers are inevitably forced to leave the comfort of what they know and jump into the unknown. They are driven by the desire to reduce pain, but they are nonetheless bounded by a difficult challenge. They must be sensitive to the fact that they, and the users of their aid, interpret reality differently and they must be capable of incorporating this truth into everything they do.

Reading between the lines of the chapters of this book, the reader will identify and become familiar with the many other ways in which humanitarian workers live in between multiple spaces; spaces that can be geographical and physical, while some other times they can be cognitive, political, cultural, spiritual, and even some other times, spaces that exist between the present and the future. The writers in this part recount fascinating stories in which humanitarian action means living and working in spaces that "are neither here nor there". Marie Anne Sliwinski brings us a nice story about her role as an interlocutor between groups of people that see the world in different ways, such as donors, those working in headquarter offices such as herself, and humanitarian ground personnel. Naomi Enns also recounts bringing together donors and aid recipients, sometimes physically, sometimes by facilitating an exchange of stories that help each understand the world of the other. Gary Shaye and Jono Anzalone share with us how the meaning of humanitarian action is affected by a life-long journey working for the same organization. Shaye is particularly concerned with bridging gaps between organizations that want to collaborate with one another. Pat Foley highlights the divide between practitioners who carry out humanitarian efforts and academic programs that take apart and study those interventions. It is a persistent and uncomfortable gap for almost everyone involved in the sector.

# 6 A behind-the-desk view of responding to a disaster

*Marie Anne Sliwinski*

## My journey to the humanitarian sector

Thursday, March 19, 2020 at 11:45pm. I stand up and step away from my laptop and stretch my arms up. I have been working non-stop all day only with a couple of hours break for dinner and to play with my toddler. It is day four of working from home as instructed by my organization. We were not to return to the office until April 20 (which has since extended to January 2021) as part of the recommended social distancing by the state of Illinois in order to prevent the spread of the COVID-19 virus.

While many who had to stay at home are bored and have binge-watched too many shows and listened to too many podcasts, I have been busy receiving requests from churches and organizations overseas for financial assistance in preparation for a coronavirus outbreak in their country. Meanwhile, our organization began to look more inward as it became clear that the pandemic will affect funding availability now and in the future. As the person who oversees the international disaster portfolio, I have to figure out how to balance the need to provide as much as we can for communities likely to be affected by the pandemic, and ensure we retain funds for other types of disasters and that our funds are not completely depleted before the summer ends.

I never thought I would be in the business of grants management and philanthropy. Growing up in the Philippines, my options were either to become a doctor or a lawyer. As a talkative and argumentative child, everyone knew I would be heading to law school. And I almost did. Except my mother, who had been living and working in the United States, called upon my younger sister and me to move to the United States and live with her. I am the typical immigrant story. We were petitioned by our mother as her dependents to live with her in the United States.

As I enrolled at a nearby community college, my mother encouraged me to pursue the hottest career at that time – computer science. But I couldn't see myself working for a for-profit company. I cannot work for "The Man". I was supposed to be a lawyer, defender of the helpless. I was in my second year as a political science major at an ultra-liberal public university in the Philippines and I did not want to switch careers. So, relocated in a Chicago suburb, I pursued and completed a bachelor's degree in political science and a master's degree in international relations.

I gave up law school as I became more interested in international development work. I was also ready to start making money and a massive student loan was not appealing. For some reason, I thought the best place to find non-profit organizations with an international portfolio was on the east coast of the United States. I was looking at possible jobs in New York City and Washington, DC. My first job following graduate school landed me in a private foundation based in Baltimore City.

Fifteen years since my first job in Baltimore, I have worked for numerous organizations in program management, specifically overseeing grants. The content of my work has varied – I managed grants for workforce development initiatives in the United States, livelihood opportunities for young people affected by the Indian Ocean tsunami, HIV prevention through peer education on adolescent reproductive health in East Africa, mobile banking research in Kenya and Malawi, agriculture and water programs in Asia, disaster response in the Philippines and Nepal, and a global portfolio on vision care. I currently oversee an international disaster response portfolio for one of the biggest church denominations in the United States. I am what the non-profit sector calls a "generalist" – I know just enough to make a critical analysis on random themes.

*Figure 6.1* Marie Anne Sliwinski working remotely from her home

Throughout my 15-year career in grants management, I was never deployed overseas. I processed grants at the headquarters of the organizations I worked for. I made recommendations on whether to support a project or not. I made recommendations on how much we should give and whether we should give again as the project continues. I organized the required documents to ensure that the implementing organization received the official grant agreements prior to receiving the funds. I issued payments to our finance department so they could send the check. I received and reviewed reports for accuracy and asked questions for clarity. I pitched stories to our communications department to make sure the projects we were supporting were shared with our donors.

Although I work behind the desk, I am still a humanitarian actor. Humanitarian actors are usually seen as on-the-ground first responders wearing baseball hats and vests – assisting men, women, and children by providing food, non-food items, and medicine. I, on the other hand, sit in a cubicle in front of the computer waiting to read the situation reports that come in and determine how many funds we can send to local non-governmental organizations (NGOs) now and later. I usually do not physically see anything until three months, six months or even one year after the catastrophe. Nevertheless, there is plenty of action and drama that can be found in an office. Here are three reflections of what I have learned in this field:

## As a grants manager, I must be multi-lingual to converse in the humanitarian sector

By multi-lingual, I do not mean the ability to speak English, Spanish, and French (though that can be beneficial too). I mean I can speak many technical languages – I am conversant in the many forms of donor speak (i.e., institutional foundations have a different "dialect" than family foundations, academia, faith denomination or individual donors), I know how to translate for finance and operations, project evaluators, and project implementers.

For example, donors from the global north or "Westerners" think and speak in a linear, logical fashion.

$$I + A = O \rightarrow Ou \rightarrow Im$$

Input (I) plus activities (A) equals output (O) which will eventually lead to outcomes (Ou) and impact (Im). Western donors believe their contribution does great things and positive change will happen to those who receive their contributions. While donors understand the success or failure of a project depends on risks and variables beyond our control (e.g., environmental changes or political instabilities), by the end of the grant period, projects must have results.

On the opposite side of the grant spectrum, beneficiaries do not think and speak in the same manner. As most projects occur in the global south, non-Westerners do not view the work in a linear fashion. They are more relational – the world is inter-connected like a web where donors are one strand among multiple strands of actors. One event is not necessarily caused by one action as it is often caused by multiple actions, by multiple layers of variables that are all intertwined.

For example, installing a water pump is a common solution for communities experiencing drought or that have limited access to potable water. Input = provisions of supplies to install water pump; Activities = install water pump in a public space; Output = water for the community; Outcome = healthy people; Impact = healthy community. For community residents, however, the lack of access to clean water is one of the many variables that prevents the community from being healthy. While a new water pump is great, without the technical knowledge, proper management, and local budget to replace parts if it breaks, the water pump becomes a community monument. Installing the water pump without an understanding of the cultural and social practices of the community can also lead to a project failure. Women, who gather water from the river, use the travel time from the village to the river to escape their husbands and children and to gossip and socialize with other women. Time to gather water may have significantly decreased, and the free time means more chores for women to accomplish. Beyond access to water, a community might also need livelihood opportunities, group formation for advocacy and access to service, education, and hygienic behavior change. A community might also want to build upon the assets they already have to be strong and healthy.

My role is to untangle the web as described by the beneficiaries and the local NGOs and turn it into a simple, neat, and linear logical framework for the donors to understand. It is a shame that donors miss out on the beauty and intricacies of the web. The relationship between donors and beneficiaries becomes transactional, a one-way street between the giver and the receiver. To untangle the web, I use narratives where I avoid the salvation arc – "poor Mr. So-and-so from a developing country did not have this, but through the support of super organization, Mr. So-and-so has been saved!" As a way to educate donors, I start from the place of dignity where communities are empowered to share their needs and how donor contribution assisted the community to achieve their needs while acknowledging the challenges to get there. For example, just because we provided tarps as temporary shelters for families affected by an earthquake did not mean we expected them to use the tarps for shelter. Families in communities have their own coping mechanisms. Because the tarps were too hot during the day and did not fully protect them from the rain at night, many families used the tarps to store their belongings and stayed with other family members whose homes were only partially damaged from the earthquake. The communities asked for the tarps and they used them where they saw fit.

On the flip side, local NGOs could learn that, sometimes, a linear way of thinking can help make things a bit easier and prevent them from falling into a trap of complexity when the answer could be simple. Many local NGOs are usually in action mode. Because they are so embedded in the community, they sometimes forget that donors halfway around the world do not know the history, culture, politics, and practices in the community.

For example, I was asked by a colleague to go to South Sudan to assist a local NGO in designing a project related to peace and reconciliation. When I arrived,

I met the leader of the organization and his staff, and after the usual formalities, he directly informed me what they would like to do and the funding they needed to get there. I replied, "That is great, but I would like us to take a pause here and reflect on why we want to do these activities". For a day and a half, I worked with them on identifying the problem they were trying to address, the result that they would like to achieve, and the process of how to get there. It was an "ah-ha!" moment – a mind-shift – for the leader of the organization. His life work had been in the community and was focused on building relationships and finding solutions. Through the problem tree and an outcome mapping exercise we were able to focus more clearly on how to achieve the results they would like to see.

In addition to program design and donor expectation, I can also speak the language of finance and evaluation. It can be a bit technical, and requires some translation for local NGOs. This is not due to lack of understanding and accountability; many of the local NGOs I have met are open to demonstrating good faith and transparency. It is more a result of my organization's own policies and procedures being passed on to local NGOs as required by donors. For example, institutional donors require an evaluation for projects at the end of the grant period. As a grants manager, it is my role to explain to the local NGOs what it means to conduct an evaluation beyond a mere verification of the output reported or activities conducted. It is important to explain how the evaluation measures the project based on different variables such as efficacy, efficiency, and relevance. And how, when we evaluate a project, it is not to question the performance of the organization per se (though sometimes lack of proper documentation does question the local NGO's capacity), but rather, how my organization, the donor, and the local NGO can learn from one another on the shared project.

The tone of translation is also important. Humility and understanding are key ingredients to ensure effective translation. As a grants manager, I know I have the upper hand when it comes to the power dynamics between the organization I represent and the local NGO. To walk into a meeting with local NGOs with a predisposition that I know how things should be done will not bode well in future relationships. All of us bring a wealth of knowledge and diverse expertise and I always take advantage of every meeting as an opportunity to learn more about how things are done in their context. As someone whose skin and hair color often matches theirs, I sense that they find me more approachable and trustworthy as compared to my fair-skinned colleagues. Women in particular are more comfortable talking to me and sharing insights on how projects are implemented and received by the communities.

In the humanitarian arena where white Europeans and Americans continue to dominate, it would be refreshing to see more people of color taking on decision-making roles in the headquarters. I believe the reason I do well in my position is because I grew up in the culture and tradition of community-centeredness. At the same time, I am professionally trained to think critically and logically. While I do see more and more diversity in central offices, I would like to see the language translated more in favor of the local NGOs and the communities we serve. I have seen many local NGOs mastering the art of donor speak, which makes work easier for me though it perpetuates the existing power dynamics between donors and the beneficiaries. Having more people from the global south (beyond tokenism) making funding decisions could be a game changer in terms of how we speak about humanitarian assistance and philanthropy.

## Funding decisions can be irrational

Designing a project and translating the proposal into a language understood by donors does not always guarantee that it will be approved and funded. The proposal goes through a vetting process where, as a grants manager, I do not have control over whether the decision will be favorable or not. For disaster grants, the vetting process is usually swift and almost always approved due to the urgency of the request. Protracted disasters or development grants go through additional scrutiny because the amount requested tends to be higher and for multiple years. When it comes to funding decisions, I have learned throughout my career not to be surprised or frustrated when questionable projects are favored over strong projects.

One reason is that donor interest and the priority of the funding organization often eclipse what is good for the community. I have encountered donors who will only fund projects in certain geographic regions even though the region is already saturated with funding contributions. I have worked for funding organizations that will only grant equipment and expects local NGOs to find other donors to support the operational costs for running the equipment. I have also worked with funding organizations who will only support certain local NGOs with which they have bilateral relationships even though other organizations have a stronger capacity to implement the project. Every funding organization has its reasons and priorities based on the composition of senior leaders – their own individual beliefs, values, and experience of what they think is the best use of the funds. Granting decisions can also be influenced by the tradition and culture of the funding organization.

It is very difficult when donors and foundations create funding parameters that undermine the ability of communities and local NGOs to innovate and design projects that are for their own good. One example in the humanitarian sector is that, years ago, there was resistance by some donors to support conditional and unconditional cash transfer programs. Donors fear that their money will be used to purchase alcohol or frivolous items like flatscreen TVs. They want to control what they think the beneficiaries need after a disaster. Studies on cash transfer programs show that it is one of the most effective forms of relief assistance during a disaster when a local market is present.[1] It offers choices for families to use the money where they see fit – paying back a loan, tuition fees for the children, or medicine for the chronically ill. It also contributes toward the local economy. As a grants manager, it is my role to lift up innovative and proven relief strategies and educate donors on effective ways to empower disaster-affected communities by giving back a sense of control to their lives.

A way to eliminate the irrationality of funding decisions is to reduce the power dynamic between funder and grantees. A new movement has begun where foundations are challenged to shift funding priorities from supporting the work or activities of the local NGOs to supporting the operations of the local NGOs. In a study commissioned by Citi Foundation,[2] they looked at four funding organizations who used flexible funding to support the general operations and building the capacities of local NGOs. They found that when foundations support the people and the organization itself, the trust between the funder and the local NGOs is strengthened. The power dynamics become more equalized into a trusted partnership. In addition, measuring success as traditionally done (i.e., I + A = O → Ou → Im) can shift into a process that is broader and less consequential. As a grants manager, I am excited at the prospect of moving toward supporting long-term general operations and capacity building for local NGOs. As I mentioned earlier, I am a generalist. I do not claim to have the expertise in the technical programming of the portfolio I oversee. I rely on the experience and expertise of local NGOs in responding to disasters. What I do know and can assess with confidence is whether the local NGO has the capacity to respond to a crisis and has the operational systems and manpower to become sustainable in the long term. Perhaps during "normal or quiet periods", funding organizations can offer operational and capacity-building support to local NGOs so that, when disasters happen, there is no need for detailed proposals to review and approve. We already know what they can do. We can ask for a situation report, send the relief funds, and in three months learn what they did and share the stories back to our donors.

## Learn about the people and entities you ultimately serve

When a grant has been approved and work has begun, I often reflect about the people and entities I serve – the donors, the local NGOs, and the beneficiaries. What is most important to them and how can I best serve them in my capacity?

We know that in the non-profit sector, donors behave in various ways. Government funders are more bureaucratic in nature and funding availabilities vary on which political party is in office. Corporate donors care primarily about their brand, their own values, and brand recognition. Family foundations and individual donors are moved to contribute by either the stories they learn or by the cause that they believe in.

Donor motivations matter to me because we use it to start a conversation and build a relationship. For example, we worked with a corporate donor who believes in youth entrepreneurship and technology because they are a telecommunications company. As I mentioned earlier, I use the language they are most familiar with such as innovations, opportunities, and results for young people. When we pitched the same program to a government agency, we pivoted the focus toward youth employability and income generation for the community. Same program but with two sources of funding where we can leverage their resources. Developing reports and stories for donors also changes depending on their needs and priorities. While I can influence the narrative and avoid the "salvation arc" in the stories I share, once the reports are in their hands, they in turn can change the narrative where they see fit.

For the beneficiaries, it is always encouraging when we encounter communities that are resilient and refuse to give up when disasters and hardships occur. However, there are also communities who have depended on handouts for years and even generations; it is disheartening when we talk to them and they cannot see or realize the assets within their communities. To help prevent or put an end to dependence, we often ask local NGOs to design initiatives which include plans for sustainability and an exit strategy. Whether the grant is for a disaster response or development work, any humanitarian assistance must include local ownership and empowerment. This means identifying ways where our response can help beneficiaries rebuild their lives, take ownership of their circumstance, and be better prepared for when the next catastrophe happens. Unfortunately, this is often easier said than done.

Throughout my career, even as we inform local NGOs that this is the last year we can support them, local NGOs often come back and ask for extended support. If there is no longer donor interest due to lack of funds or shifting interest (i.e., donor fatigue), we have to decline the request. One, two, or three years after the project ended, we usually do not look back to see if there has been any lasting impact. By that time, I would be busy managing a new portfolio with new funding at a new location. I would like to come back and check in with the community but due to institutional priorities and lack of funding, it is unfortunately not possible. In addition, it is sometimes hard to check in with the local NGO without creating expectation for new support.

I think about these three points all the time. I wonder, does humanitarian assistance have to be this complicated? Why do we need to build up so many processes, bureaucracies, and invisible gates when providing aid? Is it because we do not trust one another as humans and think our generosity will be abused? When we provide aid to those affected by disasters, it is not a one-time transaction. We enter and are welcomed into the lives of people to whom we reached out and offered assistance. We then develop a relationship and accompany one another, side-by-side, with a shared vision.[3] It would be nice if we – the donors, funding organizations, and international NGOs – could all just stay around for a while and witness the shared vision turn into reality.

## Humanitarian sector in a post-COVID world

As I finish stretching and return to my laptop, I know that my email inbox will have new requests for COVID-19 response funding. The pandemic is a game changer for us in grants management. We are providing relief assistance to so many local NGOs who have asked for help. However, the bigger concern will be how we can provide recovery assistance later in the year. We are learning that the most vulnerable population – women, children, elderly, physically disabled, ethnic minorities, rural population, migrants, and refugees – are the most at risk not only in becoming infected by the virus, but also of domestic abuse, hunger, and poverty. As the worldwide economy slows down, the pandemic will reduce and limit donor contributions we once had.

A way to temper the anxiety is to listen and gather more information from different actors in the humanitarian sector. We collect stories and information on how communities are coping, and we share stories of hope to our donors. We develop a response strategy document that is aspirational in terms of assisting families to adapt to the new normal, and pragmatic in terms of how we can support with the limited funding we have. It is up to me to facilitate the conversation within our organization and to follow through on our response plan.

I am a US immigrant whose fate has afforded me an opportunity to work in a space in the humanitarian sector that is often held by someone who doesn't look like me. Where I am now is made possible by years of learning, observing, and modeling collaborative behavior, and acknowledging that everyone brings their experience and expertise to the table. While the reflections I share are observations I have learned, they were formed because of good leaders at all levels and positions in the humanitarian sector whom I was fortunate to have worked with. I do hope that more people of color and immigrants considering a career in the humanitarian sector will also consider working in central offices and headquarters where we can be influential in disaster response.

## Notes

1  The Cash Learning Partnership. www.calpnetwork.org/.
2  *Funding from a Place of Trust*, Citi Foundation. April 2020. https://philanthropynewyork. org/news/new-citi-foundation-report-funding-place-trust.
3  *Global Mission in the Twenty-first Century*, Evangelical Lutheran Church in America. https:// download.elca.org/ELCA%20Resource%20Repository/Global_Mission_21.pdf?_ga= 2.72553491.1835854726.1604347759-1394143040.1564421835.

# 7 Ensuring shared best practices are in place

*Gary Shaye*

## My story

If I had to briefly describe myself, it would be as someone who enjoys and thrives on meeting and interacting with people from different backgrounds. I often chose to work in remote locations because of the learning opportunities presented there. I also thought that if I held a leadership position in the future, the experience gained in rural areas would build my capacity and improve my effectiveness. Moreover, working with Save the Children and living in other countries gave me an opportunity to fulfill a personal goal: wanting my four children to have similar experiences of living in other countries, learning about other cultures and languages. I was always interested in these topics and I was delighted when thanks to the Foreign Exchange Program, my high school hosted Oscar, from Costa Rica – the first person I had ever met from Latin America.

In addition, I was fascinated with Nepal, and read every *National Geographic* I could find about that mountainous kingdom. Coincidentally, in my first year at Cornell, I regularly sat next to Ashok Sharma, the first Nepalese person to study Hotel Administration. We became lifelong friends, and I had no idea I would spend more than seven years of my life working in Nepal and living just 50 meters from Ashok's home in Kathmandu.

Like many who are drawn to the humanitarian field, my first international experience was with the Peace Corps, a voluntary two-year program for U.S. citizens to work on development projects identified by the host governments, while living at the same level of the community in which they are placed. When I entered college, my older brother Jerry had just begun a two-year Peace Corps assignment in the town of Timotes in the Venezuelan Andes. I would read Jerry's letters and learn about the agricultural cooperative he was assisting with crop improvement and vegetable marketing. Friends who knew me were not at all surprised when I applied for the Peace Corps and indicated a preference to be assigned to a program in the Andes. I was driven to learn more about addressing development issues and to become fluent in another language.

I lived in Cuzco, Peru, and each month I visited artisan cooperatives between Cuzco and Puno, as well as communities around Lake Titicaca. Together with five other volunteers, we helped artisans earn supplemental income by producing and marketing high-quality sweaters, ponchos, knitted hats, and other traditional products. Eighty five percent of the sales price was paid to the artisans who were the storeowners and organized in cooperatives.

My very positive experience in Peru led me to change my plans from the career in hotel administration I envisioned when I began my studies at Cornell University to one working with an NGO. The two years in Peru demonstrated to me that the artisans with whom I worked were able to supplement the agricultural income they derived from small plots of land in the Peruvian altiplano through the sale of unique, high-quality products. I wanted to be part of work that improved the opportunities for those living in poverty, especially marginalized people living in rural areas.

When my Peace Corps assignment concluded, I returned to my hometown of Albany and I worked for two years to save funds for graduate studies. During this time, I had an opportunity to take a one-year volunteer assignment in Nepal, where I had always wanted to work. I devoted the first four months to a handicrafts development program, established by an American woman in Nepal. After she passed away, her husband asked me for advice on continuing the project; we opted to conclude it after all of the artisans were fully paid. Following that, I took a position teaching English for eight months at the American Library and was able to learn more about the culture and people by working in an entirely different environment than my experience in Peru.

My experiences in Peru reinforced my desire for a graduate degree, recognizing my need for tools and techniques for working with communities and supporting training programs. The graduate program at the School for International Training in Brattleboro, Vermont better prepared me for longer-term work with a development agency and for the career that I have had with Save the Children.

## Building a career

In order to complete my master's degree, I was required to complete an internship. In 1975, Save the Children placed me in a field assignment after an orientation at their Connecticut office, designed for me to learn more about their organization. I left for the Dominican Republic 12 weeks later.

I was assigned to Loma de Cabrera, a small rural town of about 5,000 people, a few kilometers from the Haitian border. I served four years in the Dominican Republic spending 1–3 days a week in the communities where we worked. During my six years in Nepal, I was in the communities once a month. In both countries, our initial program coverage areas were clusters of villages, in the Dominican Republic reachable by road, and in Nepal, reachable on foot. Stemming from my time back in the Peace Corps, I knew the benefit of dedicating time and energy to developing relationships with all of our team members as well as the community. This allowed me to learn about each staff member's individual skill set and where that could best be used in our program. In the humanitarian sector, a frequent conversation is about building relationships that are more effective

*Figure 7.1* Gary Shaye, Save the Children Haiti

with the community members with whom you are working and the individuals or organizations providing some of the resources.

I next spent six years in Bolivia, coincidently just 3–4 hours from the places around Lake Titicaca in southern Peru that once inspired me to become a humanitarian worker when I was in the Peace Corps. My various international assignments led me to Haiti in April of 2010, asked by Save the Children to lead our Earthquake Response Team. When I arrived in Haiti about three months after the earthquake, I was both excited and nervous about the enormity of the task ahead. The fact that we had capable staff made me also want to focus on building relationships with other NGO leaders who, as I quickly learned, faced similar implementation challenges. An NGO Coordination Group had been established, meeting weekly for the first six to eight months and I joined, quickly feeling a responsibility and a desire to participate with the broader humanitarian community. At these meetings, I thought of myself as a representative of the collective NGO community rather than as a spokesperson for my own organization and its interests. Other humanitarian leaders in this group had a similar mindset, and collectively we could see a broader vision as to the best way to approach issues in the future. I learned so much from them and together we worked to address common issues, including security, customs clearance of humanitarian materials, hurricane season preparation, and finding the most effective ways to work with the Government of Haiti.

As I look back on my years spent in the sector, I do not recall conversations specifically centered around collaboration, but I noticed all of the people who attended meetings did so because they saw a benefit in being present, receiving information, and developing contacts with other humanitarian actors. While levels of participation differ among agencies, my most recent experiences proved to me the NGO community continues to view such groupings as positive. What I have seen as different in the present-day sector is the number of consortiums that form to approach donors for program support, which will be an interesting topic for the humanitarian community to follow as it evolves.

Even though I had the position of Director in the Dominican Republic, Nepal, Bolivia, and Haiti, I learned the balance between leading while stepping back and listening. The more we could explore options together and reach agreement on program implementation, for example on drinking water or irrigation projects, the more likely it would be that projects would be maintained and sustainable. Being accompanied by staff members allowed all parties, community members, government representatives, Save the Children and other NGO staff members, to discuss next steps and even address potential challenges, an important element of humanitarian work. I was fortunate that in my early assignments in the Dominican Republic and Nepal, our staffing levels were small in number, and this provided me time to focus on these relationships and learn about their importance in terms of having better information and advice, and most of all greater knowledge of local situations.

This was something that I missed when I left the field, returning to Connecticut to serve as the Regional Director for Latin America and then as Vice President for International Programs. When I was at our Connecticut office I was tasked with critical responsibilities such as oversight of staff and program operations in the US and around the world, growing our grant-funded programs, and promoting inter-departmental collaboration. However, I always missed the enjoyment of sitting down with community members and learning about their family life, the agricultural production of their village, and their values and commitment to educating their children.

As time passed and responsibilities increased when I was in Haiti, the Director's role took more time and resulted in longer hours and less time in program locations. I often went to bed thinking about the people I didn't talk to who should have been consulted, the supporters I didn't thank, or those relationships to which I had not dedicated enough of my time and weren't tended to as I would have preferred. Perhaps it is the scale of these humanitarian emergencies that quickly humbles everyone into realizing that every agency can play a role in the response and no single agency could ever do this on its own.

## Reflections

In this section, I will share my own reflections on how both development and humanitarian staff members can focus on strengthening relationship building among communities being reached, staff of NGOs, and agency decision makers. My own experience has demonstrated to me that staff relationships with program participants and community leaders play a critical role in achieving positive results, as well as improving outcomes for children and their families.

### Travel time is not wasted time

Traveling and working in a country program put me in direct contact with the people who were actually participating in some of the services provided through our programs. During my first week in Haiti, I visited programs in both Port-au-Prince and Leogane. Travel within Port-au-Prince often took hours due to large amounts of rubble, which blocked many streets. Traveling short distances could easily take half a day, including time for a 90-minute meeting. Like the time when I was walking to villages in Nepal, this "travel time" created excellent opportunities to listen, ask questions, and get to know our staff in ways that were not always possible when I was working in our office. This was a great way to solicit ideas from staff and community members, by asking them what they thought, and refraining from doing too much talking myself. When I was in Latin America and later in Nepal, although I was fluent in Spanish and could conduct a conversation in Nepali, I became a better listener and an observer because I always learned a lot more this way. Moreover, in becoming a better listener, I was "giving importance" to their words and thoughts.

In communities, I always wanted to get a sense of the leadership and how they engaged the community members. Did they include voices of different stakeholders, including women, men, children, and families with children of different abilities? What was the role of individuals who may have left their village and lived in larger urban areas? What role did they play in their community? What about teachers, farmers, local midwives, and the nearest health workers if they were present? How did political leaders relate to the constituencies they represented? In two of the countries I worked, the local political leaders with whom I had frequent discussions and meetings were very incoherent because of their alcoholism. Yet if I met with them early in the day, they were articulate, extremely helpful, and showed the leadership qualities that were not evident later in the day.

In my work with village leaders and community members, I wanted them to know that I was listening to their concerns and issues and that I would be fair. It did not always mean I agreed with them or would approve anything that was requested. The reality was, anything I would need to approve would have to be discussed with our staff who were much closer to the situation than I was, and in a better position to make a recommendation. Over time, I felt that I did get better about discussing expectations of Save the Children with our partners, and their expectations of us.

Throughout my career, I witnessed Save the Children and other humanitarian organizations deploy staff for short periods. These experienced staff provide technical assistance to strengthen programs, assess and if necessary recommend improved security procedures, or assist with procurement. When individuals are deployed to an emergency for a very brief period, especially if they have not had prior experience in the country or the region, it can be difficult to get the full benefit of their expertise. Such assignments can have greater value and impact if the periods can be extended so those individuals can assist in putting their recommendations into practice and monitoring with a staff member how the recommendations are being addressed.

Our internal and external audit teams were good examples of individuals who came to Haiti with a tight scope of work and a detailed follow-up plan that was addressed with regular reports and conference calls. In Nepal, I was able to cultivate a relationship with Mr. C.B. Gurung, a government official who was appointed by the Queen of Nepal, and to whom I reported. Our relationship developed because the Regional Director of our Asia Programs asked me to accompany her to Nepal prior to my proposed appointment as Director of the Nepal Program. She wanted to introduce me to Mr. Gurung, and the fact that she gave him the opportunity to meet me and asked him if I was someone with whom he thought he could work was instrumental in my appointment. More importantly, it was a good example of how the Regional Director related to a government official who was critical to our work in Nepal.

In Nepal, I remember how much time was spent gathering water, a responsibility usually required of young girls. I recall one project where we provided funding so the villagers could build a storage tank for water, hoping it would take the women and girls less time to fill their water jugs. We used a few bags of cement to build a tank and were able to add some drainage ditches. After the project was completed we learned that the women actually wanted a place where they could sit next to each other to talk while others were filling their water jugs. The time spent around the water jugs was when these women and girls exchanged information, through gathering and enjoying social time in the midst of their chores. By speaking with the women, we were able to address this and build a suitable place for these important social needs at a minimal cost. These were funds well spent. If we had spoken to these women first, we would have known their needs and desires, and the social aspect of gathering water might have been more evident.

When someone such as a decision maker or a staff member within the humanitarian machine is going in and out of communities, they may only see a sliver through their lens, which is focused for a short period on community life at that point in time. I also saw this in the Dominican Republic, where I was asked to take a four-hour mule ride to the remote (by Dominican standards at the time) community of Gengebre where there was no road access. It was quite easy to understand the challenges they faced in getting their agricultural produce to market after a few hours in the sun on a small mule where my feet touched the ground. When one has the opportunity to walk with one's staff, share the same food, and drive on the same roads, every team member will have the same opportunities to see more, and through conversation, everyone will usually learn more as well.

### *Varying interests within a humanitarian response*

From very early on in the response to the earthquake that struck Haiti in January of 2010, it was apparent to everyone that Haiti was going to be a large-scale emergency. The response would require a clear roadmap of a plan that would be beneficial to everyone involved in the process, and in the case of Save the Children, was one that focused on health, nutrition, water and sanitation, education, and child protection.

Knowing Haiti was prone to other emergencies, such as another earthquake or hurricane, our strategy made sure to set aside unallocated funds for another possible humanitarian response. When the cholera outbreak came in October of 2010, we were able to respond with a contingency budget and establish three cholera clinics in different geographic areas of Haiti. I will never forget when I saw a single mother carried to one of our cholera clinics by her two children. Had she died, her children would have become orphans. At that moment, I thought about my own children, and what it would have been like if they were left as orphans. When she recovered in our clinic, I could not help but feel grateful that our reserve funds we set aside contributed partly to saving this woman's life. That woman's children, just as my own, deserve the same chances and opportunities in life. That is one of the things that continues to motivate me within humanitarian work. The experience in Haiti, as challenging as it was, encouraged me to make myself available for other deployments following emergencies in Florida in 2017, Puerto Rico in 2018, and Colombia in 2019.

Looking back at a whole career working in long-term development assignments as well as in response to a few of the world's challenging humanitarian disasters, I've discovered the importance of flexibility and improvisation. We are asked to work within the formalities of budgets and grant requirements but then something catastrophic happens and formalities must be reexamined. Whenever possible, I tried to set aside a reserve for things that would come up during the year that could not have been anticipated. The scary part was that I did not know what it would be; I just expected something else would require our attention and a response.

The response to the earthquake in Haiti drew a worldwide response. However, I could not help but recall smaller-scale emergencies in the Dominican Republic where we faced swine flu and in Bolivia where landslides and floods caused crop damage and loss of animals and homes, which were swept away, but fortunately few deaths. For those emergencies, there was little media coverage and funds were hard to identify. Many lives lost usually leads to interest by the media, paving way for greater funds to be forthcoming. I realize that the media has provided the world with a lens as to what is happening in many, but not all, locations, where large humanitarian emergencies exist. This indeed enables many NGOs to be able to respond. However, I feel we still need to address those emergencies that do not make the news, where the impact of the floods, fires, or hailstorms is not as apparent.

I remember internal discussions about what we called "forgotten emergencies" and the steps we took as an agency to build up an emergency endowment for such situations. When I was in the Dominican Republic, a drought had affected the area where I lived along the Haitian frontier. It was hardly in the news in the Dominican Republic, and in the US it was not news at all, so it was not possible to mount a response. I realize that one never has sufficient funds to address all emergencies, but you do what you can with the resources you have to address the situation you and your team are facing.

Looking back and reflecting on my experiences, I have noticed that the "decision maker" role can vary in humanitarian work. It may be a humanitarian worker at Save the Children such as myself, tasked with the responsibility of achieving results for the Haitian people impacted by an earthquake. It may be a group of NGO leaders meeting together to develop common advocacy and discussion points to share with government representatives. Alternatively, it may be a community member like the late Ramonita Reyes, a high school teacher whose volunteer work in her community and the nearby town Gengebre helped raise funds for their community school. Years later, she became governor of Dajabon Province in the Dominican Republic because of her ability to listen, lead, and achieve results.

Dynamics between the decision makers themselves and the community members are no doubt complex relationships. In many countries, there is competition for funds between various local and international NGOs, community members have certain desires that are not always met, and collaboration between them often depends on a leader's ability to harness the opinions of the majority into actionable steps. A successful humanitarian response meeting the expectations of families, communities, government officials, donors, and the NGO involved in the response depends on strong relationships between the leadership and staff of organizations, as well as a true ability to listen to the perspectives of others.

## Why my reflections matter

In the previous section, I reflected upon aspects of my experience that I wanted to share with others. Before explaining the importance of each of these areas and some of my lessons learned, I want to share the guidance I received prior to going to Nepal to start the Save the Children program.

I asked my supervisor what she felt were my top priorities. She did not hesitate at all. Devote a good amount of my time to "drinking tea", she said. By drinking tea, I would get to know people outside Save the Children as soon as possible. The purpose of this was to establish relationships with staff of the late Queen of Nepal's Coordination Council, government agencies, or NGO staff with whom I would be working. After reflecting upon my experiences working in the humanitarian sector, I feel it is also important to touch on ways in which, if given the opportunity, the sector can be improved through individual actions of those in leadership positions with an NGO.

### *Collaboration with NGOs, the UN and international agencies, and bilateral organizations*

While collaborating with other NGO, UN, and international agency staff seems like something one would do routinely, in my own experience this does not always occur. Internal demands within your own organization might lead a person to find that there is not enough time for such meetings. The "drinking tea" guidance I received in Nepal served me very well in my career, as I was able to learn not only from our own staff, but also from staff from other agencies, or from governmental agencies, who became partners in programs that we implemented together.

More and more NGO work is performed by groups of three to five distinct organizations who organize themselves in consortiums to procure grant funding. Knowing with whom to partner has become a critical skill in the matchmaking and formation of these consortiums. Another reason is getting to know NGO personnel who at some point in their career may wish to work for the organization you are representing.

Should none of the above reasons convince the reader to make a deliberate effort to meet peers in leadership positions in a country where you recently arrived, just think of the benefits of sharing security information among organizations about travel and road safety on a real-time basis. From my personal experience, I know of cases where NGO staff lives have been both saved or lost either when information was shared or not because there was no established mechanism to do so.

### Response strategy

In Haiti, our team prepared a response strategy through interviews with community members, other NGO leaders, and Haitian government officials, including mayors. The strategy allowed us to communicate our goals for the Haiti response, our geographic areas of focus, and some of the partners we would work with. We also allocated a budget based on our best understanding of what we would spend and where. Thus, program leads had the information about what funds were already secured, and what we anticipated securing. Project managers could develop their more detailed implementation plans and with a template to develop a summary of each year's accomplishments and challenges. The strategy was very transparent and provided great clarity to all.

For external audiences who wanted to know the program plan for Haiti, we had an abbreviated strategy document that highlighted the areas where we needed additional support. We also used this document as a guide for our reports to donors. Having a clear and organized response strategy, while also remaining flexible and resilient in the case of emergencies, will help you more clearly communicate what your organization is trying to achieve and where you will have its geographic footprint, and it will identify and name some of your key partners and your sectoral areas of expertise.

### Short-term deployment of staff or consultants

NGO specialists, whether they are Health, Education, Child Protection, Livelihoods, Accountability Finance, Security, Human Resources, Financial Management, Internal Audit, or Logistics, are the individuals who dedicate their lives to ensuring that best practices are in place, and innovations are sought. Many of them, before COVID-19 often traveled 50 to 75% of their time to different programs around the world. They are in great demand, so everyone wants to maximize their time. I have seen that this was most effective when the in-country staff has a dedicated technical assistance provider for a group of country programs that are normally working in the same region. In many cases, this happens, as individuals are assigned to regions. One-off visits of just a few days are not that valuable to a country team, especially with large humanitarian responses. It is hard to capture the dynamics of a situation in such a short period and develop a relationship with the staff in the office.

### Procurement of items for distribution

In an emergency situation, there are frequent staff changes and often there is a desire to stock up on supplies because of a legitimate concern that the items desired may not be available for months if not purchased immediately. In my first month in Haiti, I was asked to approve a very large purchase of specific tents, and if some staff had not spoken to me about concerns that they had about this particular tent that they felt was not optimal and appropriate for housing, I might have approved the purchase.

I also learned that procurement should only take place once the program team requesting the items has developed a comprehensive distribution plan. The distribution plan should contain a list of locations that will be reached, an estimate of the number of families who will receive the items being requested, and the dates for distribution so transport can be scheduled with the community's involvement to be certain the dates are mutually agreed. In addition, while some of these reflections seem like common sense, they are reminders of how plans should be reviewed by individuals who can ensure that all steps have been considered.

### COVID-19 pandemic

During the preparation of this document, the COVID-19 pandemic rapidly became part of all of our lives. Colleagues, friends, and some of our supporters asked me how this compared to other emergencies with which I was involved and I could think of nothing even slightly comparable.

In the case of COVID-19, all of us could easily contract the virus, and/or have family members and friends affected. Never before have I seen a situation where the entire world, perhaps with very few exceptions, has been impacted. Many of us likely know people who may have COVID-19, or who had the symptoms but may not have been tested.

I was asked how this compared to the cholera epidemic in Haiti where there were 8,183 deaths and 665,000 cases. With cholera, we knew who the patients were once they arrived at one of our clinics, or when we saw someone with symptoms in one of the areas in which we were working. If these patients could get to the clinics we operated early enough, they could recuperate and return home. In brief, there was treatment and a solution, which could provide a successful outcome in most cases.

Although I have not been directly involved in our agency COVID-19 response, I have witnessed how the worldwide Save the Children organization has mobilized when most of our staff around the world have been working from home and communicating with each other via Zoom or WhatsApp. The impact of technology and the ability to have immediate communication with many of our staff around the globe enables us to exchange information in real time.

Staff have been able to contribute their ideas on the areas where we feel we can have the greatest impact for those most impacted and that has generally focused on health, water and sanitation, education, and multi-purpose cash programs in our international programs, when available. In the United States, the programs focus on nutrition and education. Our staff in our program offices both in the United States and internationally are reaching out to community leaders and families to find out how they are doing. They also share with them the steps that Save the Children has taken to assist and support them. Our staff may have children at home, family members who are ill, and they are dealing with some of the very same issues as the people with whom we work.

My own role has been in speaking with our supporters and explaining what we are doing. I have always been very grateful for the time I have spent with many of our supporters, some who visited programs in Haiti, Nepal, and Bolivia when I lived there, and others whom I met during the years I have spent at our office in Connecticut. Many wish to remain anonymous, helping in any way that they can, often asking where their donation can have the greatest impact. The vulnerability of refugees and internally displaced persons (IDPs) to COVID-19 resonates.

In speaking with our supporters, the generosity of donors to Save the Children and many other NGOs who play such a critical role at times like this has been overwhelming. I have noticed that almost every supporter understands why we are focusing our work on COVID-19, so individuals with other priorities are supportive of the need to address COVID-19. The people with whom I have spoken have been interested in the gender impact of COVID-19 on women in particular, given the multiple roles women play in both childcare and agriculture in our international programs, as well as the situation of those who are refugees or IDPs.

What I have observed is that COVID-19 has been the priority for our organization and others and that when NGOs can bring a singular focus to an issue, our donors are supportive. Every country program and every state in which Save the Children works in the US has a COVID-19 response strategy that has enabled us to get information to those interested in supporting the organization.

# 8  Connecting both ends of the humanitarian cycle

## Engaging donors in a European context

*Naomi Enns*

## Builder of bridges, connections, and webs

Making connections. Sometimes this is an exhausting process, difficult to tend to—particularly in France in 2020, in a radically altered world where a pandemic has changed circumstances daily. For those who live in privileged countries, it feels like COVID-19 has brought life to a standstill. While always challenging, a humanitarian organization's task of making and maintaining connections among people—donors and recipients of their donations—has become even more crucial. I worry about this as I face the isolating impact of this virus storm, which means carefully mapped plans must be redrawn, narratives rewritten, and human interactions reframed to find meaning.

Accompanying, enabling, and connecting are all important elements of my job as a representative (a country director) of Mennonite Central Committee (MCC), a North American, faith-based, humanitarian, nongovernmental organization (NGO). But government restrictions on movement make me pay fresh attention to spaces, especially the one I am in. My role is like that of a slim thread in a spider's web, buffeted by a fierce wind but trying to hold the whole fragile arrangement together. People talk about a need to slow down. This sounds attractive, yet I find it hard. Knowing this pandemic will be deadly for many brings a sense of urgency. I became aware only a few days ago that my days here in Europe will be limited because of changes wrought by COVID-19—the result of an organizational reshuffling prompted by lowered funding in North America. Those who, like me, influence funding streams for vulnerable communities, are acutely aware that the daily bread and future wellbeing of recipients may be in our hands. Confinement also raises questions about how I can draw on compassion and connection to bring in desperately needed funds. If I don't pay attention, strands in this fragile web may rip; gaps may appear, demanding repair while leaving needs unmet. The humanitarian cycle may fall apart.

I'm trying to navigate through this pandemic, to keep building aid bridges between cultures and worlds. I cover 12 countries in Western Europe, building trust among communities and Europeans who donate to our international work. As a guest, I engage in donor relations with small, faith-based European Mennonite relief organizations, agencies, and church partners. I also work with local NGOs running community programs for marginalized persons. Before this, my international work included community health in an intense setting of chronic poverty in Chad, where the focus on survival was paramount. Then, I spent four years in the shadow of war with refugees and host communities in Lebanon and Syria. There, directing a large relief response, I witnessed how humanitarian care can itself be linked to trauma when we don't apply peace and conflict transformation strategies—otherwise so easily talked about by humanitarian NGOs—to how we deal with beneficiaries, staff, or even visiting donors. Today, my role has shifted. I still feel compelled to be a microphone for the voices of the most vulnerable, so they can be heard over the noise of the humanitarian architecture. But I am a 57-year-old humanitarian peacebuilder listening to the voices of donors and nurturing their patterns of giving, building a web of trust.

Each of the places where I have worked has left its mark on how I approach and engage others. Living in places of conflict and poverty has confirmed the beliefs of my Mennonite faith tradition about working for reconciliation nonviolently, about nurturing and transforming lives through building positive communities (physically, mentally, emotionally, and spiritually). I'm still not quite sure how I ended up in Europe, working in donor relations, but here I am. My 34 years of community engagement and service have been shaped through time spent on the West Coast of the United States, Canada, Central West Africa, the Middle East, and Europe. I grew up in lower middle-class America, yet I had access to higher education. This led me to nursing, community health, teaching, and overseas work in relief, development, and peacebuilding. My Christian faith and its values of caring and hospitality, often shared through stories, shape my sense of duty to help those in need. A passion for peacebuilding, righting unjust systems, and promoting healing where communities suffer from disease, poverty, trauma, and war keeps me going. Yet under COVID-19 I find myself asking: How long might this last?

Perhaps I've found myself in the humanitarian field because I have "fixer" tendencies or because of my experience as a mother. Three adult children, a grandson, and the many young adults I meet challenge me to be aware of where I am and what I can do for this planet. Their thoughts on this feel critical, because it seems the fabric of society is wearing thin. Solidarity and compassion are at risk. I have discovered that as I move from one continent to another, young people's stories of struggle, pain, and hope as they strive to build their own communities have become central to my work. Most important, I feel engaging donors has helped build collaboration between communities, an essential part of funding.

## Story builds opportunities to listen and connect

Each morning, waking up in these challenging circumstances, I think about the growing gap in the humanitarian aid cycle. I find myself asking how I can communicate what's happening in the international field with people in donor communities quickly enough to get help to where it's most needed. That's why a large part of my role in the humanitarian sector has involved gathering and sharing stories—stories that vividly present the needs and describe how lives have been benefited and touched by connections to others.

Relationships between partners here in Europe and our international NGO are strengthened by sharing stories of lives altered by the humanitarian work we do together. Personal stories that bring into focus the similarities and differences between us also raise awareness of inequality between nations and the related power dynamics. But field staff never seem fully aware of just how powerful their story may be in changing donor perspectives (I'll address that later); nor do they recognize how important timely communication is to keep the cycle intact. I find it difficult to convince them that I need relevant stories *quickly*, through email or in person. Donors are curious; they want to know what is happening *now* and how their help might empower vulnerable people, aware that, in a different universe, *they* might have been the people in need. COVID-19 has reminded all of us how fragile life is. Better communication, to and with European donors, is a vital part of my work in bearing witness to the need and building global interest in filling that need.

The stories we tell are so important. On a personal level, certain narratives have shaped and transformed me. Donors are likewise inspired by stories. In fact, I've seen many transformed into strong advocates after they listened to compelling stories. Enabling stories to be told and heard is a vital part of building interdependent relationships. In turn, personal relationships are central to rebuilding and transforming society, as I've seen in Europe in particular. Peacebuilder John Paul Lederach suggests the same.[1] Stories help people engage with the "other" in a relational moment, even at a distance. Telling stories in a way that meets the needs of those listening leads to the kind of fruitful conversation that empowers change. When I've told a story that truly connects with the audience, I see eyes light up and leaders lean in to hear more.

But how, in these times, can I share stories in that way, on behalf of poor and displaced people who are usually unseen and unheard? Coronavirus has changed our world, ripped our norms apart, broken supply chains, tightened border restrictions, altered my ability to talk to donors in person, forced us to move apart, deepened personal loss, and made it difficult to maintain connections internationally with people experiencing dire circumstances.

I'm frustrated by what has been lost, and like many I feel fragile and at times on edge. I have a vital responsibility to attend to relationships and the links that keep humanitarian work afloat during this time of stress and uncertainty—links best built through meaningful stories that foster giving. It's been difficult when I've struggled with interrupted sleep and symptoms of what might be coronavirus, isolated within the walls of our apartment. I find myself racing to catch that moment of connection when I might solidify someone's commitment to collaboration. For example, yesterday a donor was weighing his options and contemplating giving to churches in Burkina Faso where communities are suffering. He needed to know how COVID-19 is affecting vulnerable people there right now and what might be changed with help. So, to meet his need, I rushed to get him meaningful updates.

At every part of the humanitarian cycle, there are needs. You have potential donors and you need the story that can communicate, connect, and offer meaning, to help donors understand another's need or help to bring their European communities together in common cause amid changing cultures. You have the poor living among them, many of whom have fled areas of conflict, and those who are in greater need in other countries. It's all connected as I try to, first, nurture a desire to contribute something of value to others, and second, to build a new cooperative perspective that allows donors from different communities—with their own traumatized histories—the opportunity to have a transforming global impact.

Having already talked about myself and my role, I will focus on the aspect of my work which involves strengthening the humanitarian world, the sharing of stories to promote collaborative connections.

## Reflections on the power of story: humanitarian solidarity and identity

Meaningful stories are critical to the success of my work. Stories can communicate the idea that people in countries of need should not be seen as objects "out there" who need rescue, but as human beings just like us, who can be protected with financial help, just as the masks we wear daily protect our society here. Europeans and donors globally hunger for a sense of control in what seems a situation of powerlessness as we fight this virus. We also hunger for a sense of solidarity amidst isolation, to close the distance between social locations and break through systems that divide us as human beings and keep some from living well, or living at all. (Witness the sudden rise of the Black Lives Matter movement amid the pandemic, rooted in the narrative of a single man's death.)

In this time of deep financial stress particularly, stories can help build that solidarity, encouraging and increasing donor confidence in our shared values. When stories about our international work are made available quickly and explored deeply, I see increases in collaboration.

But with COVID-19 shaking financial reserves and even my job, it appears that humanitarians desperately need to provide a story people in affluent communities can feel part of, that supports transforming structures, and that will empower sustained partnerships. Initially I did not realize the full benefit of using stories to build meaning. But my experience in Europe has taught me that one needs to be willing to enter into deep conversations that link a donor imaginatively to other places, conversations that help them realize that what they (or their society) did previously and what they do now both have a wide impact. This has me asking: Is it the *way* a story is shared that empowers change, or is it the *wondering* it evokes that does this?

For international work, the European community's value is about more than the money it can bring to an organization; the stories and identities of Europeans can also teach us about change. Getting to know a broad range of Europeans has reaffirmed to me that building a resilient funding stream demands two characteristics: a) social cohesion (even in donor communities) and b) connected communities. I've found that a donor's identity can be an obstacle or a catalyst for change in either of these. I've learned that the choice to give is often sparked by a sense of self shaped by past experiences. Many times, as I've sat listening, I've heard about World War II wounds in European villages or religious differences that still cause divisions, and how being offered an opportunity to help others in similar circumstances has brought healing and cohesion by working together on a common goal. For example, groups from various European countries that once fought each other found that their common task of sewing comforters for refugees gave them a chance to heal these old divisions. Groups that included both Europeans and migrants found their common history of displacement promoted healing, fostered a sense of belonging, and decreased their fears of each other, as they focused on doing something of compassionate value together. It seems that participation and collaboration among various countries' agencies to provide aid to others has lessened the pain of their own historical wounds and built internal resiliency. If social patterns are important, then perhaps engaging donors is not only about the recipients. This is certainly part of the story here, and why we work at building relational relief partnerships.

I work in communities still haunted by the trauma of historic conflicts. Yet, as a European partner recently said of the pandemic, "In moments like these we sense how important it is to be connected." That is why we need conversations and stories that offer a chance for donors to see how they also benefit from giving. Stories can remind us that "we are at our best when we serve others," as Margaret Mead suggests.[2] I sense every response reflects a donor's identity. Relief stories often lead them to share personal trauma or a fear of the "other" lying just beneath the surface. Recently I sat with older women involved in sewing comforters (see Figure 8.1). When asked why they were participating, they shared personal stories about being World War II refugees. Their experiences of being displaced, hungry, and receiving help from someone overseas engaged them personally in the healing work of relief. I find that stories can be catalysts when they lead to a sense of shared humanity.

It is clear that both ends of the cycle benefit when stories are shared. It's etched in my mind how donors responded to the words of a recipient from Aleppo, Syria, who came to speak with our volunteers. Recognizing his similarity to them led to a new perspective of trust which has kept them donating. And as this man listened to the Europeans' own stories of suffering and resilience, and learned of their desire to help, he found a renewed sense of capacity. Recognizing that donors had not forgotten Syria, he said, "I will take this spirit back. My community can learn from your stories as we deal with our needs." So, being forced to work virtually at this time, I ask myself whether it was a recognition of similarities in a personal story or the depth of a face-to-face conversation that most helped to shift perspectives and build trust towards long-term support.

It's important to help people see beyond their borders through a positive lens. Yet I believe some people I have worked with donated out of fear, wanting with their money to keep the "other" away from Europe. This is understandable. In recent years Europe has been inundated with asylum seekers from the

*Figure 8.1* Women sewing relief comforters, sharing personal stories about being World War II refugees

Middle East, Africa, and South Asia. That migrants remain trapped in growing camps near their borders, for example in Lesbos, has had an impact on efforts to encourage donor churches to help internationally. They are mindful of terrorism and the rising, polarizing voice of nationalism. When I sense individuals are struggling with these doubts, I've found the best approach is to work through their fears first, as fear is real and can keep connections from happening. Fortunately, Europeans displaced in earlier times seem to understand the vulnerable person's realities more easily—like the women I spoke of earlier who are drawn to making relief comforters for MCC. But the migrant crisis remains; traumatized people from war-torn places need to integrate even as their presence stretches capacity during the pandemic and sparks hostility. Those I talk with worry about obtaining enough face masks or medical help. The social isolation associated with this unprecedented health crisis doesn't help, but it does teach us how much we need one another.

Amid forced confinement, I find myself seeking the comfort of human faces. Looking for life on empty streets during the short walks allowed, I see a growing number of homeless people sheltering under bridges. With our own safety nets fraying, I struggle to help supporters remain outward-looking. Funding streams for international work are drying up because of suffering economies. How do we accompany and enable others to work for positive change where the world's most vulnerable people live, when priorities are shifting? I'm reminded of the Spanish churches who asked for training in how to deal with migrant trauma and growing violence in their city, or a call from Italy asking where to donate to keep refugees from coming to their shores. As I write, I wonder whether it's important to focus first on where the need is in the donor community before pointing elsewhere. Or if one can be aware of and act on those needs, while remaining mindful that what happens here will affect what happens in another place of deep needs. COVID-19 may reinforce the idea that how we care for others in our midst predicts how we will care for others beyond our borders.

We must listen and deal with what is most important to donors in their own context. Looking back, I think it's because I have paid attention to the local context that these churches are now collaborative partners in international relief and more interested in assisting displaced people in Europe. Donors will be more engaged if we take the time to understand their own backyard, to facilitate trauma healing and to interpret what is happening in refugee camps within the constituent communities. Using story, I found it possible to highlight the implications of change in social structures (between wealthy and poor) and how donors can empower others.

Stories, it's important to note, carry the weight of identifying the power donors hold over other lives—especially in places where their forebears did great damage by colonial rule. I am seeing how stories can draw us together in solidarity, which we need now more than ever. The glue that holds a network of donors together and seals their commitment is influenced by the manner in which I have invited them into a relationship with those in need of aid. It's fostered by helping them recognize common interests and common needs: food, water, shelter, safety, belonging, and conditions to thrive. This approach sheds light on how donors might be moved from a "power over" perspective to a "power with" attitude—a shift that might help them meet their post-colonial responsibility to be part of a humanitarian movement that is building capacity in African and Middle Eastern countries to lift their societies out of poverty.

I am trying to shape change from an emergent perspective—one that leads to longer-term giving by donors because they have taken on the desire to right wrongs as their own concern, rather than because I have pushed it on them in a guilt-ridden power move. I feel we weave a stronger web of humanitarian connections when we provide a channel for compassionate giving while also nurturing health in the donor community by attending to their own social concerns.

It seems to me field staff typically aren't interested in how donors' identities and values are connected to levels of engagement. It might be helpful if they knew how the experience of fragility produced by the virus here has led to a sense of shared identity with others internationally. Or how elderly women making comforters remind me that this opportunity helps them make a difference. Since the international response to COVID-19 entered the discussion, it has motivated stronger giving to programs that are scaling up to help vulnerable people deal with the pandemic. This underscores the need to remember donors' identities and values. I've seen many examples, as I interact with Europeans, of how failing to connect our work to shared human values will mean struggling to keep donors engaged over the long haul, as their funds flow to critical needs.

While European Mennonites have a tradition of caring for others, drawn from their peace and reconciliation values, I've noticed they struggle with the idea of just sending money "out there," even if they trust the organizations involved. They abhor fancy marketing techniques. Behind their giving is a desire for relationships and dialogue. Storytelling fulfills that desire. I recall again the Syrian community leader who came to share his story. Meeting this man, whose community had received disaster aid, changed the perspective of donors. The visit had to be handled delicately, given the importance of neutrality in giving. But it may also have helped transform the guilt of colonial affluence for Europeans, whose interference historically left many societies with oppressive systems. Three years later, his visit still comes up in conversation. Commitment to giving is not just about feeling benevolent; it's also about understanding enough to see basic human similarities on a personal level. That's why I feel that, for donors, knowledge of those in need is important, and face-to-face encounters are powerful. Nothing replaces a human face, seen in real time. What makes someone far away more *human* than hearing that person's life story?

Being invested in giving helps Europeans feel a sense of solidarity with humanity. Yet shipping material resources carries risk: it gives donors power over what needs are met and how resources are received. So humility is essential, as is concern for the rights and dignity of others. I've witnessed how small issues can become extraordinarily important in maintaining respect for and peace among those who receive aid. I once coordinated a shipment of school kits with an unintended error. Not all the home-sewn kits were checked, and on 10 bags someone had placed what they thought were innocent pink six-pointed stars. I wasn't aware of this until distributing partners realized that the stars, resembling the Israeli emblem, could evoke partisan violence amid the tense Syrian conflict. It cost trust and valuable time to remove the appliques. I had the difficult job of relaying the problem at this end, where I learned that helping others recognize that what may be an innocent symbol in one place can be dangerous in another creates tension. We need to be attentive both to the emotions of donors trying to be helpful and to core humanitarian principles that put the dignity and safety of recipients first. This event highlighted the importance of honest evaluation, to build trust and develop best practices. Telling the receivers this story also helped them learn not to judge donors or assume bad intentions. It showed me the importance of recognizing differences in the spaces in which we work, as actions in one may have unintended effects elsewhere.

I've alluded to how donor conversations carry power. Power can build or destroy capacity. That is why we need to focus on *how* we share about needs. Recently, thanks to COVID-19 restrictions, I was trying to share stories about need in an exhausting seven-hour Zoom meeting of donors. I find these conversations delicate, as I represent a North American entity trying to maintain the trust of Europeans who have their own, smaller relief organizations without the same reach or global impact. Meeting virtually made it harder to sense nuances, clarify meanings, or explain assessments. Yet the technology did allow for these donors to see a partner from another organization they knew personally from visits to Kinshasa. They could hear firsthand his description of how COVID-19 was affecting his world. Afterward, the group commented that they felt closer to him after hearing his thoughts. I had wanted assistance for our work but didn't want to beg, only to offer facts and then let them decide. I felt I could influence this group.

Listening carefully, I noticed the group was being nudged towards giving by a sense of stewardship, compassion, and a compelling story. Having directly engaged with a man at the grassroots and connected with his pain, they had a stronger desire to meet his requests. They chose to send him funds.

This reinforces what I have noted often in donor conversations: their effort to understand local populations, hear about their difficulties, and visualize what is occurring in those communities, such as infant malnutrition or food insecurity. I hear from Europeans a desire to shed colonial attitudes, expressed through a deep interest in cultures, social stability, and keeping civilizations from crumbling. Stories help weave a sense of how they can do that by enabling others to build conditions where everyone can thrive. In a time of pandemic, when funders—accustomed to being in control—suddenly feel anxious, storytelling brings a welcome clarity: here is a way to reclaim justice and healing. Stories can create giving cultures.

## Why engaging cooperation through storytelling matters globally

Using stories from the field, I try to build a narrative of a more just world, with respect for human beings and our interconnectedness. Given that our organizations need multiple funders, it's time for NGOs to recognize what drives donors. My experience is that funding may not be sustained if we don't properly value the stories of both aid recipients and donors and recognize the power of these stories to engage those able to help. Our ability to gather donations, collaborate, and coordinate may depend on recognizing the power of story to creatively connect to the identities and memories of donors and inspire a desire to right the wrongs of a colonial past. As humanitarians, we recognize that collaboration and communication are key to holding communities and disaster responses together, but we need to engage donors deeply enough to transform their habits over the long term. The coronavirus crisis has shaken our world to the core. It has exposed weaknesses in European unity as member nations reinitiated borders and fought over access to resources, such as masks. It was only when solidarity values rose that aid started to flow again towards the most affected countries. Compassion calls out solidarity in donors.

The global choice to act with compassion is at risk if we don't develop consciousness of our shared humanity and help donors recognize the power of wealthy nations over the wellbeing of others. Creating that awareness takes listening by both donors and NGOs and sharing of our narratives and experiences at both ends. COVID-19 is a reminder of our shared humanity as it moves across countries, causing trauma and loss to all. As humanitarian linkers, we can use story and memory to help people imagine a post-COVID world where affluent societies realize they have much to learn from those who receive aid about maintaining the social fabric amid poverty or conflict. If we don't share the story at both ends, we lose the opportunity to move toward a better world that places high value on service to others.

The global humanitarian community, seeking European funding, needs to remember what Europeans learned through their own wars and suffering about the importance of cooperation. "Today I work your field, tomorrow you work mine," Jacques Roumain reminds us. "Cooperation is the friendship of the poor."[3] Community matters most to those who are ill or hungry, but it also matters to peace-tradition churches. Europeans, struggling with social integration of migrants, terrorism, and now the pandemic, have seen ample demonstrations of how fragile communities can be. Around the globe, in the face of COVID-19, we are realizing we need each other. Poor and rich, we need networks and ways to share our stories, to connect meaningfully.

I began to realize this when, over weeks of total confinement on my small Strasbourgan street, I participated in the nightly communal applause from balconies for people on the pandemic front lines. Humanitarians at both ends must share their stories with the other to keep the thread of connection intact and minimize hardship. Without communicating needs, we will face growing global inequality as people with resources rebound quickly while others no longer have a livelihood to return to.

Europeans yearn for ways to be human and to remove the stain of their colonial history abroad; people on the receiving end of aid yearn to be known as human beings with dignity and a right to the necessities of life. As a humanitarian organization, we need to remind both that we are in this together. We may lose the help of faith-based communities, who work at building community, if we don't remember their need to be present (in story). The "we" story is stronger than just one story.

There is debate on what level of information donors should be allowed to require. But information flow is critical in disaster responses and the key to interdependent, trusting relationships. Storytelling is a resource donor communities can draw on to strengthen collaboration and develop a culture of compassion. One (the donor) gives and two (donor and beneficiary) receive, and it is the story linking those parts that catalyzes change for the most vulnerable.

Organizations and workers need to recognize that our relationships with partners are critical to promoting assistance. Personal stories that bring people into contact, that share present needs or describe how life is experienced, or how people have been touched by assistance and connections, are a critical element of this. Strategically, if we don't keep building that connection with European donors even while social distancing, we risk losing an important funding stream—especially when many countries are headed into recession.

A final thought. A spider web hangs on my balcony. I've been reflecting on the way it swings tenaciously in the breeze. Like the wind in that slightly tattered spider web, this virus has put holes where connecting threads should be. The virus has shaken us up but also given us a chance to learn and remember what is most important in life. It can help us think about and do what makes for sustainability, resiliency, and the qualities that hold this fragile web of connection together: solidarity, trust, and willingness. So much is uncertain, but I am trying to maintain sanity, regroup, reframe loss, and focus on what is most important: human contact and compassion, in whatever way it can happen. If I may compare the spider's web to the humanitarian world, my role is that of a connector, weaving silken threads, attending to spaces, and valuing people. The art of web-weaving keeps me going. This work of accompanying, enabling, and connecting to others through compassion fosters wellbeing in all parts of the humanitarian cycle. Sharing stories is a vital way for humanitarian organizations to bridge divides. In the stories of beneficiaries and donors, we find meaning, close gaps, engage givers, and make the web of international and local assistance that much stronger.

## Notes

1 John Paul Lederach, *The Moral Imagination: The Art and Soul of Building Peace* (New York: Oxford University Press, 2005).
2 Mead, Margaret, quoted in Ira Byock, *The Best Care Possible: A Physician's Quest to Transform Care Through the End of Life* (Waterville, Maine: Thorndike Press, 2012).
3 Roumain, Jacques (1944) *Gouverneurs de la Rosée,* trans. Mercer Cook and Langston Hughes (1947) as *Masters of the Dew,* quoted in Danticat, Edwidge (2020) "This Too Shall Pass? Hope and Community amid Disaster" Regeneration, April 21, 2020.

# 9 The role of volunteers

*Jono Anzalone*

## Who are you?

Nebraska, 1978. Michael and Mary Jo Anzalone give birth to their third and last child in Omaha. Born into a middle-class family in the middle of the USA, I often reflect on the journey that would follow in becoming part of the humanitarian machine. My formative years as a child were surrounded by a large nicely balanced Italian American and Syrian American family (my mother's father an Abraham, her mom Cifuno, and my father's dad an Anzalone, and his mom a Ferris). My younger years were formed by my devout Catholic upbringing, where elementary school was spent in the Catholic system, as well as seeing the generosity and grace of my parents and Nana in caring for and respecting all people, regardless of their backgrounds.

This ambition of helping others as well as a desire to be socio-economically self-sufficient led me to working at a young age, with my sights on being a lifeguard. The prerequisites for lifeguarding in the United States are cardiopulmonary recitation (CPR) and first aid certifications. I turned to my local Red Cross to sign up for a class in 1994. This is where a milestone occurred in exposing me, a Nebraskan with limited familiarity with issues outside of the midwestern state I grew up in, to the humanitarian space. I remember walking into my local Red Cross to sign up for the classes and seeing seven posters with the words "humanity, impartiality, neutrality, independence, voluntary service, universality, and unity," as well as pictures that embodied each word. I also picked up a brochure with a clever title, "the hardest job you will never get paid for," a call to action to sign up as a member of the Red Cross Disaster Action Team (DAT).

After completing CPR and first aid and lifeguarding courses, I felt compelled to sign up as a Red Cross volunteer, as the memory of the posters in the building as well as literature on DAT was vivid and led me to believe I too could be a part of a system and organization that provided aid to those in need. As a DAT volunteer, I responded to community-based disasters, most frequently single- and multiple-family structure fires, where I was trained to work with impacted individuals and families to provide emergency food, clothing, and shelter. Being on call during my teenage years meant multiple nights and weekends where I could be awoken before classes to drive with another Red Cross volunteer to provide humanitarian assistance to those with no safety net. While the food, clothing, and shelter that was provided post-disaster was impactful, most often it was a hug or simply listening to disaster survivors that was most needed to begin their healing process.

On average, my local Red Cross was responding to nearly 600 local disasters per year, and it was evident that the neighborhoods that were impacted most frequently were those in low-income neighborhoods, typically people of color, and without insurance. While most volunteers with the Red Cross in my community were Caucasians, and most with the time and resources that allowed them to volunteer, it became evident to me how the seven posters in the lobby of the Red Cross chapter lived through action. Volunteers I deployed with did not see race, religious preference, economic status, or other categorical boxes of those impacted by disaster; they saw a human whose dignity had been impacted.

My affection for the Red Cross mission only grew, as I would find opportunities to support regional disaster deployments during my summers in high school, with aspirations to also support national disaster operations (and at the time idealizing over the dream of an international deployment). As I was discerning university choices, I yearned to expand my worldview, while balancing the deep affection and ties to my family. I decided to take my first semester of college in Madrid, Spain in 1997, a way to deepen my learning of the Spanish language which I had studied in high school.

Immediately upon return to Omaha to finish my undergraduate studies in political science at Creighton University I found myself once again volunteering with the Red Cross. This persisted until I completed my graduate studies in economics

*Figure 9.1* American Red Cross: Gran No Pi Djanm Program in Haiti

in 2006 where I then transitioned from my volunteer status with Red Cross to take the paid role of Director of Emergency Services for my chapter.

## The story

The decision to migrate from a volunteer role to a paid position was rooted in my formative years as a Red Cross youth member, as well as in Hurricane Katrina's devastating impact. It was shocking to me to know that even in the resource-rich environment of the United States there were 1,836 deaths and displacement of more than 770,000 people due to a failed safety net and that the most vulnerable were the most affected.[1]

Katrina's displacement of Louisiana residents across the US was catastrophic. I recall a flight of evacuees, nearly all African-American, arriving at the Omaha airport with nothing except what they could gather as the flood waters rose in New Orleans. As a volunteer Chairman of the Disaster Services program at the Red Cross in Omaha, I deployed to the reception and shelter center. I remember one senior citizen deboarding the plane who, as I welcomed her to Nebraska, replied "Nebraska? I thought they said we were flying to Alaska." Disoriented, with nothing but a black trash bag she was able to throw several valuables into before she was evacuated from her rooftop, she now was heading to the Omaha Civic Auditorium to join several hundred evacuees who were struggling to navigate the complex emergency management system. Among other memorable evacuees I met was a young transsexual individual.

As a gay male, although not fully out at the time, I believe I could sense her anxiety in navigating a world where there was a binary condition of men's and women' restrooms and showers. She also had to navigate the areas of the shelter which were deemed to be male dormitories or female dormitories. Trying to imagine the trauma induced by Hurricane Katrina, on top of navigating the discriminatory environment many LGBTQ individuals face, I found myself honing in on her well-being to ensure that she knew that, while with the Red Cross, those seven posters and the fundamental principles they represent were an umbrella for her, upholding human dignity. In the Red Cross volunteers working the operation, I saw unwavering action that had one principal concern: to alleviate human suffering. These seven fundamental principles, seven seemingly simple words, created the foundation for my lifelong commitment to humanitarian action: humanity, impartiality, neutrality, independence, volunteerism, unity, and universality. Even in Nebraska, a traditionally conservative state, the power of humanity could transcend political boundaries.

After Hurricane Katrina, the United States government made several recommendations for enhanced coordination of mass care (shelter, feeding, and distribution of emergency supplies) between the Federal Emergency Management Agency (FEMA) and the Red Cross. There is a rich history of the Red Cross' relationship with FEMA, dating back to 1994 when the first National Response Plan was published, listing the Red Cross as the lead agency for mass care. One of the recommendations led to Red Cross staff being embedded in FEMA Regional and Headquarter offices. I had the honor of serving as the liaison to the FEMA Regional Office in Kansas City, Missouri and there gained incredible appreciation and understanding of the role that governments, with non-profit partners, play in emergency management.

While there were significant criticisms of FEMA after Hurricane Katrina, it became evident during my tenure working with FEMA that the agency was largely filled with civil servants wanting to carry out a lifesaving mission, and that it was the enabling laws and budgets to operationalize the laws that needed to be altered. For example, US laws allow an individual impacted by a disaster to receive a maximum financial award of $25,000 from FEMA, and if eligible, an individual may qualify for a FEMA-provided temporary housing unit for up to 18 months. These units cost US taxpayers more than $250,000, are environmentally damaging, and are not scalable in housing large numbers of individuals. Instead of taking a portion of those costs and allowing individuals to rebuild or repair their homes, above the $25,000 max grant, FEMA's hands are tied without a change of the laws and regulations they are bound by.[2]

In 2006, I began exploring how I could live out my lifelong dream of working on humanitarian operations internationally by applying to become an instructor of the Red Cross International Humanitarian Law (IHL) course. This course introduces audiences from novice to legal expert on the origins of the Red Cross Red Crescent movement, as well as the rich history of the Geneva Conventions. These laws, the rules of international armed conflict, interested me as they tied back to those seven posters in the Red Cross lobby in Omaha. I was also fortunate to be accepted into the Red Cross Basic Training Course (BTC), the foundational course that would allow you to deploy internationally.

My first international assignment was as a seconded delegate to the Federation of Red Cross and Red Crescent Societies (IFRC)'s Pan American Disaster Response Unit (PADRU) based out of Panama, Panama. As a disaster management delegate, my role was to support Red Cross National Societies within the Americas and Caribbean Region. During my first response operation, I remember the awe that I felt when I walked into the headquarters branch of the Belize Red Cross in Belize City, surprised to see those same seven posters proudly displayed. Regardless of the cultural context, fundamental principles of the Red Cross Red Crescent were displayed as a reminder of the moral and ethical compass that guides 14 million volunteers and staff in 190 countries around the globe. As auxiliaries to their government, the Belize Red Cross, like other Red Cross Red Crescent National Societies, was focused on how the impacted communities from Hurricane Arthur were going to receive humanitarian assistance.[3]

This was my first international deployment where I saw the onset of humanitarian actors outside of a textbook and training; there was NEMA, CDEMA, UNOCHA, USAID/OFDA, DFID, ECHO. Alphabet soup, each with their own mandate and funding streams. "Who are these agencies? Are they all needed or are some duplicating efforts to assist disaster-impacted communities?", I thought. Working closely with the Secretary General of the Belize Red Cross, Ms. Lily Bowman, we coupled together a plan of action to mobilize the power of volunteers in Belize, despite the noise that came from the complex humanitarian machine requiring coordination with dozens of stakeholders. Our emergency appeal paid attention to those that were most vulnerable in the impacted area.

Women, single heads of household, children, elderly, and those with access and functional needs (i.e. disabled in the vernacular of many which I will intentionally avoid using in this chapter due to the lack of empowerment suggested by the word), were identified through a participatory approach. Grassroots volunteers from Red Cross chapters throughout the impacted area were mobilized for the assessment, and potential beneficiaries for assistance were made part of the plan design and execution. I recall reflecting on the various differences between US-based approaches to humanitarian assistance versus those I was witnessing (and learned about during my international training).

I found it interesting that within the broader context of emergency management in the United States, participatory approaches were less commonly used. Hurricane Katrina uprooted more than 700,000 local New Orleans residents, with no input or self-determination of their destiny. Large pots of federal funding are implemented, such as the Housing and Urban Development (HUD) Community Development Block Grants (CDBG) with little community input. It appeared (and still appears) that international humanitarian assistance had a clear lead in participatory design and accountability to affected populations.

After returning from my year in Panama working for the IFRC in 2008, I was fortunate to return to the FEMA Regional Office, this time working directly for the federal government as a Regional Voluntary Liaison (VAL). At this point in my career I knew there were these gaps in the way the emergency management ecosystem was built, and I wanted to be part of the solution. I also knew that the Red Cross principles that had guided me for 14 years were also evident in the type of work that FEMA performs: humanity as the guiding principle in particular, although as a government agency, some could argue that the agency was less than neutral and impartial. This was also immediately after the election of President Obama, whose community-based approach to governance inspired me. The VAL position was created to establish, foster, and maintain relationships among government, voluntary, faith-based, and community partners to strengthen capabilities and support the delivery of inclusive, equitable services by empowering communities to address disaster-related unmet needs. While there are many illusions of the federal government being at the forefront of disaster response, the most important asset and common denominator in disaster response and recovery are those in the communities impacted.

For nearly four years as a VAL, I had the privilege of working with countless faith-based and secular community groups and non-profits post-disaster, with one part of the job being to translate what FEMA and other government agencies do and don't do in disaster response and the other part being a sounding board for community organizing and linking best practices and resources that are part of the humanitarian machine. After the May 11, 2011 tornado, for example, I deployed for countless months working with the city treasurer and hundreds of non-governmental organizations (NGOs) that deployed to Joplin in the aftermath of the vicious F5 tornado that claimed 161 lives. A little-known US government regulation allows for city and state entities to offset the bill paid to the federal government when there is a presidential disaster declaration. States and local governments pay for up to 25% of the total cost of a disaster operation, which often can be in the millions of dollars.[4] Volunteer hours and in-kind donations can qualify to offset the state and local cost share, thus saving communities much-needed cash or cash they do not have in reserve. Through the work we performed, we documented over 610,300 volunteer hours from more than 102,000 volunteers, saving the city of Joplin $17.7 million.[5]

After nearly four years of professional growth with FEMA, my calling to come back to Red Cross arrived. I had the opportunity to serve as the Director of Government Operations in Washington, DC in 2012. My work there was as key liaison between the Red Cross and Federal Agencies, as the American Red Cross is a Congressional Chartered agency, a status that officially recognizes the Red Cross as an auxiliary to government, although independent from government.[6] Balancing neutrality, impartiality, and this independency was critical for the Red Cross to perform its mission in serving the most vulnerable, where often disaster relief can be a divisive subject. For example, during Hurricane Sandy, a large hurricane that hit New York City as well as a total of 13 states with high wind, rain, and storm surge, many immigrants and vulnerable communities were impacted. While some elected officials may wish to prioritize aid for citizens, the dignity and humanitarian imperative tells us that access to aid should be made to all those impacted and that organizations like the Red Cross are essential to ensure overlooked communities and individuals have access to key services.

My Red Cross professional journey and advancement continued as I was honored to accept a disaster executive position overseeing disaster preparedness, response, and recovery in 11 states in the central United States. This was followed by an opportunity to lead the International Services Department of the American Red Cross as Vice President in 2015, where I oversaw disaster preparedness, response, and recovery programming in more than 34 countries, including the Measles and Rubella Initiative which since 2001 has helped vaccinate more than 2 billion children and reduce global measles by 84% − more than 20.4 million lives. The universality of the Red Cross in the countries our programs supported was both inspiring and humbling, knowing that 192 countries have a Red Cross or Red Crescent within their country.

A large gap in my professional development was experience in how the private sector was making inroads in changing the way in which disaster response and recovery were taking place After a dear friend and mentor recommended that I read Elizabeth Gilbert's *Big Magic*, I knew it was time to take a leap of faith. In 2009, I met a now dear friend, Kellie Bentz, working for Points of Lights, an organization dedicated to creating a culture of volunteering. Kellie joined Airbnb in 2015 to lead their Global Disaster Response and Relief program and invited me in 2018 to join her team for a year contract. A scary move, as I had grown accustomed to the comforts of the known humanitarian sector where I had been for so long. The move was nothing short of a mega-growth opportunity for me as I had the privilege of working with a team leveraging the massive Airbnb host community across the enterprise to respond to crises and disasters that impact the Airbnb community, which includes over 4 million hosts in 190 countries. The idea of Airbnb hosts being able to offer their space for disaster survivors post-disaster was brilliant, and this outside the box thinking was much needed in the humanitarian industry, which is often encumbered by traditional thinking on the way things have always been done.

At the conclusion of my year with Airbnb, I had the opportunity to join the Airbnb team full time, and after much soul seeking, I decided to bring what I had learned about user design and innovation back to the Red Cross. After all, the fundamental principle of volunteerism had been one that hooked me into the Red Cross back in 1994. In October 2019, I was fortunate to start as the Head of Disaster and Crisis with the IFRC based in Panama, Panama, a return to the location that marked my first long-term international mission 11 years prior. This time around I was lucky to be accompanied by my wonderful husband, who worked on gender equity and social inclusion with Save the Children. In my role in the Panama Regional office, with coverage of 35 countries in the Americas and Caribbean, I lead the teams overseeing Disaster Risk Reduction, Climate Change, Shelter, Migration, Livelihoods, Disaster Response and Recovery, and International Disaster Law. Little did I know that just months after settling into this role would the world as we know it starkly change due to the COVID-19 pandemic. Suddenly, the decades of rich learnings and experiences would be challenged in a way like I nor anyone has seen since the 1918 Spanish Flu.

## Your reflections

As this book was being written in June 2020, the COVID-19 pandemic continues to unfold. Thus far, there have been more than 649,361 deaths worldwide and no country that is left untouched by the pandemic. Yet this pandemic is what I would consider a predictable surprise. Since the establishment of the World Health Organization (WHO) in 1948, experts have constantly touted the importance of maintaining investments in public health systems. Especially in a hyper-connected world as we know it today, the velocity in which virus could (and did) travel merits increased investment in public health and development, not less.

I was a guest speaker in 2018 for the Foreign Policy Association public television series *Great Decisions*, where a compelling case was trying to be made as to why investments in overseas development and aid are not only the right thing to do, but also in the best interests of the US. The video series posed a provocative question in its opening: Is the golden age of global health coming to an end, or just getting started?

At the time, the Global Health Security and Biodefense Unit, established by President Obama, had been eliminated, including the resignation of Real Admiral Timothy Ziemer, who served as a top White House official for the National Security Council. The inward-looking decision of the Trump administration mirrored the "America First" rhetoric that shaped the president's campaign, one that prioritized domestic investment over foreign spending, and strengthened hawkish investments for the US. When asked to be interviewed for the 2018 Foreign Policy Association series, I reflected long and hard about my more than 20 years of experience working disasters and humanitarian responses, and referenced my experience in responding to the 2014 West Africa Ebola epidemic, where I was deployed for a month working for the International Committee of the Red Cross (ICRC). During the interview, I told the story of the first seemingly benign news that hit the US about the virus. It was all too often that the health calamities impacting the continent of Africa could leave viewers of such news feeling callus. At first, Ebola appeared to be a health emergency like many others, where the problem was seen as one of "that is their problem, not ours." It wasn't until the first cases of the highly contagious disease started to arrive via a passenger flight to Texas that eyes began to open for many Americans.[7]

At the time, my husband and I were living in Nebraska and I would hear short-sighted statements such as "we should just close our borders" and "the US should not be getting involved with the response. Why use US taxpayer dollars when we have our own problems in the US that they can be used for?" I would explain when hearing such statements that there is a common humanity that binds us all and, most importantly, our actions as a country should be based on that humanitarian imperative.

Ebola was a wakeup call for the US. The Obama administration responded with a $5.4 billion emergency appropriation and the creation of the pandemic preparedness office in 2016 based on lessons learned from the Ebola response.[8] Yet the Trump administration's drastic dismantling of the pandemic preparedness committee also came with defunding the Global Health Security Agenda established by the Obama administration, whose belief was very much that a healthy globe can lead to a healthy America. The idea that an investment in development abroad does not rob America nor its people is a belief that guided the Obama administration, as well as aligning with my values that the basic right to life of all people everywhere is the highest priority and my belief that the artificial barriers that borders create are not only bad for those living in isolation but also a dangerous erosion of humanitarian values.

In my position as Head of Disaster and Crisis for the Americas and Caribbean of IFRC during the onset of the COVID-19 pandemic, I have carefully watched as isolationist policies have struggled to contain the pandemic. In Brazil, President Bolsonaro has referred to COVID-19 as a make-believe phenomenon, refusing to provide the WHO with data to track the spread of the virus in the country.[9] In Nicaragua, the Sandinista government is denying that the virus is spreading rapidly in the country. In the US President Trump equally refused to acknowledge the threats presented to him and his administration in December, calling the threat totally under control in January 2020. Yet the realities of the impacts of the virus were being seen by myself and my peers working for the Red Cross. The Ebola response was less than seven years prior, and public health professionals were warning that by not taking the response to COVID-19 seriously, we were placing the world's population in grave danger. Have we not learned from the

Ebola response? Does the fundamental principle of unity not have a role to play in bringing together countries during times of crisis to transcend political difference and rather to find solutions that can benefit humanity?

As a humanitarian, deeply alarming was also seeing US domestic policies enacted through the pandemic response which reversed fundamental humanitarian principles and human rights. In January of 2020 the Trump administration proposed nine federal regulations that would enable federal agencies and programs receiving federal funding from them to discriminate against LGBTQ people, women, religious minorities, and other vulnerable communities if they believe serving those populations in any context would go against the program's personal beliefs. Departments of Labor, Education, Justice, Housing and Urban Development, Veterans Affairs, Homeland Security, and Agriculture were soon able to legally engage in discriminatory behaviors. This also included the US Agency for International Development, which accounts for more than half of all US foreign assistance. The regulation would empower organizations receiving federal funds to discriminate against LGBTQ people and other vulnerable communities. I was gravely alarmed by this needless and cruel attack on marginalized people.

These executive orders would allow federal agencies to engage in activities that would expose vulnerable populations in the aftermath of disaster, pandemics, and in fragile socio-economic contexts to be given an immoral, unethical, and potentially unconstitutional choice: that of engaging in religious practice or not receiving lifesaving or sustaining federal services. Long-standing academic research has demonstrated that such conditionality placed on aid is harmful to individuals. We know that scholars such as Dr. Jeannette Sutton, a leading expert in disaster and risk communication, point out that "proselytizing, victim blaming and giving answers to questions about human suffering in disaster were described as forms of exploitation in which the minister attempts to convert the victim in his or her own time of greatest vulnerability…" and "could cause more damage to the already fragile mental health status."[10]

Yes, faith-based organizations do play a critical part in the provision of humanitarian aid both domestically and internationally. Yet prior frameworks for funding such faith-based organizations both domestically and internationally have ensured that services provided are not subject to proselytizing behaviors. An enormous undertaking took place in 1994, the year I first came in contact with the Red Cross and knew I wanted to be part of the movement, when 546 parties signed the 1994 Code of Conduct for the International Red Cross and Red Crescent movement and non-governmental organizations in disaster relief. This code, among other things, made clear that "Aid will not be used to further a particular political or religious standpoint." Additionally, the code forbids "proselytizing," as it is clearly an unethical condition to receive aid under the framework of "embracing or acceptance of a particular political or religious creed."[11]

Within the humanitarian aid sector, the imperative to aid impacted individuals and communities should come first, as affirmed in the Red Cross fundamental principles of humanity and impartiality. Faith-based organizations are already protected from religious discrimination in federal law, including by the Free Speech and Free Exercise Clauses of the Constitution. The proposed regulation does nothing to bolster these protections, but instead invites faith-based organizations to institutionally discriminate and proselytize using federal funds. The well-established standard in the 1994 Code of Conduct for the International Red Cross and Red Crescent provides that Red Cross components (national Red Cross and Red Crescent societies, the International Committee of the Red Cross and the International Federation of Red Cross and Red Crescent Societies) and non-governmental organizations in disaster relief do not forbid organizations or individuals within them from publicly or privately celebrating their faith. This expression of faith is well protected within both the United States Constitution and international bodies such as Article 18 of the United Nations Declaration of Human Rights, which was passed unanimously (48–0) in 1948.

The regulations passed by the Trump administration open the door to discrimination against LGBTQ people and other vulnerable populations. It amounts to baked-in discriminatory rights for faith-based organizations to deny services to vulnerable communities. Further, at the Red Cross we recognize that non-discrimination workplace policies not only foster a diverse workforce, but support our employees to bring their full, authentic selves to work. This improves the services that we are able to provide to individuals and communities in crisis.

Should tax-payer dollars fund organizations that can choose to only serve individuals who are subject to undergoing religiously based service options in order to access their assistance? Socio-economically vulnerable communities deserve better and as both a taxpayer and humanitarian professional, I strongly oppose the implementation of this proposed regulation. The US federal government, particularly the Trump administration, must revisit the basic humanitarian principle of "do no harm" before such implementation, which would be ethically disastrous and potentially put lives in harm's way. Forcing an individual to undergo religiously based service options in order to receive service or allowing faith-based organizations to use discriminatory employment practices is unethical, illegal, and immoral.

## Why your reflections matter

Since 1994, the spirit of volunteerism and principles of the Red Cross Movement have been guiding my professional journey. After 26 years as a volunteer and paid staff member in the humanitarian space, I remain conflicted about what the future will bring. There is a part of me that sees the COVID-19 pandemic, coupled with persistent inequality, growth in ultra-conservative regimes, and inequality that we see globally as a boiling point that could lead to significant instability of the global systems that are known to most of the world's inhabitants today. The optimist in me sees incredible opportunity and an awakening of the world's citizens to say "no more." In the US, we are seeing this with the Black Lives Matter movement, in Hong Kong where pro-democracy demonstrations are standing up, or in Costa Rica which recently passed legislation allowing for gay marriages. Popular uprisings that demand equality and social justice present hope.

As I reflect on my experience within the humanitarian machine, I hope that my story presents a lived experience that underscores the value of guiding humanitarian principles: humanity, impartiality, neutrality, independence, volunteerism, unity, and universality. These seven fundamental principles have not only guided the international Red Cross Red Crescent Movement since its origin, but also my life within this field. The official adoption of the seven fundamental principles took place in 1965 at the 20th International Red Cross Conference and the principles have since been influential in influencing humanitarian action in more than 864 organizations that have signed the code of conduct based on these principles.[12]

The COVID-19 pandemic is an aperture for us to reflect on our common humanity and to question isolationist rhetoric. As a 70-something-year-old fellow volunteer wrote to me after our disaster deployment in Hamburg, Iowa back in 1998, "You have to give yourself to life, before you really live; it is foolish hoarding love or wealth, those lose who never give."

## Notes

1 US Government. 2006. *The Federal Response to Hurricane Katrina: Lessons Learned*. Washington, DC: US Government.
2 US Government. 2006. *The Federal Response to Hurricane Katrina: Lessons Learned*. Washington, DC: US Government.
3 IFRC. 2008. "Belize: Tropical." https://reliefweb.int/sites/reliefweb.int/files/resources/DA6469D73C7B4C2E8525745D006702DE-Full_Report.pdf.
4 FEMA. 2020. "Federal vs. Non-Federal Cost Share." https://emilms.fema.gov/IS1020/groups/17.html.
5 Woodin, Debby. 2012. "The Joplin Globe." www.joplinglobe.com/news/local_news/volunteers-donations-saved-city-million/article_0f338294-41a2-58bb-a46d-2b0999945c53.html.
6 American Red Cross. n.d. "Our Federal Charter: Our Relationshop with the Federal Government." www.redcross.org/about-us/who-we-are/history/federal-charter.html.
7 Center for Disease Control. n.d. "2014–2016 Ebola Outbreak in West Africa." www.cdc.gov/vhf/ebola/history/2014-2016-outbreak/index.html#:~:text=On%20September%2030%2C%202014%2C%20CDC,Dallas%20tested%20positive%20for%20EVD.
8 CSIS. 2018. "Health Security Downgraded at the White House." www.csis.org/analysis/health-security-downgraded-white-house.
9 Human Rights Watch. 2020. "How Authoritarians Are Exploiting the COVID-19 Crisis to Grab Power." www.hrw.org/news/2020/04/03/how-authoritarians-are-exploiting-covid-19-crisis-grab-power. April 3.
10 Sutton, Jeannette. 2006. "Convergence of the Faithful: Spiritual Care Response to Disaster and Mass Casualty Events." *Journal of Pastoral Theology* 16(2): 18–29.
11 IFRC. n.d. "Signatories to the Code of Conduct." https://media.ifrc.org/ifrc/who-we-are/the-movement/code-of-conduct/signatories-to-the-code-of-conduct/.
12 IFRC. n.d. "Signatories to the Code of Conduct." https://media.ifrc.org/ifrc/who-we-are/the-movement/code-of-conduct/signatories-to-the-code-of-conduct/.

# 10 Action learning in the Anthropocene

*Pat Foley*

## Prelude

Imagine creating your own three-dimensional puzzle, figuring how to solve it, then reflecting on the creation and solution experience. This story is about an analogous discovery process linking field and classroom experience. It begins with a nongovernmental organisation (NGO) programme in Uganda that stretched from 2009 to 2016, then shifts to 2016–17 when I taught introductory and advanced courses in humanitarian affairs as adjunct faculty for three semesters in New York City.

I am an anthropologist, dedicated to international cooperation since coordinating a development education programme between New Zealand, Sri Lanka, and India between 1995 and 1997. I have worked throughout the ecosystem, from grassroots to government, freelance since 2004. I facilitate research around gendered risk, resilience, and economic security for humanitarian and development programming. I also facilitate technical workshops and on-the-job learning, largely with change agents at the interface of communities and institutions. I am interested in how we learn from our work, and how that contributes to better work. Such reflection is not typically encouraged in the rapid, dynamic world of humanitarian response, despite the fact that we promote evaluation and learning as industry ideals. I am interested in how we train professionals, how we convene meaningful (and mutual) learning without scripts and slideshows. I also think practitioners and academics can create more collaborative, more complementary middle ground to improve our work further still.

The opportunity of university work was more intellectual than financial. Beyond so-called "teaching" it was a chance to revisit my education through the perspective of accumulated experience, and to reflect on my work with the help of younger idealists. Deep field experience earned me legitimacy among students, but brought little currency with a university that was increasingly dependent on external contingent staff. Adjuncts at the time were actively pursuing the right to unionise for an increased stipend from the reluctant institution, which was better than the state's minimum hourly wage but part time and without healthcare or stability. These terms discouraged some adjuncts from investing themselves into their courses; some were open about keeping assignments short and easy to grade (in addition to research, preparation, teaching, office hours, and maintaining other income sources). Like a hardship post, adjuncts accept the job for what it is. That's the gig: We revisit our practice; students learn through our experience; and the university supplies affordable, marketable expertise.

But there is distance between academics and practitioners, between inquiry and delivery, theory and practice. There is also a tension within gritty fieldworker communities that anything resembling academia is divorced from practical reality. (Can I use this on the ground?) We scarcely pause to consult secondary sources, let alone validate findings. Conversely, to academics, practitioner literature is inherently sophomoric, lacking rigour and peer review. Grey. This polarity inhibits our complementarity.

This chapter explores some of these dynamics. It is part of an ongoing conversation with peers and former students, written in Spain during the 2020 coronavirus lockdown. It follows a trail of breadcrumbs left in 2018, when a simpler version was presented at a conference of the International Humanitarian Studies Association. The story also tries to set new trail, seeding food for further thought. It explores a humanitarian classroom, a personal reflection on preparing tomorrow's young leadership for our common, uncertain future.

## Theme

I taught introductory and advanced courses. The introductory course surveyed the humanitarian scene, actors, and narratives, while the advanced course delved further into dynamics and polemics, and expected students to challenge their own assumptions and motivations. We encouraged introspection, and contrasted the introductory and advanced courses as a transition from matters of fact to matters of concern.[1] We did not pretend to train aid workers; we assumed that student career paths would be as diverse as their backgrounds and double majors. Instead, we tried to enrich critical capacity and an informed sense of personal responsibility that would apply to any globally conscious vocation.

The advanced course was also distinct from its prerequisite in that we contextualised humanitarian affairs within a larger problematic of world power. We critiqued the colonial legacy of humanitarian action and asked whether systemic limitations of the industry are symptomatic of global political economy and therefore inherently unable to address root causes. We also drew inspiration from a growing body of literature about the Anthropocene, interpreted here as our current geological epoch and characterised by disruptive human influence against social, economic, and biospheric systems.[2] By situating ourselves in the Anthropocene, our concerns were not simply emergency and development, but how the humanitarian enterprise is entangled in the "inequalities, alienation, and violence inscribed in modernity's strategic relations of power and production."[3] With reflection as a core principle, we were interested in how knowledge is generated and structured, how it is legitimised and alternatives are delegitimised, and how such knowledge transforms nature and society.[4]

We used the Anthropocene as an analytical umbrella to critique humanitarian affairs, without getting distracted by the concept itself. The course was more specifically concerned with three themes—conflict, disasters, and capital—without prescribing how these themes related to each other or to the Anthropocene in general. We worked with hypotheses of relationships, rather than a theory of change; gradually developing and linking our ideas. This semi-structured approach was cultivated throughout the semester, culminating with individual research in which students unravelled an analytical knot of their own design. Embracing uncertainty was part of the process, encouraging students to work with unknowns and interpret multiple information types and sources.

All students used the same Uganda livelihood programme as a departure point (discussed below), but each pursued independent lines of enquiry. Students chose their own adventures, with significant freedom for individual interests and creativity. Extensive data and reporting from the Uganda programme were shared with students in a curated case file that included maps, matrices, baselines, spreadsheets, diagrams, evaluations, photographs, participant stories, and secondary literature. Current and previous NGO staff also participated as respondents, joining us in person or by videoconference to discuss their work, elaborate specific data, and answer student questions.

The case study was a real programme implemented by an NGO in northern Uganda from 2009 to 2016. Originally it was a one-year project for households returning to their places of origin after being displaced by conflict between the Lord's Resistance Army and the Uganda People's Defence Force. It was a country pilot on the programmatic use of cash with 1,500 households reinvesting in rural production. Over eight years and four funding cycles, it expanded from a single year project into a multi-year programme. It started with a focus on short-term household access to cash, then evolved into long-term socio-economic empowerment of women and girls as a means of countering vulnerability to gender-based violence.

I led the original design team in 2009, after living two years in Uganda. The design was the last thing I did before leaving, and I was not involved in the implementation or ongoing research that followed. Although it was a pilot project approved by government and financed by an embassy in the capital, very little time was allowed between announcing the tender and accepting proposals for one year of funding. In fact, we did not even have time to conduct fieldwork for the design, so we improvised with data and experience from the agency's earlier work in the same area (in nutrition, water, sanitation, crops, and livestock). Our design was as informed as possible, but we never anticipated that the project would iterate over so many years. Despite the unknowns of rapid design (or because of them), the original strategy included a learning objective. The budget and workflow included a final evaluation and specific commitments to research and share programme lessons. Therefore the original project and its metamorphosis were unusually well documented with baselines, evaluations, case studies, and complementary research in an effort by the NGO and donor to learn from their work and contribute to a wider community of practice.

As the NGO programme had evolved through successive cycles with changing activities and outcomes, there was scope for each student to shape their paper in remarkably different ways, such as focusing on a single cycle, comparing one cycle with another, concentrating on a particular technical sector, and more. They typically chose topics that spoke to a combination of individual interests and professional growth, and had to review additional literature to widen their perspective. Without compromising academic research or critique, the assignment tried to build practical skills in analysis, synthesis, evaluation, and professional report writing. Students had to demonstrate their command of course content, but the assignment let them do this in a way that could be replicated in their internships, senior theses, and other work. The assignment encouraged embracing risk and creativity, along with presenting their study as a real-world report, as if inter-agency managers would use the research to make evidence-based decisions.

The collection of final papers is impressive in its breadth and insight. Students all wrote about the same overall programme, but each paper is distinct. For example, one paper compared qualitative and quantitative analysis of nutritional change; one analysed water-sanitation targeting criteria as they related to livelihoods programming; several discussed context analysis and adaptive management; others explored cash-based programming in relation to gender and economic security; and one explored how seasonality intersected these same themes.

*Figure 10.1* Evaluation participants assess relative wealth among programme participants, ranking on a scale of 0–3 (unknown to high) and illustrating the messy reality of subjective perceptions

Even within a theme, such as gender, students took unique approaches to challenging the "myth of community" that we had proposed earlier in the semester.[5] Some students compared sociological dynamics between women and men, while others analysed the causes and effects of gender-based violence. One student analysed programme impact on crop production and the consequences of receiving cash grants from the NGO, concluding that prioritising women's participation over men's did not address the root causes of gendered inequality. Another student analysed definitions of equality to compare programme cycles engaging "gender" generally and gender-based violence more directly, concluding that contributing to empowerment depended on how explicitly gender was addressed in programme planning.

The papers are also remarkable for their insight into the messy, well-intended humanitarian business and its intrinsic tensions between theory and practice. For example, in this photograph from an evaluation in the Uganda programme area (Figure 10.1), participants are comparing relative wealth within a farmer field school group. Respondents were asked to rank how they perceived the wealth of member households on a scale of 0–3, independent of each other's opinion. The twist in the photo is that the three respondents each scored the same household differently. It is a simple example, but with students such questions helped illustrate tangible challenges of real work, such as how to interpret and report divergent, anecdotal findings. It is no surprise that our humanitarian documentation is inherently grey, easily dismissed from systematic reviews.

## Reflection

We called the assignment action learning, exercising course content while pursuing individual learning interests that could contribute to employability and professional relevance, not simply enhancing critical capacity in isolation of its application. Pursuing tailored objectives helped make the assignment real for each student, which in turn informed their reflection and contributed to their sense of global citizenship. The tangibility of the programme and its case study material also instilled an unexpected sense of empathy with NGO programme participants. Although removed in time, space, and power, the programme participants were not seen as anonymous subjects; they were actual people engaged in active choices and constructive change. Students took the research seriously. It would have been ideal for them to hear programme participants speak their own truths and voice their own reflections, in some cases over 10 years later. How, for example, would participants analyse the NGO if there were a way to reverse the roles? What would they think of us, in the classroom, learning from them—or from what was written about them in absentia?

The paper and course encouraged reflexivity, but students across all semesters maintained a running joke about their individual, impending "existential crises". The concerns were valid, but many students mocked their own earnestness, their periodically fragile balance of ambition and uncertainty. All wanted "to contribute" but did not yet know how. We struggled throughout every semester with the weight of geopolitical history. In pursuing internationally conscious careers, we questioned our complicity in humanitarian mission as a legacy of Empire.[6] We questioned whether we could influence solutions, not embody problems. Indeed, some resigned from the course and even the degree programme. Some also grappled with their privilege at an expensive university, accumulating debt that undermined their agency, during a period of dissonant campus debate on the value of adjuncts in place of doctored professors.

We therefore tried to make the paper and the course not only as practical as possible, but also as constructive as possible. We fostered critique, not cynicism. We considered process as important as product, and prioritised individually meaningful learning outcomes above standardised messages predefined by the course, along with the ability to articulate that learning. We encouraged creative risk by concentrating on depth of engagement with the material, rather than the ability to produce a document that outwardly looked the part. We also acknowledged limitations of the assignment and its façade of reality. For example, the various Uganda programme teams had all moved on, and we had neither means nor mandate to try contacting former participants in the field. In their analysis and synthesis, students acknowledged that the evaluation results they cited were not their own, and that as secondary users we could only take reported programme outcomes at face value. There was no way to verify our findings, or hear participants discuss their version of reality. In recognising the limits of our work, we tried to introduce humility and allow for critical self-reflection. We hypothesised that less hubris and self-certainty could increase the relevance of what we produced.

Beyond individual topics and conclusions, in the final section of all papers, students reflected freely on the assignment, the course, their studies, work, and lives. These reflexive paragraphs brought the assignment full circle to the course rationale and its introspective objectives. These closing paragraphs encouraged students to explore their personal praxis, which we interpreted as the individual interplay of theory and practice, iterative and infinite. Their reflection is poignant, captured in the illustrative quotations in Box 10.1.

By acknowledging the limitations of an aspirational, competitive humanitarian enterprise reacting to global disorder, students found constructive, contemplative space to consider how they, as inspired youth, might contribute to an uncertain future, even in their own neighbourhoods. For example, one student was clear in bringing humanitarian studies to her borough high school teaching; another remains active in her community through city participatory budgeting and COVID-19 voluntarism; another writes for an NGO headquarters; and another works for his embassy.

Their reflection validates the relevance of teaching how to think instead of teaching what to think, the necessity of cultivating skills for lifelong learning that can contribute to global sustainable development.[7] This inversion of pedagogic power is more a question of commitment than artful technique. For example, within the institute I gained instant and undeserved notoriety for Socratic method through the simple, symbolic act of starting every session with a plenary

## Box 10.1 Student reflections on personal praxis

- "Quality education transcends the technical."
- "I learned a lot about my humanitarian goals … Cash programs work, but what role do I have in implementing them?"
- "My conclusions broadened my interpretation of humanitarian *good enough*."
- "This study turned me off from getting involved in international development."
- "I've realized I wouldn't apply to a position that requires logical frameworks … I want to create changes in the institutional framework."
- "This paper helped me understand the nuances that occur throughout the project cycle and the unpredictability that comes with even the most meticulous plans."
- "For me this paper was a real-world exercise in the evaluation of humanitarian programming … it offered students the opportunity to ask how aid works in practice, to delve into the nitty-gritty of project cycle management."
- "Most humanitarian projects have serious issues, or core contradictions, flawed priorities, complex or even 'wicked' problems, and yet I still believe in the humanitarian mission as a valuable enterprise."
- "This case study allowed me to go beyond education and analyse different structures to combat gender inequality. Without economic empowerment, advocacy and awareness do not go a long way."
- "I have felt as though much of the time evaluations are conducted then forgotten about, but here, I could visualize where someone took the original program and completely transformed it into a new, gender-based program."
- "This research awakened me that gender awareness and women's empowerment often get ignored in project planning, even when they may have relevance to the programme. I feel more prepared to incorporate gender awareness into humanitarian action and development."
- "I believe men must also feel empowered through gendered programming, which is something I feel has lacked, and I would want to provide my own input on the challenge."
- "I have become more interested in how cash-based programs could be better integrated into improving livelihoods of impoverished groups within the United States."
- "Researching [this] programme has further sparked my interests in nutrition, infectious diseases, and global health … The research has connected my community outreach and passion for fighting health disparities in the Bronx."

rearranging of seats from parallel rows to interactive circle. It was an instinctive gesture to allow students intellectual room to manoeuvre, yet every semester they were surprised.

We all struggled with power. Students were generally unaccustomed to the freedom to make active learning choices, instead of being treated as mature children who could learn what teachers dictated. Students complained of lecturing throughout their education, with professors "drowning us in the text of their own published work."[8] Some students struggled with the uncertainty of empowerment, but they appreciated the course's disrupted power dynamic despite the additional energy and accountability it entailed. I too struggled with power, the role's automatic authority and indelible hierarchy, the contradiction of professing to disempower myself in class while scoring and reporting their performance up the food chain.

I still hear from many; I receive updates and sign recommendations to employers and graduate schools. (One recently wrote, "People finally understand what my major of Humanitarian Studies is, thanks to this pandemic.") These are bright, intelligent people, but consider the precarity of their inheritance, worse than graduating with debt: A quantum bomb of fossil hedonism, capital agglomeration, and species complacency. Are we equipping these graduates with the right tools, despite their glaring comparative advantage? Are we educating them for uncertainty?

Here we return to the opportunity of better collaboration between academics and practitioners. In this case, our critique of humanitarian affairs was augmented with deeper concerns of the Anthropocene. Without that broader perspective, much of our narrative would have been limited to tropes from the field, hackneyed oral history from a middle-aged adjunct. There are deep pools of academic thought that can inform, inspire, and connect us as activists. There is established empirical practice in ecology, economics, pedagogy, anthropology, and more that is already mobilised against the Anthropocene but unknown or underappreciated in our responsive, action-oriented field.

As practitioners, as outwardly neutral idealists, we do not have a culture of reflecting critically on the history, norms, or implications of what we do. We are more familiar with promoting our work (and our brand) than we are with thinking aloud or inviting divergent perspectives. In a recent email to a community of practice, a contributor apologises for reflection during emergency: "sorry for driving this discussion into the theoretical realm, we are supposed to be discussing practical analysis and responses to COVID-19!"[9] Why is there stigma in pause? We jam like rockers that take pride in not knowing scales or theory, autodidactic and playing by ear (unlike jazz musicians, for whom technique liberates expression). We can learn from academics, classicists, expert in the written score but not necessarily renowned for their groove. From us they could learn about making uncertain decisions with incomplete information; translating concepts into activities; delivering under pressure, under the gun, or on the fly. Anyone who has spent years in the business has met incredible people achieving amazing things in remarkable environments. But if we dismiss each other's work, then we are simply learning less. Otherwise we are each writing reports to ourselves, maintaining and multiplying our own systems.

For me, writing this story in pandemic has sparked an additional, unexpected learning loop beyond the intended chapter blueprint. The scope expanded as current events highlighted differences between pandemic symptoms and endemic root causes. Our chaotic new normal affirms the ongoing introspection of the advanced course, its interest with unsustainable global systems, and the proximity of disorder. The Anthropocene and state of nature demand new ways of teaching and thinking so that leaders and teachers both have conceptual navigation tools to "educate humanity out of the current planetary crisis."[10] More than ever, we finally risk sailing off the precipice. Consider how easily COVID-19 rattled supply chains, how readily the United Nations Security Council paralysed. Consider too the unanticipated outcomes, such as waves in the USA against its original, capital sins of genocide and slavery, and how that impetus spread. There are new conversations and new optimism alongside imminent risk. But is it inconceivable that the United Nations could have failed altogether, like the League of Nations assembled after our first world war? What about limitless growth and the market-based response ahead of us: How neoliberal and biopolitical is our common future? Will we gift a COVID-19 vaccine freely to humanity, as we did with polio after another world war?

## Implications

Like the research assigned to students, this story would be incomplete without questioning our praxis, beginning with a coda to the 2016 World Humanitarian Summit. In a statement of six commitments from humanitarian scholars, signatories say that a strong knowledge base is essential in the face of future threats to human security. They say that research and education are part of "critically engaging with forces and factors that create positive change in order to imagine and achieve a different future for the world."[11] The commitments are meaningful, but they overlook the catalytic influence an engaged classroom offers in cultivating ethical, empathetic praxis at home (see Box 10.2).

The vision is as appropriately aspirational as the humanitarian endeavour itself. However, the commitments miss scholars' importance as educators, "a sad reminder of the way teaching is seen as a duller, less valuable aspect of the academic profession."[12] The commitments embrace relevance and so-called localisation, but are external and unidirectional. What would they say if crafted by the localised? Are these commitments the counterpoint of multiple, independent voices—or are they homogenised preaching from the choir? Beyond what scholars pledge to research, what is committed to their students?

---

**Box 10.2 Statement of commitments from humanitarian scholars at the World Humanitarian Summit (WHS) (abridged)**

1. Make humanitarian research more collaborative and inclusive…
2. Research the positive and negative impacts of the WHS…
3. Develop and adopt evidence-based approaches to relevant humanitarian research…
4. Localise humanitarian research and education within the regions and communities affected by emergencies…
5. Improve the impact and increase the use of humanitarian research…
6. Protect academic freedom, uphold scientific ethics, and be accountable for our research and its use…

---

Academics are bound by institutional "publish or perish" dharma, with different career incentives than practitioners, who are judged by technical competencies and the crises we have weathered. The field-facing scholar commitments neglect the quotidian, transformative influence academics can foster locally with tomorrow's aid, trade, and civil society actors—in this case tomorrow's globalisers and localisers. The classroom is "a location of possibility,"[13] and can help channel the energy and intentionality of young minds. I accept the conceit of thinking I have contributed to someone's intellectual or professional development, but am equally conscious of my fingerprints on possible futures. Some former students are in fact now humanitarian practitioners, but many more are doing similarly constructive things in law, education, media, medicine, diplomacy, and more. As educators we are complicit.

Purposive assignments like the Uganda case study are not contingent on previous involvement or networks. They are part of my story here and obviously helped the concept to germinate, but they are not essential. For example, in the introductory humanitarian affairs course (prerequisite to the advanced course discussed above), 37 students over two semesters mined a curated file of secondary material around Myanmar, Cyclone Nargis (2008), sovereignty, human rights, and humanitarian standards. I had no prior experience with the Nargis case, and adapted the assignment with insight from the Uganda papers. Lines of enquiry were equally diverse, and all papers concluded with questions of reflection and accountability. It was another powerful learning process, and Nargis seemed the perfect storm for entry-level students to apply humanitarian principles and normative frameworks. In retrospect, insight from the Uganda papers also suggested that we should have focused on the USA's 2005 hurricane Katrina instead of Nargis. Like contrasting humanitarian affairs against its geopolitical history, Katrina illustrates differences between an event and the structural inequalities that exacerbate its impact. Nargis also speaks to these concerns, but Katrina informs humanitarian action and political economy closer to campus. Localisation. Even at the time of writing, this same student community is marching for social justice within a block of the university.

Meanwhile, pandemic is redefining work and interaction. As we speculate windows of opportunity, there is renewed speak of supporting localisation by sharing more responsibility with colleagues in situ. The term itself is loaded and inherently exogenous, but if stuck with it I would suggest localisation transcends subcontracting more work to more locals, especially if compelled by an inability to despatch expats. Instead, to borrow from literature, what if localisation is about silence, about what we opt not to say? How well can we listen? Borrowing from music, what could we learn from an audacious composition named for its duration, wherein a pianist sits silently at the instrument, precisely four minutes and thirty-three seconds?[15] Every performance is unique, a function of audience and environment, attitudes and behaviour. Each person hears what they would have overlooked otherwise (like birdsong in lockdown), accepting uncertainty and acknowledging diversity, refusing to confine concepts to single interpretations governed by unassailable truths.[16]

Which returns us to the reason of the advanced course: Backstopping young humans (not just humanitarians) in critical, reflexive thinking about real-world challenges. This includes the ability to learn iteratively, differentiate symptoms from causes, and continuously apply learning to practice. For me, locating humanitarian affairs in the Anthropocene provides a subjective missing link, a metaphor that intersects experience, experimentation, and intentionality. I am not suggesting it is a useful concept for everyone, nor am I calling for humanitarians to subscribe. Quite the opposite, especially when as a community we still struggle with older essential jargon like gender, resilience, and participation (distinct from women, vulnerability, and consultation). I have never used Anthropocene on the job or in the field; only around the campfire and only in safe company. Like with students, I am more concerned here with whether or not we as practitioners maintain our own metaphors, our own heuristic models for problem solving and self-discovery, rather than standardise definitions and approaches. In this case the Anthropocene is a provocative example, but we equally could have grounded ourselves in other abstracts like sustainability or political economy, among others. A similar logic applies to banal stereotyping of academics and practitioners, convenient for a story but not necessarily conducive for collaborative, contrapuntal harmony.

More visceral than peak oil or coral bleaching, the pandemic present is one example of how system failure could unfold, an errant sneeze in lieu of nuclear winter. But just as humanitarian affairs are symptomatic of deeper disorder, so too is this novel virus both cause and effect. Other examples are a stone's throw away, such as pigs dying from another member of the coronavirus family currently running amok in Asia and Melanesia at the time of writing. In one affected island state, government reportedly can neither afford to test which swine fever virus is prevalent (there are two!) nor finance a response, while licit and illicit trade amplify the problem.[17] Markets, contagion, permeable borders, vulnerable livelihoods ... sound familiar?

The Anthropocene is our nature and creation, seen equally in pandemic as endemic inequality and species lust for capital, the ghosts in our machines. From a rational, risk-based perspective this suggests "that we have squandered the past decades, and that preparing for a collapsing global system could be even more important than trying to avoid collapse."[18] If we are truly sapient, then let us graduate from *homo economicus* to *homo illuminus*. Let us be great apes, not monkeys.

## Notes

1 Bruno Latour, "Why Has Critique Run Out of Steam? From Matters of Fact to Matters of Concern," *Critical Inquiry* 30 (Winter 2014), 225–248.
2 Carl Folke, Reinette Biggs, Albert Norström, Belinda Reyers, Johan Rockström, "Social-ecological Resilience and Biosphere-based Sustainability Science," *Ecology and Society* 21(3), 41.
3 Jason Moore, *Capitalism in the Web of Life: Ecology and the Accumulation of Capital* (London: Verso, 2015), 170.
4 Vandana Shiva, "Monocultures of the Mind," in *The Vandana Shiva Reader* (London: Zed Books, 2014), 71–112.
5 Irene Guijt and Meera Kaul Shah, eds., *The Myth of Community: Gender Issues in Participatory Development* (London: Intermediate Technology Publications, 1998).
6 Antonio Donini, "Through a Glass, Darkly: Humanitarianism and Empire," in *Capitalizing on Catastrophe: Neoliberal Strategies in Disaster Reconstruction*, eds. Nandini Gunawardena and Mark Schuller (Plymouth: AltaMira, 2008), 29–44.
7 Stephanie Bengtsson, Bilal Barakat, Raya Muttarak, *The Role of Education in Enabling the Sustainable Development Agenda* (Abingdon: Routledge, 2018).
8 Personal communication, 2020.
9 Personal communication, 2020.
10 Jonas Andreasen Lysgaard, Stefan Bengtsson, Martin Hauberg-Lund Laugesen, *Dark Pedagogy: Education, Horror, and the Anthropocene* (Cham: Palgrave, 2019), 15.
11 Statement of Commitments from Humanitarian Scholars at World Humanitarian Summit (The Hague: International Humanitarian Studies Association, 2016).
12 bell hooks, *Teaching to Transgress: Education as the Practice of Freedom* (New York: Routledge, 1994), 12.
13 Ibid., 207.
14 Virginia Woolf, *The Voyage Out* (London: Duckworth, 1915).
15 John Cage, *4'33"* (New York: Henmar Press, 1952).
16 Elizabeth Atkinson, "The Responsible Anarchist: Postmodernism and Social Change," *British Journal of Sociology of Education* 23(1) (March 2002), 73–87.
17 Personal communication, 2020.
18 Graham Turner, *Is Global Collapse Imminent?* (Melbourne Sustainable Society Institute, University of Melbourne, 2014), 16.

# Extending the conversation

Humanitarian action is a global phenomenon – humanitarian workers hail from all countries and carry out their work all over the globe. The contributors in this book alone come from eight countries and their stories are set in many different and faraway places. The organizations they work for make up the biggest portion of the entire humanitarian machine. They are often grouped into a category known as international nongovernmental organizations (INGOs) or international humanitarian organizations.

We have entitled this part "Bridging the divide: neither here nor there." The title points out that the humanitarian machine exists in a space that is difficult to define with precision. Being neither business, nor government, it occupies an arena that is often characterized as a third sector. Its way of being has developed over the last 50 or so years, as it came to be seen by its constituents as a way to respond to human need and by various governments as a viable alternative at a time when governments' trust in others was eroding.[1]

It functions according to its own norms and customs and it follows its own understanding of how things must be done. Part of the bygone lore of the organization where Daryl worked was the story of delivering a container of pinto beans to Central America to relieve a drought-caused food shortage. To the Americans and Canadians who had put together the shipment, the beans were an obvious choice for a humanitarian shipment. They knew that beans are a major part of the Central American diet. But while a bean is a bean in the United States and Canada, that is not true in Central America, where they prefer small red or black beans and do not like pinto beans. The pinto beans in that shipment did little to alleviate the need for food. The story stands as an enduring lesson to not ignore the culture gap.

Almost every humanitarian worker can tell of similar organizational faux pas. There are countless stories of misunderstandings that can make for hours of entertaining conversation in the coffee shops and bars where humanitarian workers go after finishing their responsibilities. But there are other divides highlighted in this part, and present throughout the book. Marie Anne Sliwinski aptly describes one part of the gap as a language issue. But Marie Anne is talking about another kind of language translation, more similar to the way that Dorothea Hilhorst speaks about it when she points out in her description of NGOs that "actors strategically deploy a multiplicity of development languages, such as when relating to development interveners and to funding agencies."[2] She compares her role as a grant manager to that of a translator between donors and partners: not the type of translator that a French speaker would need to communicate with an Arabic speaker, but rather a translator who moves between the way of doing business of donors, aid workers, and the recipients of aid. Conventional Western businesses emphasize a particular way of looking at the world. Management textbooks teach concepts and tools like how to carry out evaluations, log frames, and cost–benefit analyses,[3] which are undergirded by a specific outlook. One of its manifestations is the underlying assumption that can be summed up as a simple formula – humanitarian action X will lead to result Y, a linear outlook that is not shared by all within the humanitarian space. Aid workers usually act as links, translating divergent points of view, so that aid can make a smooth journey from one pair of hands to another.

Humanitarian workers are aware that giving aid is not straightforward. Providing aid to alleviate suffering is a complicated business. That is made clear by the "do no harm" principle which the humanitarian aid sector has borrowed from the medical profession's Hippocratic oath. Several writers in other parts repeat this theme. When they reflect on this principle, it brings into focus the distance between ideals and reality, an uncomfortable divide that all humanitarian workers must at least acknowledge. This particular divide is essential to the conversation, because it emphasizes the possibility that even the best intentions to help someone can hurt and inflict pain. Humanitarian workers get energy from a belief that the world can be made a better place, even though, to do so, they must have their feet in a messy reality.

There are other divides that characterize the humanitarian, some of which exist in the realm of beliefs or philosophy. All chapters in this book are written by individual humanitarian workers telling their story from their unique, individual perspectives. None of them, however, work alone. Humanitarian workers very often make fun of the stereotypical worker depicted in movies as a lonely cowboy, surrounded by an aura of heroism, who travels the world to save communities all on his or her own. The real humanitarian worker is far different from this. They carry out their work on the scale necessary, through strong associations with one another. Isolated individuals could not possibly confront on their own the overwhelming amount of need that exists in our world. But that stereotype nonetheless exists. And it exists because, even thought it might be difficult for humanitarian workers to be fully aware of it, that belief that humanitarian providers are saviors to those who without them would suffer extensively is an idea that is widely present.

The space between blind allegiance and complete loyalty to one single organization on one end, and engaging with many different organizations on the other, is another kind of gap that humanitarian aid workers bridge. A few contributors have spent entire careers immersed in the work of one organization. Other writers describe moving from one organization to another or engaging in consulting work with several. Underneath what is visible in this intermediate space, humanitarian workers struggle with the conflicting idea of having to choose between models.

The first one, one could argue, represents a model based on traditional values of loyalty, in which the humanitarian worker chooses to engage in a life-long commitment to fight a single cause. In the second model, on the contrary, the cause itself is less important than the idea of suffering and pain. In this model, the humanitarian worker navigates multiple organizations and engages in multiple causes, where they believe they can make a contribution.

Organizations pay attention to, and respond to, different conditions than do individuals. Individuals, for example, often do not feel the same fealty to large donors that organizations do. Organizations make decisions at a different level than individuals, tending to look at the bigger picture when they decide where to put funding and energy. At that level it is challenging to distinguish differences in the details on the ground. Pulling funding from one place in favor of another may meet big-picture concerns, but it cannot consider the costs or benefits that those decisions will have on countless people taking advantage of the aid. In contrast, individual workers often know very well what organizational big-picture decisions mean to the realities on the ground in front of them. The dissonance that can result from being the link between the experience of people in crisis and the organizations and governments whose big-picture decision makers are often far from the scene is at the heart of many of the accounts our contributors write about, even though the individuals involved at every level may claim the same set of values are grounding their decisions.

Many of our contributors have pointed out the many spaces in which the humanitarian machine operates – between one culture and another, plans and implementations, donors and recipients, theory and praxis. One understanding of social systems holds that the best, most creative, decisions are made when organizations teeter right on the edge of chaos. Living and working in gaps means humanitarian workers are often at that spot. It means constant interpretation, weighing how words are used, considering how society's values and cultural markers are understood, deciding which society's markers take priority and comparing them all with one's own understanding and values. The result can be brilliant humanitarian work; there is also a chance of failure. It is a risk always present in the minds of humanitarian workers.

Considering all the gaps present in humanitarian work brings up the question of power and how the sector uses the power it has. This is the essence of the following part.

## Notes

1  Nicola Banks and David Hulme, "The Role of NGOs and Civil Society in Development and Poverty Reduction," *SSRN Electronic Journal*, no. BWPI Working Paper 171 (2012), www.academia.edu/12245756/The_role_of_NGOs_and_civil_society_in_development_and_poverty_reduction.

2  Dorothea Hilhorst, *The Real World of NGOs: Discourses, Diversity, and Development* (London; New York: Zed Books, 2003) p. 220.

3  Ronald D. Sylvia and Kathleen M. Sylvia, *Program Planning and Evaluation for the Public Manager* (Long Grove, Illinois: Waveland Press, 2012).

# Part 3

# Culture and power

The value of humanitarian interventions

# Introduction to the conversation

At its most basic, humanitarian action is a global scale transfer of resources. Therefore, it is forced to contend with perceptions of power differences. All humanitarian workers are acutely mindful of this, aid recipients even more so. This is one of the threads that weaves its way through many chapters in this book and is the focus of this third and last part.

At a superficial level, the issue of power appears to be related by the contrasts among the various cultures and subcultures of those involved. But underneath the surface of all humanitarian interventions, power is mostly related to the relative ability to influence groups, and, more generally, to the possibility of defining how interventions are implemented and how relief is distributed. The power Western states wield looms large in humanitarian action. Often organizations possess power to influence simply by virtue of the world's perceived hierarchy of nations and the weight given to wealth. This type of innate, almost natural power is the essence of the discussion on localization, which has been mentioned over and over again by the authors throughout this book.

Writers in this part point out various ways in which power is part of the humanitarian experience, and the readers will feel them struggling with these issues. Kendra Pospychalla presents the power of hierarchy by sharing with us a story in which we can see the dilemmas faced when the realities on the ground are simply not shared by the leadership. Andrew Cunningham draws attention to a different type of power. His story recounts the possibility of international workers leaving the field of operations under the presence of excessive risk, while their local counterparts must stay to face the danger. Rami Shamma also focuses on a completely different kind of power, that which humanitarian workers exercise over their own bodies. The dedication that humanitarian workers feel to meeting the needs means they often work longer and harder than humanely possible. Matthew Levinger highlights an interesting reality which is not always entirely acknowledged by all – humanitarian work is not neutral, aid will always have a political element to it, and thus humanitarian agencies have power over others.

# 11 Invisible to systems, invisible to help

*Kendra Pospychalla*

## About me

I grew up in a small, rural town in the United States. With a population of roughly a thousand people, it didn't offer great diversity or cultural understanding. After my mother became a travelling nurse, we moved across country a few times to similarly small towns until we settled in Northern California. Two weeks after I graduated from high school, I began basic training in the US Marine Corps. I left the military after my first term due to a brain tumor and to pursue my first degree. I obtained a Bachelor of Arts in International Studies with the goal of working in international development. I sought this field because I am both curious about people and cultures I am unfamiliar with and I just generally wanted to make the world a better place somehow. As a small-town girl, the world felt so big. I wanted to be part of it.

Unfortunately, I struggled to find work upon graduation with my bachelor's. After heavy rain flooded a garden shed I was living in, I lived in my car a few months until I finally moved back to my parents' house while I continued to seek work. Those months led to other challenges, ranging from debt to health issues. During the months in my car, I tried to find organizations that could at least help me get a shower for job interviews. While I found programs for those in drug abuse recovery, victims of domestic violence, and other criteria to which I didn't classify, I couldn't find anything for a young, white, female veteran with a recent college degree.

Eventually, I found an opportunity in AmeriCorps serving in a disaster relief program for the American Red Cross in Los Angeles. Because AmeriCorps members lived on stipends below poverty level, I had continued experience first-hand with a life on a razor's edge. During most of my term, I couldn't afford gas for the stove, a refrigerator, or a bed to sleep on. One day of overspending on grocery expenses meant my electric was shut off or I didn't have money for gas to get to work. Once, I missed a sign notifying residents of a parade planned through my neighborhood. My car was impounded for being parked in the parade route. The fees cost me my rent that month and I almost lost my apartment, which would have risked a catastrophic chain reaction to losing my job and car.

While I don't believe these experiences unilaterally inspired my interest in the field, I do think they contributed. I fell in love with the field of disaster relief. Admittedly, I loved the urgency of the response phase but ultimately found career interest in the complexities involved. Disasters open a moment when a myriad of variables and systems converge into a wickedly complicated science. This science is what keeps my intellectual curiosity engaged. Not least, I understood how one bad day could cause catastrophic and irreparable damage to someone's livelihood. I also understood the importance of social networks since my family likely saved my life. My experience, pale in consideration to others', at least allowed me to understand the multiplex of challenges involved in such situations. Further, I had some amazing mentors in my early career to whom I owe so much inspiration.

After five years with the Red Cross, I left to pursue a graduate degree in Disaster Science and Management at the University of Delaware (UD). This program challenged many of my philosophies on "good services" in disaster relief. My experience in practice had focused so heavily on providing relief at the onset of a sudden disaster. Emphasizing the importance of social systems and pre-existing vulnerabilities, UD had the biggest influence in helping me understand the complexity of our work. Nearing the end of my graduate program, I began working with Team Rubicon. I've since continued to volunteer consulting in disaster relief program design, disaster planning, and field operations on larger relief efforts for a few additional organizations.

My career is a personal passion, but it is not without its ethical challenges. Over the years, I have frequently heard highly oversimplified explanations of needs and even more simplified ideas for solutions. As I believe this story will illustrate, there is a temptation for us to oversimplify for convenience, self-assurance, and story-telling. Most organizations view the human through the lens of the service they provide, but we are so much more complicated than that. I am an adamant proponent of establishing a targeted impact, a vision of the future, for *every* humanitarian program. Then, we must assess if we are truly meeting that vision.

I do not hold my allegiance to the organizations or institutions for which I work or volunteer. I hold my allegiance to those they serve. Institutionally, measuring progress to this vision is how we ensure our claimed purpose for existing is honest.

I have largely chosen a career in the non-government realm thus far for this reason as well. NGOs (nongovernmental organizations) have a powerful advantage to public programs: they can choose differently and reach broader. They can help in ways policy has missed. I believe the arguments on immigration, land use, legalization of marijuana, or other controversial challenges discussed herein are for policy makers and politicians to solve. I have no interest in giving value to any side of political arguments as this is not my interest area and I recognize how complicated those topics are alone. I am a humanitarian. I have chosen a career in serving humans, not constituents.

However, the challenges they create do exist, and my interest is in finding avenues for change despite public policy, and not being frozen by it. I believe law doesn't have to always be the answer, and people can change our world voluntarily when given the vehicles to do so.

*Figure 11.1* Photograph of Kendra Pospychalla

## The story

I will begin by telling you a story of a response to a wildfire in the western United States. In the next section, I will discuss how this story serves as a great example of many challenges I have observed in my career thus far in the humanitarian sector.

My story began on the second or third day of a relief operation after a wildfire in the western United States. As would appear to the superficial eye, the town was largely homogenous, mainly comprising farmers, and was of lower socioeconomic status. It had a population of less than a couple thousand people. Although it had a small main street and an unexpectedly large fairground, many homes were spread throughout the thick forests of the mountainous terrain. These mountains spanned thousands of square miles and had only a few communities but many marijuana fields nestled throughout. Local politics on the topic of the fields were tense because the farmers were accused of releasing harsh polluting chemicals into public soil, causing erosions from the cleared vegetation and triggering mudslides, exacerbating drought conditions, and even stealing water from fire departments. Some locals argued the marijuana business was immoral and detrimental to the community as well.

The wildfire was a conflagration developed from more than a hundred small fires started by a severe lightning storm in the area. Mandatory evacuations were widespread. A local church had volunteered their tiny building for use as a service site on the first night of the fire. Our service site offered a few different services by our organization as well as some locals, such as sheltering, fire-related information, animal food, and hot meals.

On that day, I stood at the service site as a man angrily scolded us for leaving people hungry. The site supervisor had called me when he found he was not able to assuage the man's frustration.

"There are people sleeping in the dirt! They haven't eaten. I dropped off some water and food for some of them, but *someone* needs to get out there and actually help them. Why aren't you doing anything?" he irritably explained.

After the man left, I began making phone calls to local authorities I had been coordinating with to seek more information, but they had none. Because of the road closures, we were unable to access the area to look for ourselves. In lieu of our own assessments, I asked local authorities to share their reports of damages with us. Those authorities reported less than ten homes lost, and some of those homes were large, vacant vacation homes. Yet the locals continued to refer to many people sleeping on the ground in the burned area. Our team was restricted from these areas for partially unknown reasons, but we were told there were ongoing firefighting efforts in some parts and concerns of hazardous waste in the soil. Intelligence on the humanitarian demands continued to rely on rumor. The local anecdote of need and the official reports weren't telling the same story. Meanwhile, I received pressure from my supervisor to close the operation due to the low population of the area and the low counts of visitors at our service site.

Finally, I was able to convince local authorities to allow our assessment team into the area. Once they had access, they reported that there were many, many people living in the burned communities in the mountains. A local volunteer fire department had explained that large families of non-English speaking, Hmong migrant workers (many said to be undocumented) lived in shacks on the marijuana farms. They claimed the terrain and high fences prevented them from seeing the full extent of the destruction. It appeared no one had a good understanding of the number of people living on these farms and their current condition.

I decided to go up to the burned area myself. Even though the trees and under-brush were lost to the fire, the high berms along the road made it impossible to see the land behind it without climbing onto the property. In some areas, parts of the fences hiding the land behind it still stood. Everything was blackened with soot. As we continued to drive through the dusty roads up the mountain, we came upon the little, volunteer, fire department our team had referred to.

The chief told the story of how the fire came through the area. He escorted us to the small fire department's building. It had the bay open and tables were lined up, covered with various bowls of food. Cases of water were stacked at the ends of the tables. "This is from people in the area," he explained. People were coming to the fire department to leave food and supplies in an effort to help the people rumored to be living in the fields. "They don't usually come get it though. The Hmong, I mean," he clarified.

We followed him to a large particle board lifted upright by hastily nailed two-by-fours. A large map was stapled on the board. "This is the community and these lines are the borders of the parcels." As he continued to explain the geography and how the fire moved through the land parcels, I began to realize how significant what he was telling me was. "This is thousands of people," I said, almost as a gasp.

"Oh, yes. It's hard to say how many thousands. I'd guess anywhere from two to four thousand though," he said casually. I asked why the government reports and media were only reporting a handful of homes lost. He said that they could only count legally built homes. Anything the farm workers were living in was classified as an "outbuilding" – not a home.

We thanked him and promised to return. As we headed back down the steep dirt road, my mind was spinning. As I began to try to understand what to do next, two young men appeared ahead along the side of the road. We pulled up to them and chatted with them. They spoke English and walked over to a fence and opened it to unveil a few other gentlemen sitting on the tailgate of an old pickup truck. A blue tarp was fixed across the bed of the truck and the blankets laying throughout indicated they slept in it. A small campfire was set up next to the truck where one man sat on the ground.

I looked at Raquel, the volunteer who had come with me, and said "I need to call my boss." My phone wasn't picking up any signals, so we decided to try to find a high point. When I had a small signal, she pulled the truck over and I climbed out. I retold the story that the fire chief had told us to my supervisor.

"So you are telling me there are thousands of people out there?" His tone almost sounded patronizing. It was clear he didn't believe it.

"Yes."

"Look around you! What do you see?" he asked flatly. I was quiet for a moment as I looked around. I saw dusty berms along the dusty, dirt road in which I stood. I could see glimpses of the mountaintops miles away over some of the blackened mounds. In a few hundred yards in front of me, a deer slowly came from over a hill. He pressed, "Do you see *thousands* of people?"

"No, I don't."

"Where are all of these people, Kendra?"

I raced to find an answer but I didn't have one. I just knew he was wrong. My thoughts were broken and tumbling over themselves. My head was pounding. I had had a cumulative total of less than six hours of sleep in the five days since the fire began. I hadn't showered nor had I changed my clothes in days, and I had barely eaten. My days were spent running our operations and my nights were spent planning and completing paperwork required by headquarters. I had been denied most of my staff requests, and had no staff who had adequate training in administrative functions. So I had to compensate by working through the nights. Cigarettes and coffee were the only things keeping me standing.

He continued, "So, what do you need?"

"They need supplies. Food, for a start."

"How much?"

I hadn't prepared to answer this, although I should have. I tried to quickly develop a plan to assuage his growing impatience with me. Knowing the average serving of the organization's truck loads I tried rapidly calculating against the populations we were estimating. "Five trucks," I blurted.

"*Five trucks?*" he almost shrieked.

My mind was in hyperdrive trying to calculate what to do with his reaction and it felt like it was crumbling in my skull. I even began to feel slightly dizzy. I am convinced I was borderline delirious during this conversation, but I am positive my judgment was sound.

I don't recall how the conversation ended. I only remember getting back into the truck and telling Raquel that I needed to take a nap before I made any more decisions. Needless to say, we didn't get the five trucks.

I began trying to figure out a plan to help the migrant workers in the fields after that day. There was a local English-speaking Hmong woman, Mei, who agreed to work with us. She was well-trusted among the Hmong community that worked in the fields. She helped us understand the barriers we were facing in our efforts to reach the affected people. Many of them trusted the little fire department and would come for water and supplies as they could. However, some of the food at the fire department upset their stomachs and wasn't culturally fitting. They wanted nonperishable, canned vegetables and rice so they could cook it themselves. She told us of a rumor among them that the fires were started intentionally by the locals to "burn them out" of the community. The politics of the marijuana crops made them fearful of everyone, and was a primary reason they wouldn't leave the property (even under mandatory evacuation orders). They were afraid they wouldn't be able to get back in. They also had lost most of their cars in the fire, and many were worried they would struggle getting back if they left. Many were also undocumented and couldn't speak English. They feared government officials, and they thought we were government as well.

Language was another barrier. In order for our organization to provide services to them, they had to fill out paperwork. As was explained to us, the Hmong language had no standard written form. We couldn't find any translation services for written materials for them. We couldn't put our documents in writing nor could we use signage to help spread the word of our services. After almost a week of searching, we found two volunteers who travelled six hours to serve as translators for us.

Local government agencies agreed to work with our organization to provide what social services they could. There were programs that could help the affected Hmong people, if they so chose to use them. We organized a plan with Mei and the local social programs. Under pressure to close the sites and end the operation from my supervisor and his chain above him, I asked him to let us try this last effort. He agreed.

Our strategy was to hold a day where we distributed canned vegetables and rice at the fire department. We stocked enough to give each family one day of food. When the families came to get the supplies, our translators would help explain the other services and resources that awaited at the service center. The government officials who wanted to attend the event and discuss the services in which they represented agreed not to wear anything that would indicate they were government officials; they were only invited under the premise of helping the families. Mei's role was to spread the word in the community. She informed the families of the event and vouched for the trustworthiness of our organization. She assured them no harm would come.

It worked, mostly. People came, took the food, and heard about all the services they could get in town. Further, many agreed to let our assessment teams see their burned dwellings so we could get counts of destroyed homes over the next few days.

But no one came to the service sites in town after that day. It wasn't enough that they took the food. They had to come down from the mountains and check in at our site so they could be reflected in official numbers. Mei encouraged us to bring it all up to the fire department. However, we didn't have the resources to set up the services on the mountain. We had no reception, power, facilities, or equipment to set them up ourselves.

My boss ordered the operation shut down shortly after that, citing costs as a pressure, in addition to no clientele. The assessment team had barely finished their data collection. At the closing, data from the assessment team's count of destroyed homes finally caught up and the budget was retroactively updated. It now showed that our operation should have been doubled in budget.

I was commended up the chain because I came in so under budget and had some of the most impressive paperwork in my division.

But people still slept in the dirt.

## Reflection

The primary topic I would like to reflect on is the concept of "success". As a humanitarian organization, would one call our efforts in this wildfire "successful"? We *did* provide meals to close to a hundred people for a week. We strengthened relationships between our organization and the local government. A handful people who couldn't get to their homes during evacuations did find shelter, showers, water, medical care, information, pet food, and clean air at our HEPA-filtered service site. Although there weren't many, a few Hmong families did come receive some assistance, clothes, and other supplies. So, was this successful?

Considering "success", there are three points on which I want to focus. First, I would like to explore how success was *defined*. The second point is how success was *measured*. The third was on *who* determined what was considered successful.

When our response to this wildfire began, I admittedly didn't have a definition of success beyond providing the services of the organization for which I worked within an expected timeframe. There was no goal or vision for what the desired state of the human would be when we left that town. The goal was merely to provide services. So, is a service in providing meals successful if you leave people hungry? Is a sheltering operation successful if people are back on the streets after you close the doors? Is a program to rebuild homes from flooding successful if it is destroyed again the following year in the next flood?

It takes a self-reflection of the organizations providing services to ask themselves what they are ultimately trying to do with these services. What is the end state we are looking for from the program? *That* should be the definition of success. As a sector, we will continually argue in circles about what is "working" and what isn't if we haven't planted a flag in the ground to clearly articulate what we are shooting for.

To this end, the definition of success should be defined through the lens of a human, not an organization. As I stated in my introduction, we are a complex creature and our social, environmental, and political constructs make addressing the total human more complex. Looking at success through the provision of a single service doesn't adequately align to reality. Our lives comprise a variety of needs that interplay with each other. One vulnerability or barrier from recovery is likely causing another or is being caused by another. Think of the farmers in my story. Imagine you lost your home, crops, and most farming equipment to this fire. Not only did you lose your home, but you lost a significant income. This eventually means you may lose your car, making it harder to find alternative work or get your kids to school. This eventually leads to greater stresses on the family that potentially cause additional, generational challenges. Even if someone offers to rebuild your home for free, it isn't a comprehensive enough solution to keep you from losing the entire farm (with the home) anyway.

In my story, no meals, furniture, or bags of clothes would have realistically had much impact on the Hmong families. What does one do with a new lamp when they have no table to set it on or outlet to plug into? I'm not proposing that transitional programs have no importance. Transitional programs (those that seek as temporary solutions until longer-term interventions can be implemented) are critical in the response phase. However, even they need a vision for success.

This is why we must not define success by the provision of a service instead of the desired condition of a human, family, or community at a given stage or milestone. Success shouldn't be to provide services for the sake of providing that service. Further, our program goals shouldn't be to hope for the best.

Secondly, how we measure success matters. The supervisor in this story used to say, "If you can't count it, it doesn't count." This is a horrible truth that unfolded on this operation. What you measure indicates what matters to you. In my story, the organization counted how many people they served, not how many people needed help and weren't unserved. They didn't measure how many people were hungry. They measured how many meals were provided.

Once we know what we want success to look like, we must measure to make sure we are reaching it. What gets reported and measured is also what becomes naturally incentivized.

I guarantee that any volunteer-led organization can provide numbers on how many people they mobilize. When the number of people you deploy is what you boast, you are creating an environment that encourages the deployment of more volunteers. Common understanding in the sector is that outside volunteer activities are finicky in their impacts. In some situations, they are ideal. In others, they potentially displace job markets, lack understanding of local dynamics that cause issues, do not contribute to local resilience building, and can detract funds from affected families and communities. However, if you are measuring the number of volunteers mobilized instead of the desired state of the community, you are incentivizing the wrong behavior.

What is measured is an indication of the values of the organization as well. If there is a genuine curiosity in how a service is impacting someone's life, it is fair to expect *some* efforts to measure or evaluate it. My values and ethics are pressed as a practitioner when I see no interest, or even a distaste, for thinking in this vein by my employer.

There is an amazing book on this topic, *Lean Impact.*[1] The author has an incredibly comprehensive discussion on the importance of impact and how it is measured. I do not wish to be too redundant to her pleas, so I encourage those interested to read it as well.

An angle to this conversation that highly influences the first two points on success is *who* defines it. The key is to understand who makes the rules of what counts and which stories get told. My definition of success for you, the reader, may not be the same as the definition you would illustrate for yourself. This conversation is highly interdependent on social systems, systematic oppressions, policy implications, culture, and values. There are likely more factors at play that I am not even identifying.

In my experience, these decisions are most primarily made by straight, white men. This is likely not a surprise to anyone, but I do want to highlight how it plays into the success of humanitarian programs.

In this case, consider the assumptions of the organization's needs assessment. Our budget for the operation was computed using a pre-existing template. The formulas for estimating things like the budget or number of families and individuals needing help was based on the assumptions such as average numbers of individuals in households in American culture. For these Hmong families, they had at least two times the number of people per household than the formula used. It also assumed that families lived in legally built structures, that they had transportation to come to services, and that they would be able to read or write. There was also a considerable assumption of innate trust of our organization.

I even reflect on the meals that had been provided by the local community, partner organizations, and our own organization. They were quite American, country-favorite dishes. I remember a few times in my career when food provided to a community was completely different than their cultural diet, chosen diet, or medical-required diet. When the mismatch was pointed out, I have *frequently* heard people say, "if they are actually hungry, they will eat anything." On another operation years before this fire, I personally witnessed a group of Mandarin-speaking, elderly Chinese folks fed McDonald's for breakfast. Many were ill all that day.

Imagine if the Hmong families had designed our services. Imagine how differently they would look. So much of how our humanitarian programs are designed rest on assumptions that reflect those that make them, and they often show their privilege. This is why inclusion of locals in the decision-making of not just how to define success, but in the strategies to reach it is imperative. This is also a good example of why diversity is important.

The conversation of who gets even more complex when you dissect organizational structures and dynamics. Who in the organization designs the programs or prioritizes what gets attention? Statistically speaking, straight, young, white men of middle income in America are least likely to need the services provided by humanitarian organizations. So we need to be honest with ourselves about the limitations of a homogenous group of these gentlemen driving the programming for people different than them. In my experience, the decisions made in haste are never inclusive. "Not enough time" or "perfection is the enemy of good" are frustrating phrases I hear to justify impulsive decisions that invited no perspective or local incorporation.

## Importance

What makes the conversation of impact and measuring success so important is existential to the sector (or to an organization). The impact our services have on improving the current state for those disadvantaged is why we exist. Period. If an organization doesn't have the interest to know where their services contribute to this effort, they are a costly detraction of resources from those who do.

This brings me to a secondary note of importance: humility. If my supervisor in this story had more of it, he would have listened beyond the media reports. Even if we had the services that could've helped those families, my supervisor had presumed higher understanding than I of what I saw before my eyes. So those services would've likely not been at my grasp to the degree needed. He oversimplified the situation considerably.

We oversimplify because we are human. It makes the complex less challenging. It makes us feel smarter and more confident in our decisions. However, it takes humility to recognize what is too complex for one to solve alone. It takes even more humility to recognize the lacking omnipotence of our ideas and limited perfection of our own programming enough to want to measure it. As in this story, there wasn't a question asked about the community we left behind.

However, humility works both ways. It is easy for me to become self-righteous on this topic at times. As this story helped me recall, it wasn't too long ago when I thought the same oversimplified philosophy: "If I intend good things, good things will just happen." This is a point of self-reflection I encourage of academics and scholars in this field as well. There are a considerable number of pressures and challenges organizations face in making these actions commonplace. More than anything, they often are not staffed with adequately trained and experienced personnel. So the organizational learning curve takes longer. Educating those who don't see these dynamics for what they are and supporting their improvement should be the objective of these conversations.

This brings me to a final note on the importance of leadership within the sector. Before my role ever became involved in this fire, I was set up for such an underwhelming outcome. Someone, long ago within the organization, determined the services I would have to offer and how I could offer them. Someone else determined the authorities I would have in the field, and the resources I could use to respond. What culminated to become that story began long ago with leadership decision and program design. Who was at the table when those decisions were made? How diverse were the faces and minds at that table? How representative were they of those being served?

During this COVID-19 response, African-American and the elderly have been identified as particularly vulnerable and affected. For those developing services to address the impact of COVID-19, we have an opportunity to make sure those voices are foremost in the development of solutions. However, it is not what I have witnessed. Even amidst a widely supported social justice movement for black communities, we neglect to put them at the center of decision-making regarding services for black communities. Everyone around me making the decisions of what services we offer, how we offer them, and when we offer them are young, white men.

The humanitarian sector serves those that have been historically underrepresented in decision-making. They have been marginalized and disadvantaged by systems, habits, and behaviors. If we do not ensure they are the drivers of the solutions, we contribute to the damaging systems that create the vulnerabilities we seek to fight.

We become part of the problem we are fighting.

## Note

1   Ann Mei Chang, *Lean Impact* (Wiley, 2018).

# 12 Security management

## Local responsibility, local engagement

*Andrew Cunningham*

### Reflections and questions

I find that reflections often start with a set of questions, and these initial questions invariably bring forth others. This is what I have learned from humanitarian work – it is a series of questions with few concrete answers. I have found that in the business of aid work reflection is sometimes frowned upon – the point is to do, not go around in abstract circles. But I believe that as practitioners we should allow ourselves to ask questions, and think about these deeply, even if the result is simply asking more questions. We improve practice if we question why and how we do things and challenge ourselves to do better. Our trajectories as humanitarians are informed by our past experiences and how they have been interpreted and integrated into our world view.

After a couple of years in working with a development agency in Burundi teaching farmers how to build small-scale fish farms, my trajectory in the humanitarian business was to focus on working in emergency interventions, starting with the Rwandan refugee camps in Tanzania in the mid-1990s. I spent most of my time after this working with Médecins Sans Frontières (MSF) managing programmes and security in various highly insecure contexts around the world. My focus was on places such as Somalia, Pakistan, Afghanistan, Iraq, South Sudan and Nigeria, but I worked in many other places as well. I spent quite a few years in the former Soviet Union – working throughout Central Asia, in Moldova, and in the North Caucasus of Russia, including Dagestan, Chechnya, Ingushetia, and North Ossetia.

I worked as a logistician, in the water and sanitation sector, and then went on to project management, emergency team roles, and country director positions. I liked being in the thick of things and seeing the immediate impact of the work we did. Working in humanitarian crises combined my desire to work in other countries with the need to do something useful while being there. Even if the need to be useful becomes the dominant motivation we must admit that there is always a residual romanticism to the work.

To me emergencies were the bread and butter of humanitarian action, but crucially I learned that emergencies were rarely short and that they were always difficult to understand. Increasingly I was interested in trying to understand the causes

*Figure 12.1* Akhmad Kadyrov Mosque, Chechnya

of these crises and the multi-faceted ways in which they affected populations and communities and, most importantly, how humanitarian aid contributed, or not, to responding to the needs of these populations.

After I stopped working in the field I moved to headquarters and worked on context analysis and humanitarian affairs issues – trying to understand how we could do our jobs better by gaining a deeper understanding of the contexts within which we worked, the limitations of humanitarian action, and the principles by which we operated. This led to an interest in how humanitarian international non-governmental organisations (INGOs) and states interacted, which lead to a PhD in War Studies and a professional book on the subject. This must be a typical trajectory – field work leads to jobs managing operations, to time in the headquarters, to further study, and finally to writing.

## Remote security management

Whilst still in the field, one of the key elements of the type of work I preferred was that it was direct programme implementation and hands-on security management – on the ground, with our staff, in a top-down management structure. Quick decision-making was the name of the game and hierarchical lines were simple and short. Importantly, I was part of the management of programmes which could access the at-risk populations and the areas where the programmes were being implemented. In other words, I could get my hands dirty.

This is not to say that negotiating humanitarian access was simple – it was tricky to negotiate, often with state and non-state armed actors and in areas with many security restrictions. There was always a threat of violence and we had to tread carefully. We expected that at least minimal access was possible and the skills I learned revolved around this process of analysis and negotiation. We could find work-arounds and compromises to allow programme staff to reach the populations being assisted, and in fact this was normally a prerequisite. This begs the question, though – what is humanitarian access?

Access is a physical act – access by the populations to aid materials or access by aid workers to the populations. Most humanitarian aid is material aid, and even non-material aid demands a certain level of physical access. Here I am thinking of the benefits of proximity and solidarity and many protection activities which aim to uphold people's rights and keep them safe. There must be some form of physical contact with the people being aided by aid agencies – to understand what the needs are, to show support, to witness and communicate.

But access by whom? For most emergency-oriented international humanitarian organisations, access implies physical access by expatriates (also known as 'international staff' as opposed to 'national staff' who are from the place itself). As mentioned, this was my experience for many years. Compromises were made to always allow physical access by expatriates, even to the point of being forced to use armed guards or to drive two days out of the way to safely reach a project site. Inconceivable was a situation where I could never travel to the programme site and interact with the populations seeking aid. How would such a system even work?

The story I tell here remains sensitive to those involved and so I cannot be too specific in the details. The context was highly insecure, with a high risk of kidnapping for all staff, especially for expatriates. There was massive violence against the civilian population, many disappearances, and an oppressive regime of intimidation, arrests, and torture. It was, quite frankly, a brutal context where mistakes were not tolerated, and dozens of kidnappings were the result of bad judgement calls. We had one overriding issue that defined all acts and decisions – security. This was not only the case for humanitarian organisations but for the civilian population as well – we all struggled to stay safe. One 'solution' to access constraints was to facilitate local actors to implement programmes in a way that best suited the security limitations of the context. This became known as a 'remote control' and later a 'remote management' system.

To be more precise, in this context the international team was based a few hours away from the project site, in a location that was much safer than where the programmes were being implemented. There was proximity between local staff and international staff managers, as we could all 'meet in the middle' at locations safe for everyone, but as the boss I was not on site. National staff implemented the activities and support was provided remotely.

The remote-control label was a curious formulation, as I could picture myself safely sitting in an office many kilometres away with an actual remote control and

TV monitor, changing the channel to find the reality I wanted to see. This was obviously never the case. Was it even remote management, the later conceptualisation? This implied a certain standard management structure but directed from a remote location. Neither conceptualisation quite hit the mark. One reason was the perspective taken. Maybe management was the problematic term and a better way to look at it was that I was there to facilitate local actors – to help a local structure implement activities; to provide resources to them. We had to develop a working relationship between 'us' and the local staff through negotiation and discussion. We found ways to work together, to share responsibilities – not through job descriptions or formal contractual obligations, but through trust, communication and adaptation. The aim was to work together to get the work done.

This system was not a traditional hierarchical construct of top-down management and direct expatriate supervision of local staff, but involved many compromises and adaptations. We had to find a balance between facilitating the work and managing the various agendas stated and unstated by all those involved. Agendas included personal needs and desires – related to jobs, careers and professional obligations, as well as obligations to communities, families and organisations. Not to over-generalise, but expatriates tended to prioritise organisational needs and national staff local needs. In this way the humanitarian act was a negotiation – local priorities and perspectives had to be balanced against the agenda of the international organisation.

This was not the way I was used to working and it took mental adaptation. Such a system focuses the mind on the interworking of the context and humanitarian needs. It also focuses the mind on the idea that national staff were not just mechanisms in the humanitarian machine but were essential components of decision-making and humanitarian action. Crucially, as members of the communities themselves they are not outside the context.

Let me here focus for a bit on security management. A fine balance must exist between interests and risks, and each part of the group will have a different perspective on what these are. Local staff have better local knowledge, better engagement with local state and non-state authorities, and can engage as individuals in society – they are more than their INGO affiliation and have their own reputations, relationships and professions. Therefore, local engagement and, implicitly, local responsibility for humanitarian action become key aspects of the humanitarian act.

## Who brings what to the table?

But what does the humanitarian organisation itself bring to the table? As a manager of the humanitarian operations, what am I bringing to the table? Resources, of course, as any set of humanitarian activities takes cash and materials to implement. But who determines what is an acceptable risk – is it also a negotiation? Colleagues on the ground for the most part managed their own security – as an expatriate manager I could not do so from a distance, especially for a place I rarely visited. This all had to be worked out clearly for the system to work; in security management a lack of clarity can get people killed. Everything and everybody must be in balance between risks and benefits.

An INGO can put things out of balance based on its interests. An INGO will focus on a variety of issues, and not all of these issues are directly relevant to the implementation of aid. Information collection for use outside the country is one such issue. An INGO is on the outside and can communicate, can tell the world what is happening, can speak for those unable to tell their own stories, and can advocate for certain things to be done or not be done. This is valuable and an important role an INGO can play. This is a concrete activity, something that can be done even in the environment of remote management. But we could not do it alone, not without agreement of colleagues on the ground, not without their active participation, and not without them taking on added risk. Safe ways had to be found to collect useful information, information that was authoritative and factual. Thus, the idea developed to collect information from medical facilities about war trauma cases to be able to paint a better picture of the violence faced by the civilian population. The idea was to show the effects of violence on the people we were working with.

But something went wrong – a local staff member got into serious trouble. The incident involved sensitive information being discovered by armed troops at a checkpoint – a staff member was transporting compromising papers describing cases of war trauma. The staff member was arrested but thankfully incarceration lasted only a short time and no prison sentence was given. Regardless, exile was the result – the colleague could not go home again for a very long time as it became too dangerous to return. Our colleague paid a high personal cost, but what, if any, was the cost to the organisation, and what was the value added by the exercise?

Boiling it down, the issue at hand revolved around divergent risks associated with divergent interests. The ultimate goals were not in question – everyone involved, expatriates and nationals, were committed to assisting the population living in difficult circumstances. This could be accomplished in different ways, however. The added value for our INGO contribution was surely in providing a public voice and capitalising on the proximity the organisation had via the national staff to the population. Something had to be said about the situation to the outside world. But this was a sensitive issue, and it was potentially dangerous for anyone to be connected with such information. Interests then diverged at the level of actual engagement, meaning the practical ways in which all of us involved were involved with the exercise. It should always be remembered that organisational interests are carried out by real people, not by positions. Organisational and individual interests will often be at variance.

I am often reminded of this story when I think of the role of the 'local' in humanitarian aid operations – ideas such as local engagement, local responsibility, international support for local responses. There are dangers and there are dilemmas to encouraging a larger local response, but I am not convinced enough is said about these. These dilemmas do not all relate to security issues and stories do not always end with people not being able to go home. But sometimes the starkest of examples help clarify the issues that need to be thought through and dealt with, and deconstructing security incidents tends to help with this. The aid environment is full of relationships, of all types and complexity, with all the related power dynamics and assumptions built into these complicated engagements. Not every situation is so dangerous, not every situation is so highly insecure, but every situation has its own risks and complications. Those supported on the ground to provide aid are people, with lives intertwined in their own environments of power, interests, needs and risks.

I recall this story especially when I encounter talk about localisation, which is about acknowledging and strengthening the independence of local aid actors and respecting their decision-making to best meet the needs of crisis-affected populations. This is the new buzzword for these complex engagements but as has been noted (at least in conversations I have had with colleagues), the moral component is somewhat missing from the discussions. Sometimes it seems that the localisation agenda is a way for international actors to abdicate their responsibilities and let the national actors take not only more responsibility but the risks that come with local engagement. There are limits to localisation – a balance must be kept between the interests and risks taken by the international and the national. Here I make a comparison between the story and the sort of local partners to which localisation refers. This lesson taught me long ago to be wary of the promise of the localisation of engagement and to question the limits of responsibility. Red lines do exist. Localisation should not lead to disengagement on security realities. Care should be put on balancing personal care versus organisational values, objectives and prioritisation.

This is not meant to be a rejection of the localisation idea, but simply a chance to relate a stored-up story which may apply to current debates and discussions and ways of thinking about how humanitarian aid is implemented. This is the way of things. My 'humanitarian' mind keeps ideas tucked away, and they pop up periodically. A story from long ago stays with me, is always there, and resurfaces when needed, or when prompted. Different times, different places, different flavours of the month, but some things remain the same. This is in and of itself an interesting finding, as how often do things fundamentally change? In my humble opinion, lessons stick because things do not really change, but often old lessons get thrown out with new perspectives and rationalisations. What changes is how we package concepts into narratives we are comfortable telling ourselves.

I often wonder about this, as I have been in the aid business for 30 years now, but I am not sure anything fundamentally new has occurred, although as individuals we do change our views. Three points stand out for me in this progression. One is that I progressively started to slow down, and I have begun to take greater care to understand the context within which I am working. Second, I have developed a greater appreciation for the local side of the equation – the thoughts and perspective and concerns of those embedded in the context. And third, I now see much more clearly the limitations of organisations themselves – they are merely tools to be used and are not the most important factor in deciding how aid should be delivered.

That is me and my changing views, but as a sector why must we so often change how stories are interpreted and revise the narratives we write to explain to ourselves what we do and why? Why so many new buzzwords? Are we really so unsure of what we are meant to be doing?

## Future perfect

This story was remembered and reflected upon in the midst of the Covid-19 pandemic. There are at this time (late 2020) many blogs, webinars, articles, press statements and interviews floating in the ether which all have a common theme – that the pandemic has fundamentally changed this or that. I want here to be a contrarian and respectfully disagree. Yes, there are effects to how we work and live and some of these will last into the future. Some, I hope, will last far into the future, such as the lessening of air pollution and the decrease in flying. It would be great if everyone slowed down a bit and businesses and organisations could finally see the value in working from home.

But in terms of humanitarian action, I am not so convinced that much has, or indeed will change beyond some logistical issues which will be solved over time. Except for one aspect, and that is what I have heard called 'localisation by default'. This is the case where international aid workers cannot travel, internationally or domestically, and people are locked down in their homes and communities, and so aid, as with so much disrupted by the pandemic, becomes local by default. Covid-19 has made life for so many as local as life can be, locking millions in their homes for a time. This is surely changing the complexion of humanitarian aid. But how fundamental of a change will this be and how long-lasting?

Let me go back to the story these reflections revolve around. In my story the norm was expatriate presence, the exception was remote management, and…what happened next? The organisation eventually reverted to the norm – expatriate presence on the ground, once it was again feasible. That is, the organisation felt much more comfortable working with expatriate staff on site and once security allowed it this way of working was re-established. A full expat team was put into the field once security had improved and the role of local staff was severely diminished as a result. The power and decision-making dynamic reverted to the norm.

Old instincts are hard to shake. More disturbingly, old stories lose their meaning as they are no longer considered relevant. That is, until they suddenly are again. Localisation by default is like remote management – a system temporarily put into place to fit the needs of the time. The question is: If the needs of the time change back to the norm, won't the system change back with it? In the case of Covid-19 I believe that it will.

What does a pandemic change, and what does it not? What it will not fundamentally change is the dominance of international aid actors, nor the predominance of northern aid monies in the aid system, nor the power dynamics created by the geo-political realities of the world as it is. These will someday change, but it will not be because of Covid-19 and it will be long in the future that true change happens. The response to the pandemic, however, will create short-term disruption in certain aspects of how the world works and some of these lessons may be slowly taken up over time – necessity is the mother of invention and local response capacities will be adapted to meet the changed environment.

I think that it is appropriate to focus on what local actors can do outside the normal power dynamics which have been temporarily disrupted. I am anxious to discover what is possible within a disrupted system and without the direct intervention of international actors. I will be curious, after the fact, to analyse what the practical, on the ground, consequences of what is basically a logistical disruption will be. The virtual aspects of communications and the ability to wire money instead of shipping materials will be important aspects to watch.

On a higher scale, current developments may link to the recent trend of governments limiting the field access of international actors, especially expatriates. Indonesia and the Philippines are good examples, where the governments have used the frame of local action and sovereignty to take better control over aid interventions during a sudden-onset crisis. But these have related more to the physical access of international organisations rather than disrupting the flow of resources, which are still appreciated. In these cases the system has been adapted to relate to local circumstances, but the exceptions prove the rule, which is the 'normal' way of operating, which is for international organisations to have their own access, with expatriates, to emergency contexts. It may over time become the norm for states and local communities to take full charge of humanitarian operations with only support in the form of resources coming from international actors, but I argue that this will be a long time in coming. It may, however, be the case that the Covid-19 pandemic accelerates this pre-existing trend.

Not to be forgotten is the relationship between governments and their own local communities and the potential disruptions to these relationships. It will be interesting to see how the social contract between state and civil society will be affected. How will individual governments respond to the pandemic and how much will local civil society organisations feel either supported or abandoned? Each region, each country, or even each sub-region within a country, may have a different experience.

A comparison can be made between the story these reflections have discussed and the changing relationship between states, local aid actors and international aid organisations. This is obviously not a direct comparison but only a way to point to a pattern of moving away from, and then back to, norms of behaviour. The periphery may change based on certain contingencies, but the fundamentals may not. The pandemic may change the periphery for a time, and may add to on-going trends, but the fundamentals of the international aid system will probably not change; or, if small changes do occur, they will be on the edges and will only point to a very long-term reengineering of the aid system and its geo-political underpinnings.

Therefore, and in conclusion, let it be said that the old stories will continue to be relevant and we should not be afraid of relating them to current situations.

# 13 Starting from within

*Rami Shamma*

## Plugged into humanitarian work

My journey started back in 2006, when Lebanon entered into a 33-day war with Israel, which resulted in destruction of the infrastructure and in people's lives being lost. As a background, my small family includes a mix of nationalities. My father is Lebanese and my mother is Ukrainian. They met in Ukraine back in the 80s when my father studied there. They agreed together that they wanted to live in Lebanon and so they moved to Lebanon in 1985.

I was lucky in 2006, as I had the option to be deported outside Lebanon during this 33-day war. We were deported to Ukraine and lived for a short period of time with my grandparents. However, my father stayed in Lebanon as he was a member of the local government and was responding to the needs of the members of our village.

I came back to Lebanon on September 17, 2006. Two days later I started my first job in the humanitarian field as a field officer for an emergency response project that DPNA (Development for People and Nature Association) was implementing to respond to the needs of the affected people in South Lebanon.

At that time, I still had to finish the last semester of my BS degree in Computer and Communication Engineering. I knew that my job was not related to any humanitarian work at that time but this had been my dream since I was 13 years old, as my father is a computer engineer. So even though it was my last semester, my focus was fully on the activities that I was engaged in within the response. I enjoyed the work and I enjoyed most of all the support we were providing for the people in need.

As soon as I was done with my exams, I fully dedicated myself to my work with DPNA, and for a period of four months I had very little contact with anyone except my work colleagues and the communities we served. At that time I took part in more than 80 recreational activities for the well-being of children and youth, held different distributions of basic needs to affected people, and linked up with various decision makers (mayors, UN agencies, local organizations, etc.) in the villages we were working in.

This experience is the one which 'plugged' me into the humanitarian field for good. I changed my career aspirations from being an engineer to being an active member in the civil society field and within the humanitarian system in Lebanon. It took me some time to make this decision to shift directions but I finally made this choice in the summer of 2007. For many years I used to speak up with passion and I used to work with complete commitment to our mission as humanitarians, but I never really knew the deep meaning of "why".

When my first son was born in 2014, we were undergoing strategic thinking and planning for DPNA and I was asked the reason why I was in this field. This is when I fast forwarded my imagination to a scenario 15 years down the line, where my son was in school and he was asked by his teacher: "what did your father do for your country?" This is when I truly understood that I want my son to have an answer to this question. This is where my passion and commitment lies and this is where I want to pursue my dreams in contributing to change in the world.

## My journey with profound stress

My experience with stress began in 2006 when I began working in this field, even though I did not clearly understand what was happening then. We used to come to the office between 6 and 7 a.m. and come back from the field at 10 p.m., only to resume preparatory work until 1 a.m.

*Figure 13.1* World Vision group photo from field visit to the food parcel distribution in South Lebanon during COVID-19 response interventions

At that time, I didn't feel tiredness, I didn't feel I was overwhelmed, I didn't feel the need to rest. Instead, I felt drive, passion, and commitment to the work that I did. Because of the constant field visits and activities, I was mostly relying on junk food and chocolate, since they were easy to have access to; the chocolate provided me with the energy I needed.

With this lifestyle, my digestive system was affected and I started to have the health problems that still plague me up to this day, especially when I am under lots of pressure. I didn't have much information on what I was going through except for what I needed to do from the medical perspective to resolve the immediate complications.

My work with DPNA continued after 2007 but in different roles and responsibilities, which were not humanitarian as there were no natural or man-made disasters to respond to. During this phase, I managed a program that trains and builds the capacities of young people to run for municipal office, so that they can impact the lives of other young people living in their village/city. This was a program that I worked on throughout the whole of Lebanon and it gave me exposure to many areas which I didn't even know of. This gave me an idea that NGOs do have a role even if there is no crisis present.

In 2011, the Syrian conflict started (here I am referring to it in the non-political terminology so as not to get into the political discussion on this). Lebanon had a huge influx of refugees, which resulted in more than 1.5 million refugees displaced to Lebanon in what is said to be the largest refugee crisis in the world.

In 2011, we started responding to the needs of these refugees and this continued under different fields of interventions. I was able to build my experience in being part of DPNA, but also with other organizations where I would support their work as a consultant. This required me to put in more time than I used to, resulting in 15–20 hours of work per day when there were too many tasks to accomplish.

In the summer of 2014, the story of understanding the consequences of stress started to come into play. I had two consultancy jobs in addition to my regular job with DPNA. I had to take on extra jobs in my free time to be able to secure a better quality of life for my family. National and local NGOs in the humanitarian field normally don't get the same salaries as UN or international NGO staff. Moreover, the networking that one needs to do in order to keep up with the developments in Lebanon and the region require time, effort, and financial investment on different levels. So, throughout my work in DPNA, I had the chance and luxury to actually benefit from the opportunities to use my skills to improve my financial situation.

Although I was able to achieve my tasks in an effective way, it was at the expense of my health. I started developing symptoms that were new to me. I used to feel weakness in my legs, constant back pain, numbness in my forehead, a taste of iron whenever I was eating food, and various digestive irritations. I had the necessary tests done but they all came out normal. I used to develop these symptoms mostly on the weekend, my "normal" work weekdays having been productively full. This caused my family members to notice since I was not able to be there for my spouse or my child (who was less than one year old at that time). This created stress in our home, which of course added an extra layer to the already existing stress from work.

Three months later, and after consulting with a family doctor, I registered at a gym based on the doctor's recommendation that I change my lifestyle. The symptoms were gone in three days, which was quite unusual for me and for many people around me. I didn't understand what had happened at that time but was happy with the result.

In 2015, I was invited to participate in the Training for Trainers (ToT) on Profound Stress and Attunement in Jordan, as a member of a regional program that implements this methodology with young adolescents. It was also a stressful period of time with job responsibilities but also with my family since my wife and I were expecting our second child. I started developing the same symptoms but fortunately it was convenient since the trainer helped me understand the complications of stress and how it can affect the individual.

I was able to also get through this, but this time it was more intentional and with the correct mindset for a long-term strategy to deal with stress.

Many reasons cause stress to a humanitarian aid worker, starting from the fact that we are working in a crisis, to the number of hours we put in to supporting others, to the lack of staff care in many instances, to the external pressure we get from family and friends to give them time but without our ability to do so, and so it is just a matter of time before we burn out. Everyone who is part of an emergency response goes through this. The different levels of stress we pass through in our field are different from what people go through in other sectors.

The international organizations have reached a point where these levels of stress are acknowledged by the organization and often this extra support is provided to people in the humanitarian response. The international organizations even give attention when required to the international staff who are not working in their own country, since there is the extra level of stress where you are working in a context that is different from the one you are used to. Unfortunately, this is not widely practiced in the local NGOs, and they are at the forefront of any response.

This is how and why I started my journey in introducing profound stress in my meetings, trainings, humanitarian work with other organizations or individuals, government entities, and even personal friends/family.

## My reflections on profound stress

### *Reflection 1*

I learned that the first level is to know yourself. I need to be aware of what is happening with my body and my heart. I need to know my feelings and the symptoms that are strange to my body. One of the actions I have taken is that I have developed an understanding of the triggers that impact me. I do this by three different steps:

1)   Identify the triggers – this is a learn-as-you-go task that you should start immediately if you have not done so already. This requires high levels of alertness

and you should know the different feelings that develop when passing through different experiences. Every day, in the different situations I pass through, I spend time analyzing how I felt about these situations. What were the different sentences, words, actions that people said or did that triggered the feelings inside me?

2) Develop ways of dealing with the triggers – after identifying the triggers, I started developing ways of dealing with those triggers, sometimes in the feelings that I developed and sometimes in the actions that I made. For example, one of the practical actions I developed is walking around the office. It was clearly explained to me at a later stage that walking actually decreases the level of cortisol hormone dripping in your brain. For those people who like results, I had really remarkable results when I used to walk while going through stressful situations.

3) Create an internal library of those triggers – over the course of time, I developed a number of triggers that are mostly related to my past as an individual, with the feelings that I normally get when these triggers materialize. I noticed that not every trigger can be dealt with in the same way in different situations. Thus, there was a need for me to think all of these through and create a list internally in my mind of those triggers and the ways I would be able to deal with them. This is a life-time exercise and I really recommend every single person to put in the time and effort needed to reach this.

Profound stress relies on the two systems of thinking in our brains. The triggers that affect our well-being because of stress have the same thinking. Whenever I am fully in control of my actions/reactions, it means that I am taking my time, concentrating, constructing thoughts, analyzing, and acting/reacting with more reason; I am using System 2. Whenever the trigger interrupts my thinking, I go back into a fast action/reaction based on intuition, involuntary control, effortlessness, and my innate skills; I am using System 1.

When I am under profound stress, the brain moves into System 1 of thinking. This is why my reactions become uncontrollable and I notice that I make more mistakes than when I am not under stress.

## *Reflection 2*

Another thing I learned is that I used to practice shaming in my daily life, mostly without the awareness of it happening. As humanitarians, we are often unaware of the words and sentences we use with our peers, stakeholders, and communities we interact with.

In our daily interaction, we shame and get shamed. But what does this really mean and how does this impact our well-being?

One of the important definitions for shame that I rely on a lot is: "Shame is an inner sense of feeling diminished or insufficient as a person. It is the self judging the self."[1] One of the main reasons why we shouldn't shame is that shaming stops emotional growth, which is the development of emotional intelligence. As a father during the periods when I was passing through profound stress, this was one of the highlights for me and truly it is a learning journey with my children to be able to understand their feelings and from where they develop their actions, and try to stop any shaming that might be done. The first step that I was definitely able to accomplish is the awareness of different words or actions that resemble shaming.

We often take on the stress we pass through in the place where we are comfortable the most, considering that our family should be able to understand what we are going through. Indirectly, we practice shaming to people around us and often we end up hurting their feelings and affecting the relationship. One of the additional reflections on shaming is the indirect way stress influences our interaction, causing us to shame others without us knowing about it or recognizing what we have done.

I developed some strategies to deal with the stress I was going through, without going into shaming mode.

I tried to break down the components related to shaming, for example the reason behind the shaming – is it a cultural difference? Is it an age difference? Is it a way to try and control? Is it related to an experience the person passed through where they were shamed? etc.

I attempted to understand the reason that we talked about above. I don't need to accept it but the least I can do is to understand where it is coming from.

I talked to the person and let them know what they had done. Most importantly, I explained to them what I was feeling since feelings are always relative to the person experiencing them. They have to know that they have shamed me and what it means for my own well-being.

A good strategy which I have tried myself is to write a letter. Write the letter to this certain someone and you could always actually give it to this person. Sometimes I sent out a message using the different digital platforms. The important part here is that I needed to express why this was causing me stress.

One of the principles that I used during this period is "it doesn't really matter if the person thinks it is okay and allowed, what really matters is how you felt and the importance of this person knowing about it".

The better I was able to express this, the more I was able to take off the concern from my shoulder/back. The more I have experiences that I have been shamed in and that were not resolved, the more I had stress accumulating over the years, and it was just a matter of time before it exploded and caused me greater harm.

### Reflection 3

My final reflection is about life–work balance.

This was definitely not only related to me but also to the people around me. One can actually work on the fact that if your life inside your home is not working well then this definitely adds an extra layer of stress in your life and to your work responsibilities.

The more I was able to minimize this level of stress, the more I was able to perform well in my job. Thus, working with my family on understanding my work responsibilities was key to having this layer of stress decrease. This doesn't mean that this level of stress will fade away, because it will not. It is important to keep this in mind.

Another aspect of this is not letting my stress affect the relationship between myself and my spouse/children. This is still learning in progress and I can only say that, at this stage, I am able to understand what I am going through and help my family know about this as well, so that we can all work together on dealing with this issue that affects the dynamics in our home.

It is important to note as well that I went through different priorities in my life, as did other people. My family members needed to understand these priorities but they were not able to understand them if I didn't communicate it to them. I made sure to inform my family members of the change in priorities and thus I was able to give time to those priorities with their support. I have two boys and one of the main lessons learned from my side is to give quality time to my children and help them understand what I am going through, since this will help a lot in shaping the expectations they have from me in my responsibilities.

When I was under profound stress, I felt really bad. I had negative vibes all the time, negative thinking about all the situations I was going though, and negative perceptions of all interactions that I was part of. I didn't have a reason to wake up in the morning since I felt that I didn't want to do anything in my life. In one way or another, I had lost hope that my life had an added value.

After I reflect on these days, I understand more that all my passion for helping others, all the commitment I have towards putting the lives of people ahead of mine and my family's, all the dedication I have to contributing to change in the communities, and all the values I believe in; they had no meaning at all when I was under profound stress.

The experiences that I went through with profound stress interrupted all my relationships with my family my co-workers, and the people in the communities I was working with. I was not able to give them the support they needed, nor was I able to think clearly of ways they could work around the challenges they were facing. My communication was not healthy anymore, and the more interaction I had, the more problems I faced, since every conversation resulted in a negative outcome and increased the gap I had in my different relationships.

## What does it mean to us as humanitarians?

We hear many people say, ' If you are not OK, you cannot help others be OK". What does this really mean? Is it true? Is it something that we need to put as a priority?

What it really meant to me is that I will not be able to deal with the problems in a correct way and thus I cannot meet the needs of the vulnerable communities. Not being able to meet the needs of the vulnerable communities jeopardizes the humanitarian work and what I want to achieve. I simply will not be able to serve others.

Is it really true? Some people argue that it is not, in the sense that we are OK if we see others doing OK. It is always the question of which came first, the chicken or the egg? Similarly, it depends here on how I was viewing the case, but it works both ways: If I am not feeling well, I am not able to give from my heart and with the energy needed AND if I see others going through rough times, I forget how I am feeling and suddenly I have the power it takes to make them feel better or change their lives for the better.

I understood that we all have needs that we either communicate with others or choose to deal with by ourselves. Understanding our own needs, as well as the needs of others, will help us formulate who we are and facilitate a healthy interaction with the people around us.

With my experience, I will divide the impact stress has on us as humanitarians into three layers: as leaders, as humanitarians, and from the beneficiaries' perspective.

On a leadership level, we as humanitarians should understand the needs of our teams, of our peers, and of the communities we serve; basically the needs of all stakeholders involved. If all of those needs are not met then there will be a missing component in the way we are dealing with the crises we are trying to help alleviate. We often tend to give priority to one of those groups while marginalizing the other groups. One of the main things I learned is understanding the importance of giving time and efforts to my team members, so that they are able to give more and support more. In one of the phases of my management career, I was able to give all my time during the day to internal support for the teams. This has given them a noticeable boost in skills, attitude, and passion towards our mission as humanitarians. In turn, it helped in the projects we were implementing and definitely enriched the support we were providing for the vulnerable.

There is another aspect in the leadership that needs to be taken. We need to ensure that the knowledge we have is transferred to our peers and colleagues. We need to ensure that all information leaders have is passed on to all team members. In my experience, I ensured that my team knew about profound stress and how they could get themselves out of it, which helped in turn in their performance and in achieving the tasks well. Even with other peer agencies, I was able to transfer this knowledge. I have friends who work in other organizations who have told me how much understanding about their well-being has helped them in their work and also in their life decisions.

As humanitarians, we know that in every intervention we make there is a division of tasks and responsibilities among team members. Imagine that you have a car and one of its parts doesn't work. It means that you are putting your life at risk while driving it. The same concept can be applied to any humanitarian intervention. Any team member who is under profound stress and has to perform a task will not be able to do so if they are not dealing well with the stress they experience. If their unresolved stress jeopardizes the task itself it will either cause harm in the community or delay in the implementation, which often will risk life-saving activities not being carried out.

There are two levels on which stress can affect the communities receiving humanitarian assistance. The first is related to humanitarian aid workers going through profound stress, which affect their work with people, and the second is related to the communities themselves going through profound stress.

I have explained the first level and how it relates to our role as humanitarians.

As for the communities we are working with that are experiencing profound stress, they might act in ways that may not be accepted easily by many of the team members. It is our role to know what they are going through and to make sure that our staff and volunteers are able to deal with them in a proper way. This is where attunement comes into play and where the knowledge in how to attune should be part of the capacity building that we provide to all staff working in the humanitarian field. Attunement is when you work on decreasing the levels of stress and go back to improving your well-being to be able to continue your work in a good way.

NGOs need to work not only on the levels of stress and introducing this concept to their staff/volunteers but also on how to deal with it, how to decrease it, how to overcome it, and how to feel better.

We are humanitarians, we have to have hope for a better future, and we have to learn how to transmit this hope to others. Many people's lives depend on us and our well-being. It starts with oneself and then we are able to change people's lives for the better.

## Note

1  Gershen Kaufman, *Shame: The Power of Caring* (Schenkman Publishing Company, 1980).

# 14 The politics of genocide prevention and the limits of humanitarian neutrality

*Matthew Levinger*

## How I came to study genocide

As a child, I perceived myself as living on the margins of catastrophe. Growing up in the 1960s in the placid suburbs of Cleveland, Ohio, and on the outskirts of a Massachusetts college town, I had little personal exposure to violence. But scenes of violence came over our grainy black-and-white TV screen every night—body counts from Vietnam, riots in American inner cities, police dogs attacking civil rights protesters in the Deep South. And the unspoken memories of violence lurked silently in the background—both those of my father, whose Jewish family had fled Nazi Germany in the 1930s, and of my mother, a privileged Southern Presbyterian daughter of Jim Crow Mississippi.

Before their marriage, the two of them had settled on the pacifist faith of Quakerism as a mutually agreeable religious middle ground. But in the 1960s, the Quakers were angry. In our Sunday morning meetings for worship, congregants would rise mournfully to bear witness to the scourge of nuclear weapons that threatened to destroy all life on earth 13 times over—as if once were not enough. We would stage anti-war vigils on our town common and protests outside the gates of the nearby Air Force base. And yet we did not acknowledge our own rage: we saw ourselves as pure vessels of peace, unlike the angry warmongers on the other side.

In college and graduate school, I was drawn to studying ideologies of violence: the political doctrines of revolutionary and nationalist leaders, from Robespierre to Hitler, who justified the extermination of rival groups in the pursuit of utopian dreams. I sought to comprehend the logic of the profoundly irrational mass movements that have destroyed hundreds of millions of human lives in recent centuries. After a decade teaching history at a liberal arts college in the Pacific Northwest, I gave up my tenured professorship to help launch a new Academy for Genocide Prevention at the U.S. Holocaust Memorial Museum in Washington, DC.

For the past 15 years, I have worked at the intersection of academia and the policy world, teaching international conflict management skills to government officials and other practitioners through executive education programs at the Holocaust Museum, the United States Institute of Peace, and George Washington

University. My students include military officers, diplomats, and humanitarian and development assistance workers, among other professionals. In these jobs, I have worked both as a teacher and as an advocate for more robust and effective policies to address one of the world's most pressing humanitarian challenges: the prevention of genocide and mass atrocities in conflict-afflicted countries around the globe.

Most of the chapters in this book present reflections by practitioners who have spent their careers working for humanitarian NGOs or international organizations. The story I tell here, by contrast, focuses on my work at the intersection between the U.S. government and independent nonprofit organizations. This is an important topic to include in a volume on the "humanitarian machine" for multiple reasons. Not only is the U.S. government itself an important player in the delivery of humanitarian assistance, through organizations such as the U.S. Agency for International Development (USAID), but it also provides significant funding to UN humanitarian agencies and international NGOs. Moreover, my story highlights the tensions between the concept of "national interest," which undergirds foreign policy decision-making by the U.S. and other governments, and "humanitarian neutrality," which is a guiding principle for humanitarian NGOs. I seek here to bridge the gap between these two principles. I argue that the prevention of genocide and mass atrocities must be understood not only as a humanitarian concern but also as a key national security interest for the U.S. and other governments. Conversely, I contend that UN agencies and international NGOs need to move beyond the principle of strict humanitarian neutrality in order to protect vulnerable populations from mass killing by predatory groups.

## How genocide can elude both diplomatic and humanitarian responses

By temperament, I am a cautious person, and I have always held a profoundly ambivalent attitude toward utopian ideals and movements. Over the past two centuries, communist revolutionaries promising harmonious workers' paradises have created dictatorships that imprisoned dissidents and massacred millions of their citizens, while right-wing demagogues pledging to return their nations to a glorious imaginary past have unleashed racist violence and catastrophic wars. Although the pursuit of utopian visions can lead to disaster, we also need such visions in order to expand our imaginations and our sense of the boundaries of possibility. Sir Thomas More, the author of the 16th-century novel *Utopia*, coined this word as a pun on two Greek phrases: "*ou-topos*," meaning "no place," and "*eu-topos*," meaning "good place." In other words, a utopia is a good place that is nowhere to be found.

The utopian vision that has guided my work in Washington, DC has been the dream of a world without genocide or mass atrocities. I first moved to Washington in January 2003, as part of a year-long fellowship program for visiting academics at the U.S. Department of State. While most of my colleagues were absorbed in managing the diplomatic fallout from the U.S. invasion of Iraq that began two months after the start of my fellowship, I worked to organize a series of conferences exploring strategies for interagency and international cooperation to prevent mass atrocities in vulnerable countries around the world.[1]

One key finding of these conferences was that the U.S. government lacked both the bureaucratic structures and the institutional culture that were required for effective atrocity prevention and response. Although the State Department and CIA both had small intelligence units focusing on atrocity early warning and war crimes prosecutions, there was no established policy apparatus for evaluating atrocity risks and formulating coordinated whole-of-government responses.

Even more important than these bureaucratic deficits were the cultural biases and blind spots that pervaded the formulation of U.S. foreign policy. Foreign Service Officers at the U.S. State Department are taught that their mission is to "advance the national security interests of the United States," and that they must avoid becoming distracted by activities that are peripheral or contrary to this core objective. And yet the State Department's leadership rarely encourages systematic reflection about the nature and requirements of U.S. national security, which can result in a cramped and narrow conception of its institutional mission. For example, when the Rwandan genocide erupted in April 1994, the State Department and Defense Department sprang into action to evacuate nearly all of the 258 U.S. citizens living in Rwanda within the first three days. Having accomplished this mission, however, the U.S. government stood idly by as Hutu extremists slaughtered between 500,000 and one million of their fellow Rwandan citizens over the next three months. During this time, the State Department convened an endless round of interagency meetings to deliberate over legalistic questions such as whether the violence in Rwanda constituted "genocide" under the terms of the UN Genocide Convention or merely "crimes against humanity" or individual "acts of genocide" that did not require a robust U.S. response.

The American government's inaction in the face of the Rwandan genocide reflected a "realist" calculus concerning the nature of U.S. national security: Rwanda was a poor and remote East African country, peripheral to geopolitical competition and disconnected from the U.S. alliance system, possessing no strategic minerals and insignificant from the standpoint of global trade. Based on these criteria, political events in such a country seemed largely irrelevant to U.S. interests.

Yet, as President Bill Clinton himself acknowledged in his apology speech at Kigali's airport four years later, this narrow conception of national security was flawed. Beyond the human cost of permitting this vast blood-letting to proceed unchecked, the U.S. government called into question its own moral authority at a historical moment when it was triumphantly proclaiming itself to be the world's last remaining superpower; and by rejecting a robust multilateral response, it also undermined the credibility of the United Nations as a guarantor of global peace and security. The Rwandan genocide also had larger economic and geopolitical reverberations that persist to this day. Many members of the Hutu militias that had perpetrated the genocide in Rwanda fled just across the border into eastern Zaire (subsequently the Democratic Republic of the Congo), where they were sustained by international humanitarian assistance in newly erected refugee camps, enabling them to threaten the stability of the new Tutsi-led Rwandan government. In 1996, seeking to destroy these militias, the Rwandan army invaded Zaire, sparking a quarter-century-long conflict that has come to be called "Africa's World War" and, by some estimates, has resulted in more than 5 million deaths.[2]

Just as U.S. government officials failed to reflect deeply enough about the national security implications of the Rwandan genocide, the leaders of many humanitarian and development organizations working in Rwanda also failed to reflect systematically on the political context and consequences of their own work—clinging instead to a flawed concept of "humanitarian neutrality." In *Aiding Violence: The Development Enterprise in Rwanda*, Peter Uvin observes that "NGOs and bilateral and multilateral aid agencies" shared a "rosy image of Rwanda" during the 1980s and early 1990s. Indeed, "No aid agency ever denounced the official racism or the quota system or the ethnic IDs—not even in the 1990s, when it was clear that they were being used to prepare for mass killings."[3] Father William Headley, who directed the programs of Catholic Relief Services (CRS) in Rwanda during the years leading up to the genocide, has observed:

> In truth, Rwanda was not a case of mysteriously appearing genocide. There had been major societal and ethnic rifts as well as related injustices for years. These were not hidden. They were considered to be outside CRS' development mandate. Our traditional programming improved socioeconomic life. It did not touch the country's latent conflict. CRS' projects were wiped out in minutes; the people we served became "the well-fed dead."[4]

Much of my work on genocide prevention has focused on the challenge of storytelling. I have sought to help recast the narratives that American leaders tell about their foreign policy objectives, so as to recognize the importance of the protection of human lives and human rights in advancing national and global security. As founding director of the Academy for Genocide Prevention at the U.S. Holocaust Memorial Museum, I helped launch a bipartisan Genocide Prevention Task Force, chaired by former Secretary of State Madeleine Albright and former Secretary of Defense William Cohen, which issued its report in December 2008, shortly after Barack Obama's election as U.S. President.

In my initial concept paper for the Genocide Prevention Task Force in early 2007, I wrote that the Task Force would seek to "spotlight the challenge of genocide prevention as a core foreign policy priority for the U.S. government, and to move this issue from the margins to the center of mainstream U.S. foreign policy deliberations." I pointed out that

> [e]ven when genocide occurs in territories remote from the United States, it creates devastating regional spillover effects including the expansion of armed conflicts, the spread of extremist political ideologies, the propagation of pandemic diseases, and the disruption of international trade. When the U.S. and other nations permit genocidal violence to continue unchecked,

they undermine their own moral authority and their capacity to productively shape the international order of the twenty-first century.

Some of the points from my concept paper made it into the Task Force's final report, as well as into President Obama's Presidential Study Directive 10 (PSD-10) of August 2011, which declared the prevention of mass atrocities and genocide to be a "core national security interest and core moral responsibility" of the United States and created a U.S. interagency Atrocities Prevention Board (APB). The APB included U.S. officials from the National Security Council and the Departments of State, Defense, Justice, and Treasury, along with the U.S. Agency for International Development and the intelligence community; it met on a monthly basis to assess emerging threats of atrocities around the world and to recommend coordinated U.S. policy responses.

Theoretically, the establishment of the APB remedied many of the key defects in the U.S. government's atrocity prevention capacity that had been identified by the State Department conferences I had organized in 2003. From an institutional perspective, PSD-10 created a standing interagency mechanism for assessing atrocity risks and formulating integrated whole-of-government policy responses. From the perspective of bureaucratic culture, it included a formal statement that atrocity prevention must be seen as a central goal of U.S. foreign policy, rather than as a subordinate issue that was principally of concern to human rights advocates and other do-gooders.

In practice, however, the track record of the APB and its successor organization was mixed—even before the advent of the Trump administration's America First foreign policy, with its scornful attitude toward human rights. Under President Obama, the APB was able to carve out zones of influence to help shape policy toward conflict-affected countries of peripheral interest to other U.S. government stakeholders, such as the Central African Republic. But, in dealing with marquee foreign policy challenges such as the Syrian civil war or the Saudi military offensive in Yemen, the APB frequently found itself shut out of the action—exposing President Obama's declaration that atrocity prevention was a "core national security interest" of the United States as little more than lip service.

## How humanitarianism and *Realpolitik* intersect

This story of my frustrating 17-year-long (and still running) struggle to elevate the cause of genocide prevention as a U.S. government foreign policy priority brings me to the central argument of this chapter. One reason why it is so difficult to mobilize effective multilateral action to prevent and respond to campaigns of genocide and mass atrocities, I believe, is that the task of atrocity prevention falls into an uncomfortable gray zone between humanitarian action and traditional diplomacy. The actions that are required to prevent atrocities are seen as too political for humanitarian organizations to undertake, while they are seen as not political enough and frequently too costly in terms of time, blood, and treasure to appeal to the arbiters of great power foreign policy.

Even today, U.S. government leaders (along with the leaders of other major powers) tend to divide their national foreign policy priorities into "hard" and "soft" objectives. The "hard" objectives are seen as self-interested and political: for example, securing vital resources in order to preserve America's economic power and prosperity, protecting the homeland from attack by terrorists or hostile nations, and maintaining a global alliance system as a force multiplier and geographic buffer against foreign aggression. The "soft" objectives are conceived as altruistic and apolitical: for example, supporting initiatives for disaster and humanitarian relief, global public health, and development assistance, along with the protection of human rights and the promotion of democracy. Such programs aim to improve the lot of suffering people around the world. From a national security perspective, U.S. leaders justify the relatively modest annual expenditure on these causes by asserting that they elevate America's moral standing in the world and increase its "soft power" by helping build international partnerships and good will.

In the councils of power within the U.S. government, the so-called "hard" objectives of foreign policy almost invariably take precedence over the "soft" ones. To this day, the prevention of genocide and mass atrocities is widely seen as a "soft" objective—a humanitarian concern rather than a vital national interest. Thus, to take a recent example, when government-backed forces in Cameroon began committing atrocities against separatists in the country's Anglophone western provinces in 2017–2018, the U.S. government was slow to take action to try to halt this violence—in part because it did not want to jeopardize Cameroonian support for the U.S.-backed counterinsurgency and counterterrorism operation against the terrorist organization Boko Haram, an Al Qaeda affiliate infiltrating the country's far north, which was seen as a more urgent foreign policy priority for the United States.

In my view, this dichotomy between "hard" and "soft" foreign policy goals and activities is misguided, because humanitarian suffering in vulnerable countries can have devastating effects on the so-called "hard" national security interests of external powers. For example, an extreme drought in Syria in the years 2007–2010 drove as many as 1.5 million rural Syrians into urban centers, creating resource shortages and social stresses that helped precipitate the Syrian civil war.[5] The subsequent military campaigns against civilian populations perpetrated by Syrian and Russian military forces provoked millions of Syrian refugees to flee into Western Europe, undermining the cohesion of the North Atlantic Treaty Organization (NATO) and the European Union and contributing to the passage of the Brexit referendum in 2016. These indirect effects of the Syrian civil war have caused profound and lasting damage to the Western alliance system.

Likewise, in the case of Cameroon, even from the standpoint of *Realpolitik* it is a mistake for the U.S. government to elevate the priority of counterterrorism and counterinsurgency operations against Boko Haram in the north over the prevention of mass atrocities in the western Anglophone provinces. Boko Haram operates principally in Borno State, a remote and desolate region of Northeast Nigeria, and (at least to date) it has not carried out any terrorist operations directly against the American homeland. Cameroon's Anglophone provinces, by contrast, border on Eastern Nigeria's oil-rich Niger Delta, one of the principal drivers of the Nigerian economy, and a region that fought its own secessionist war against the Nigerian government in the late 1960s. These factors suggest that the eruption of civil war in western Cameroon has the potential to produce far more disruptive political and economic spillover effects than the expansion of Boko Haram into northern Cameroon.

A straw man argument that has frequently been raised to justify inaction in the face of genocidal violence is that "America is not the world's policeman," and that the Department of Defense cannot afford to dispatch the 82nd Airborne to patrol the streets of conflict-prone countries around the world at the first sign of trouble. While of course true, this argument overlooks the fact that the majority of the instruments of leverage that need to be mobilized to prevent genocide and mass atrocities are non-military in nature: for example, quiet diplomacy, public "naming and shaming," programs to combat corruption and to promote good governance and rule of law, initiatives for security sector reform, the granting or withholding of economic aid and trade concessions, targeted sanctions, and threats of war crimes prosecutions.

Another important tool for atrocity prevention is the strategic use of humanitarian and development assistance programs in order to discourage intercommunal violence and encourage cooperation across group lines. Ideally, government-funded agencies such as USAID would work together with inter-governmental organizations and humanitarian NGOs to mitigate the risks of mass killings. Traditionally, however, humanitarian and development assistance providers have sought to guard against the "politicization" of aid programs. The four humanitarian principles endorsed by the United Nations are *humanity*, *neutrality*, *impartiality*, and *independence*. According to UN General Assembly Resolution 58/114 of 2004, humanitarian actors "must not take sides in hostilities or engage in controversies of a political, racial, religious, or ideological nature." Rather, humanitarian action "must be carried out on the basis of need alone, giving priority to the most urgent cases in distress"; and it "must be autonomous from the political, economic, military or other objectives that any actor may hold with regard to areas where humanitarian action is being implemented."[6]

Although the UN humanitarian principles express laudable ideals, in practice they can have negative unintended consequences. When humanitarian actors uncritically presume that they are operating in an altruistic and apolitical manner, they may ignore the political dimensions and impact of their own activities. The distribution of scarce resources within any community is an inherently political activity, and the politicization of aid distribution is heightened in conflict environments where multiple factions are fighting for dominance or survival. Humanitarian assistance providers—even those working for independent NGOs without their own political agenda—need to understand the political contexts within which they are operating, through the use of conflict analysis tools such as the "Do No Harm" framework, to ensure that their assistance programs are having a constructive rather than a destructive impact.

The cases of the Rwandan genocide and the Syrian civil war again offer instructive illustrations. As noted above, in the aftermath of the Rwandan genocide, many members of the Hutu militias that had perpetrated genocidal violence fled into Eastern Zaire, where they commandeered food and other resources supplied by international humanitarian organizations. In effect, humanitarian aid enabled the militias to transform refugee camps near the Rwandan border into armed bases for continuing their struggle and threatening the stability of the new Tutsi-led Rwandan government. The militarization of these refugee camps created an impossible dilemma for humanitarian aid workers. As unarmed civilians, the humanitarian workers did not have the ability to prevent the theft of aid by the militias; their only viable alternative would have been to shut down or relocate the refugee camps, which could have put thousands of victims of the conflict at risk of starvation.

In the case of Syria, the World Health Organization (WHO) and other UN agencies are currently delivering medicine, water sanitation and hygiene (WASH), and food aid to millions of desperately vulnerable displaced persons in Syria, whose peril has become even more acute since the eruption of the COVID-19 pandemic. But, as a condition for obtaining humanitarian access within the country, UN agencies have agreed to base their relief operations in Damascus, which has not only bolstered the international legitimacy of the Assad regime but also enabled the Syrian government to divert humanitarian funds for its own uses. According to a 2018 analysis in *Foreign Affairs*,

> UN agencies such as the WHO have permitted the Assad regime to take control of the $30 billion international humanitarian response, using donor funds to skirt sanctions and subsidize the government's war effort... . The best estimate is that only between two and 18 percent of UN aid actually reaches needy Syrians. That aid, moreover, rarely goes to those most in need: the Syrians suffering in opposition-held areas, often under siege. Rather than helping at-risk civilians, the bulk of the aid has bolstered the Syrian government.[7]

As in the case of the refugee camps in Zaire, there is no easy solution to this conundrum. If UN agencies refuse to collaborate with the Syrian government, they may be denied humanitarian access to millions of vulnerable civilians. As Ambassador William B. Wood has noted,

> [t]he WHO is the weakest player at the table, absolutely dependent on governments for contributions and for the cooperation necessary for its work.... Dealing with populations ruled by evil governments poses a dilemma.... To assist the people, we must accept that some benefits will leak to the government. Politicizing humanitarian work will only make it worse.[8]

Yet to dismiss this dilemma altogether, based on blanket assertions about the neutrality of humanitarian assistance, is too simplistic. Reasonable observers might agree that if 90% of the aid reaches its intended recipients, while the Syrian government steals 10%, this is a price worth paying. But if only 10% of the aid gets through to vulnerable communities, while the Syrian government diverts the remaining 90% to fund a savage war against its own citizens, the case for continuing humanitarian aid programs in government-controlled regions of Syria becomes much less persuasive.

In recent decades, development assistance professionals have focused increasingly on the imperative of "conflict-sensitive development," which seeks to mitigate potential negative impacts of assistance programs in conflict-afflicted environments. A key figure in this movement is Mary B. Anderson, author of the seminal book *Do No Harm: How Aid Can Support Peace—Or War.* Anderson begins her book by observing:

> When international assistance is given in the context of a violent conflict, it becomes a part of that context and thus also of the conflict. Although aid agencies often seek to be neutral or nonpartisan toward the winners and losers of a war, the impact of their aid is not neutral regarding whether conflict worsens or abates.[9]

Anderson's Do No Harm analytical framework seeks to help development practitioners anticipate and prevent unintended negative consequences of their programs, as well as to identify unrecognized opportunities for a given program to help mitigate conflict.

Organizations engaged in the delivery of urgent humanitarian assistance have made some moves toward incorporating the Do No Harm concept into their work—but these steps are still tentative and underdeveloped. For example, the 2018 *Sphere Handbook* on "Minimum Standards in Disaster Response" includes a guidance note on "Negative Effects and 'Do No Harm'":

> The high value of aid resources and the powerful position of humanitarian workers can lead to exploitation and abuse, competition, conflict, and misuse or misappropriation of aid. Aid can undermine livelihoods and market systems, drive resource conflict and amplify unequal power relations between different groups.

The *Sphere Handbook* urges humanitarian workers to "[a]nticipate these potential negative effects, monitor and take actions to prevent them if possible,"[10] but provides no further details about how to achieve these objectives.

## Making the case for prevention

In my 2007 concept paper proposing the creation of the Genocide Prevention Task Force, I identified "the propagation of pandemic diseases" as one of the devastating spillover effects of genocidal violence. With the outbreak of the COVID-19 pandemic, this warning has become timelier than ever. During the first months of the pandemic, experts predicted that it could cause a death toll dwarfing the worst human catastrophes of the past century—potentially greater than that of the Rwandan genocide, the Holocaust, and both World Wars combined. Probably only a minority of those deaths, they believed, would be caused directly by the disease; the vast majority would come from indirect effects of the pandemic such as the loss of livelihoods and food shortages leading to mass starvation. In April 2020, David Beasley, Executive Director of the UN World Food Programme, warned that "we are not only facing a global health pandemic but also a global humanitarian catastrophe." The food program, he said, was currently feeding "30 million people who literally depend on us to stay alive," with over a hundred million more facing "crisis levels of hunger." Moreover, "an additional 130 million people could be pushed to the brink of starvation by the end of 2020" as a result of the coronavirus pandemic.[11]

Although Beasley's worst fears about COVID-induced famines have fortunately not materialized, COVID-19 is unlikely to be the last pandemic that the world confronts. Widespread violence stemming from wars, civil unrest, or mass atrocities could make evolving strains of COVID-19 or potential future novel viruses far more lethal and difficult to contain. Some such viruses can move back and forth between the northern and southern hemispheres on a seasonal basis, which means that the health security of the richest and most stable countries is dependent on public health conditions in the world's poorest and most volatile regions.

Rather than ending this essay with apocalyptic warnings of future global suffering, I would like to close by emphasizing the possibilities of this pivotal moment in world history. What puts hundreds of millions of people at risk of starvation during the current pandemic is not a global shortage of food, but rather a global shortage of political will to ensure that the most vulnerable among us have enough to eat. A coming wave of global famine is not inevitable; it will occur only if our political leaders today make the same calculation as U.S. leaders made in 1994 with respect to the Rwandan genocide: namely, that the deaths of innocent civilians in distant lands have little relevance to our own national security.

Since 2012, I have returned to academia as a research professor at George Washington University's Elliott School of International Affairs. In this role, I teach executive education programs on national security leadership for senior military and civilian officials from the U.S. and its international partners; and I also direct the Elliott School's mid-career Master of International Policy and Practice (MIPP) program, both on-campus and online. Most of the students in my executive education programs are colonels and civilian equivalents from the U.S. Department of Defense; in the MIPP program, I teach many Army captains and majors who are training to become defense attachés or security cooperation officers in U.S. embassies overseas.

From my conversations with hundreds of senior and mid-grade U.S. military officials over the past eight years, I have learned a great deal about the challenges confronting U.S. defense strategy during this volatile era in global history. Many of these soldiers express frustration over the never-ending quagmire of counter-terrorism and counterinsurgency operations over the past two decades, in which an endless string of tactical successes have added up to strategic failure. At the time of the World Trade Center and Pentagon attacks on September 11, 2001, Al Qaeda had fewer than 200 members in its core group.[12] After nearly 20 years of the Global War on Terror and its various spinoff operations, at an aggregate cost approaching $5 trillion,[13] the ranks of Al Qaeda and its successors have metastasized, with violent extremists around the world numbering in the tens or hundreds of thousands. As counterinsurgency expert David Kilcullen observes,

> [o]ur repeated failure to convert battlefield victory into strategic success or to translate that success into a better peace... is a key reason for the seemingly endless string of continuous, inconclusive wars that have sapped our energy while our rivals prospered, tied us down while new threats gathered, and contributed to internal unrest around the world.[14]

Recently, the U.S. government has refocused its national security strategy on the resurgent imperative of Great Power Competition against China and Russia, both of which are seeking to undermine American hegemony by building up their own military power and working to disrupt America's global alliance system. But the U.S. faces equally daunting challenges in the realm of conventional warfare as in its continuing counterterrorism operations. According to the recent book *The Kill Chain*, in U.S.–China war games exercises run by the Pentagon over the past decade, China has won nearly every time.[15] In the modern era, America's way of war depends heavily on capital-intensive weapons systems like the F-35 fighter jet, hundreds of billions of dollars over budget and still not fully operational, and aircraft carrier groups that are vulnerable to destruction by far cheaper weapons such as hypersonic glide vehicles. Even with the bountiful defense budgets of the past two decades, the Defense Department has been hard-pressed to fund its weapons acquisitions programs, and the funding shortfalls will likely become even more challenging in the post-pandemic era of budgetary austerity.

Where the U.S. still retains a decisive strategic advantage is in the much-maligned arena of "soft power." One of my Elliott School colleagues who is a leading China expert quips that the Chinese version of a "win–win" negotiation is: "We win, we win." Shortly after the COVID-19 pandemic struck Europe in early 2020, the Chinese government made a show of sending a plane load of personal protective equipment to Italy. The luster of this humanitarian gesture was tarnished when it turned out that China had not donated the PPE, but rather sold it to the Italian government at a hefty markup. When it was subsequently revealed that the same PPE had several weeks previously been donated by Italy to China, the Italians were enraged.[16]

As for Russia under President Vladimir Putin, its primary export products (along with greenhouse gas producing fossil fuels) are chaos and corruption. In its near abroad, Russia actively provokes domestic unrest and even civil war in countries including Ukraine, Moldova, Georgia, and Azerbaijan in order to prevent them from effectively resisting Russian expansionism. Further afield, it seeks to destabilize the European Union by funding both right-wing and left-wing extremist parties, meddles in American elections, perpetrates war crimes in Syria, and dispatches paramilitary organizations like the Wagner Group to shore up corrupt authoritarian regimes in Africa.

The chances of either China or Russia leading a global multilateral campaign to prevent famine or mass atrocities are somewhere between slim and nil. This type of ambitious effort, designed to benefit humanity while also serving our own nation's enlightened self-interest, is in the traditional wheelhouse of American diplomacy, not that of America's Great Power rivals. In the midst of the current global economic and public health crises, the U.S. has a rare opportunity to reassess the ends, ways, and means of American foreign policy, and to better align its strategies for pursuing the "hard" and "soft" dimensions of its national interests. It is tempting to dismiss the platitude "We're all in this together" as a facile cliché. Nonetheless, the COVID-19 pandemic has exposed as never before the interconnectedness of our fragile global community. Working vigorously to prevent atrocities and other humanitarian disasters is an essential step toward building a more secure, prosperous, and healthy world.

## Notes

1  I would like to thank the many supervisors, colleagues, and friends who have supported and informed my work on genocide and atrocity prevention during and since my fellowship at the U.S. Department of State, and who have inspired me through their vital leadership in this field. I am especially grateful to Giovanni Snidle, who brought me to the State Department as a William C. Foster Fellow in 2003; to Lee Schwartz and Sheri Sprigg, my supervisors in the Department's Bureau of Intelligence and Research (INR), who provided sponsorship and guidance for the 2003 conference series on atrocities prevention that I helped organize; to Susan Nelson of INR and Stewart Patrick, then of the State Department's Policy Planning Staff, who devoted their energy and expertise to the task of realizing our vision for these events; and to Amb. David Scheffer, whose pioneering work on this issue during President Bill Clinton's second term created the initial road map for the 2003 conference series. I would also like to express my gratitude to Jerry Fowler, former Staff Director of the U.S. Holocaust Memorial Museum's Committee on Conscience, who developed the plan for the Museum's Academy for Genocide Prevention and hired me to help bring it to fruition; to Sara Bloomfield, Director of the U.S. Holocaust Memorial Museum, who provided unflagging support for Jerry's bold vision; to John Heffernan and Ann-Louise Colgan of the Museum's Committee on Conscience, Lawrence Woocher of the U.S. Institute of Peace, and Amb. Brandon Grove of the American Academy of Diplomacy, who were my principal collaborators in mapping out the plan for the Genocide Prevention Task Force; to Amb. Samantha Power, who, as Senior Director for Multilateral Affairs and Human Rights at the National Security Council during President Obama's first term, was the driving force behind the efforts to translate the Task Force's recommendations into the presidential directive establishing the interagency Atrocities Prevention Board; and to Jim Finkel, who in retirement from government leads the Washington, DC-based Atrocity Prevention Study Group, and who has taught me most of what I know about atrocity prevention.

2  Joint Evaluation of Emergency Assistance to Rwanda, The International Response to Conflict and Genocide: Lessons from the Rwanda Experience, Study 3: Humanitarian

Aid and Effects (Copenhagen: Steering Committee of the Joint Evaluation of Emergency Assistance to Rwanda, 1996), 143; John Borton, "The Joint Evaluation of Emergency Assistance to Rwanda," *Humanitarian Exchange*, no. 26 (March 2004), 17–18, https://odihpn.org/wp-content/uploads/2004/04/humanitarianexchange026.pdf; International Rescue Committee, *Mortality in the Democratic Republic of Congo: An Ongoing Crisis*, Jan. 22, 2008, https://reliefweb.int/report/democratic-republic-congo/mortality-democratic-republic-congo-ongoing-crisis.

3  Peter Uvin, *Aiding Violence: The Development Enterprise in Rwanda* (West Hartford, CT: Kumarian Press, 1998), 44–45.

4  Quoted in Matthew Levinger, *Conflict Analysis: Understanding Causes, Unlocking Solutions* (Washington, DC: United States Institute of Peace Press, 2013), 20.

5  Colin P. Kelley, et al., "Climate Change in the Fertile Crescent and Implications of the Recent Syrian Drought," *Proceedings of the National Academy of Sciences of the United States of America* 112, no. 11 (March 2015): 3241–3246.

6  UN Office for the Coordination of Humanitarian Assistance, "OCHA On Message: Humanitarian Principles," June 2012, www.unocha.org/sites/dms/Documents/OOM-humanitarianprinciples_eng_June12.pdf.

7  Annie Sparrow, "How UN Humanitarian Aid Has Propped Up Assad," *Foreign Affairs*, September 20, 2018. See also Christian Eis, Kholoud Mansour, and Nils Carstensen, "Funding to National and Local Humanitarian Actors in Syria: Between Sub-contracting and Partnerships," Local to Global Protection, May 2016, www.local2global.info/wp-content/uploads/L2GP_funding_Syria_May_2016.pdf; and Simone Jeger, "UN Agencies Have Surrendered to Assad Regime—and Syrians Are Paying the Price," *EA Worldview*, May 29, 2019, https://eaworldview.com/2019/05/un-agencies-have-surrendered-to-assad-regime-and-syrians-are-paying-the-price/.

8  Amb. William B. Wood, letter to the editor, *Washington Post*, April 22, 2020, A26.

9  Mary B. Anderson, *Do No Harm: How Aid Can Support Peace—Or War* (Boulder: Lynne Rienner, 1999), 1.

10  The Sphere Project, "Humanitarian Charter and Minimum Standards in Disaster Response" (Geneva, 2018), 61.

11  David Beasley, "WFP Chief Warns of Hunger Pandemic as COVID-19 Spreads," UN World Food Programme, April 21, 2020, www.wfp.org/news/wfp-chief-warns-hunger-pandemic-covid-19-spreads-statement-un-security-council.

12  Leah Farrall, "How al Qaeda Works: What the Organization's Subsidiaries Say About Its Strength," *Foreign Affairs* 90, no. 2 (March/April 2011): 128–138.

13  Neta C. Crawford, "United States Budgetary Costs of the Post-9/11 Wars Through FY2019: $5.9 Trillion Spent and Obligated," *Costs of War Project* (Boston University), November 2018. For a lower estimate of $2.8 trillion, see Stimson Study Group on Counterterrorism Spending, *Protecting America While Promoting Efficiencies and Accountability* (Washington, DC: Stimson Center, 2018), 5.

14  David Kilcullen, *The Dragons and the Snakes: How the Rest Learned to Fight the West* (New York: Oxford University Press, 2020), 254.

15  Christian Brose, *The Kill Chain: Defending America in the Future of High-Tech Warfare* (New York: Hachette Books, 2020), xii.

16  Ross Ibbetson, "China 'Forces Italy to BUY Back Masks and Coronavirus Supplies It Had DONATED to Beijing Just Weeks Earlier," *DailyMail.com*, April 6, 2020, www.dailymail.co.uk/news/article-8193197/China-forces-Italy-BUY-masks-coronavirus-supplies-donated-Beijing.html.

# 15 Between coordination and communities

## Navigating competing perspectives after Hurricane Matthew in Haiti (2016–2019)

*Paul Shetler Fast*

### How I came to humanitarianism and a bias toward local solutions

When I arrived in Haiti in 2015, I was new to "the field" – just five years out of a Master of International Development and freshly graduated with a Master of Public Health (both from the University of Pittsburgh). While my education had been focused on supporting community-level efforts, and I knew all the academic reasons why a community perspective can lead to more effective and efficient work, it was my family experience and faith background that most deeply biased me towards local solutions and local ownership.

I was born into a family committed to supporting an unusual style of local-level community development and humanitarian work abroad. My grandparents served with Mennonite Central Committee (MCC) in the 1950s and 60s, helping to develop a rural clinic in northern Haiti in cooperation with the Haitian government, which was successfully turned over to local management after decades of partnership. I was born and grew up in rural Tanzania where my parents (also working for MCC) supported micro-level community development projects with local churches. Prior to that, they had worked with local groups in humanitarian response to famine in Ethiopia and what would become the Democratic Republic of the Congo. I grew up in East Africa as HIV/AIDS cases first surged through these communities. My memories of this era are not of heroic humanitarians, but of sitting with childhood friends at their parents' funerals, feeling the fear of an unspoken threat stalking my town and seeing communities come together with what they had, long before external groups ever decided HIV/AIDS was a priority for major international funding and action.

As a Mennonite, my faith calls me to give priority to those marginalized by society, and to always be skeptical of the priorities and perspectives of governments and the powerful, even in the humanitarian sector. It is a faith that does not have functional central coordination and was born in resistance to the centralized top-down dictates of governments and religious leaders in 16th-century Europe. MCC, as a ministry of Anabaptist churches, embodies this tradition through a widely decentralized structure (MCC's global work, for example, is overseen by

11 semi-independent boards across the US and Canada) and a long-term part-nership model which strives to give local partners more equal voice and drive deeper localization and local ownership. This skepticism of governments and being beholden to major powerbrokers and their agendas is also a primary reason MCC has often been hesitant to accept major government and founda-tion contracts.

So when I arrived in Haiti with my wife as new Representatives for MCC (i.e. directors), I came with skepticism toward the major humanitarian coordination groups in the capital, the large-scale projects implemented by and for USAID and other major donors, and even the reports from these groups which frame the con-versation among major powerbrokers about what was happening in Haiti, what the real problems and priorities were, and what solutions were most appropriate. True to MCC's emphasis on local knowledge and grassroots action, our orienta-tion in country consisted not of meetings with high-level officials, participating in NGO coordination groups, or reading official reports. Instead, our orientation to Haiti consisted of months of homestays with rural families, local language study (Creole instead of French), and meeting mostly with project participants in their homes and fields.

Ever since those first months in late 2015, I had been trying to reconcile how often official perspectives in the capital clashed with the perspectives and realities of everyday Haitians I was seeing and hearing from firsthand in the communities we worked in across the country. However, it was only after Hurricane Matthew struck Haiti in late 2016 and the massive humanitarian mobilization and coord-ination of response afterward that I began to understand that this gap between powerbroker perspectives in the capital, represented by NGO coordination

*Figure 15.1* Mountain village of Wopisa, Haiti after Hurricane Matthew

mechanisms (the UN Cluster System particularly), and local communities was not an anomaly. Instead, this structural gap between coordination mechanisms and the communities we serve is where humanitarians in the field must work, constantly navigating, translating, and attempting to bridge these competing perspectives and priorities.

## Crisis reveals the gap in perspectives

As Hurricane Matthew veered north towards Haiti across the Caribbean Sea, major NGOs, embassies, the Haitian government, and the media announced that the country was preparing for its landfall and that the emergency systems developed after the earthquake had been activated; deploying over 18,000 government staff across the country to prepare. The UN Cluster System, a system for coordinating government and NGO action during humanitarian emergencies, began to organize and hold its first preparatory meetings. Haiti would be as ready as it could be. But from before the storm even hit, gaps began to emerge between that official perspective in the capital and reality on the ground. When I made phone contact with rural community-based partner organizations, including local government officials and members of the supposedly prepared emergency response teams, it was often the first time they heard a storm was coming. As I topped off our NGO's Land Cruiser with diesel one last time before hunkering down to wait out the storm, I asked the woman trying to sell me mangoes on the street if she had heard on the radio about the need to prepare. "The big men talk, but they don't understand. They keep saying 'prepare,' but there is nothing I can do ... Their plans are not for people like me," she said laughing. "It is when the wind blows that you see a chicken's backside," she scoffed, quoting a Haitian proverb about how crises often reveal uncomfortable truths.

In the morning after the storm, unconfirmed reports started coming in and an official narrative began to take hold. According to these reports, the damage was largely confined to the southern peninsula, and mostly to the cities accessible by road where NGO and media representatives happened to be. Our organization's primary focus areas in the mountains of the Artibonite and central plateau were said to have been spared. The official reports showed no deaths, little damage, and no response justified in these areas. The official UN Cluster maps did not even show the country beyond the southern peninsula. Heated arguments broke out in Cluster meetings about which NGO would get priority to work in the cities in the south that had made the news. Governments, major donors, and the biggest NGOs were setting the direction fast through the Cluster System and humanitarian groups were falling in line. Coordination was working. At least the scandal-ridden chaos of uncoordinated NGO responses that many experienced after the 2010 earthquake in Haiti would not be repeated. I remember leaving that first Cluster meeting feeling relieved; there was a clear, coherent, and coordinated plan. Decisions were being made rationally, resources were being prioritized where they could have the most impact, and everyone was rowing in the same direction. It was an internally consistent and powerful message of coordinated response.

However, our staff and partners on the ground spoke of a very different reality. Less than 18 hours after the eye of the storm passed, with the rain still falling, I was high up in the mountains of the Artibonite Department with our team of Haitian staff assessing damage and meeting with people whose homes and livelihoods had been destroyed. People were still bleeding from walls that had collapsed on them in the night. Others had lost loved ones in the storm. Others had awoken to flattened fields and dead livestock. In the small commune of Verrettes, we and our partners confirmed 542 homes and thousands of acres of crops destroyed, multiple deaths, and thousands of livestock killed. We and our local partners, including local governments, submitted these reports of damage, but none of it ever made the official statistics or maps. The consensus coordination narrative was already set. When I showed the latest UN and government maps and statistics showing "minimal impact" in the area to a local government leader, he grew exasperated.

> How would they even know? No one has come up to look! No one has even asked us! What are they basing these plans on? Has anyone on those coordination groups ever gotten out of their white Toyotas and touched the dirt in our communities?

Similarly, there were clear differences between Cluster-identified priorities and what the communities we worked in were asking for. Based on early assessments of southern cities, Clusters put priority on emergency food distributions and shelter. However, when we conducted focus groups and interviews across the communities we worked in, we consistently heard different priorities being expressed. In the high mountain village of Lakwa, inaccessible by car, a 75-year-old woman was typical of her community when she said,

> I was born in Lakwa, and life has been getting harder each year. My husband has died, and I have eight children I care for … the storm destroyed our homes and gardens, I lost hope. I lost everything … I can rebuild my home, it is only mud and stones and grass…but without a garden and seeds … how will we live again? How will I feed these eight children after this food is gone? How will we begin to rebuild a life?

Eight miles away, in another mountain village only reachable on foot, we heard different prioritization, despite the areas looking identical on paper. Adrenya Charl, 36 years old, summed up the predominant perspective in her community when she said,

> For me, the health of our children is what me must protect first now. What good is rebuilding a house and a little food if I lose it all to medical bills, or another child dies from diarrhea and cholera? … I have two children now, 7 and 11, and I cannot see them get sick again. We need latrines more than anything.

In the communities we worked in across Haiti, we heard repeatedly that priority investments needed to be in long-term assets like restoring gardens and livestock, and building durable community health infrastructure like simple latrines, clean water systems, and community child malnutrition treatment systems. Emergency food was appreciated and needed, but it was not enough. Haitians in these communities had seen too many disasters to think that a short-term band-aid solution like tarps and food rations should be the top priority.

## Whose perspective gets prioritized

From the first reports of damage after Hurricane Matthew through needs assessments and priority setting, there were persistent structural disconnects between high-level coordination groups and what our team saw and heard on the ground. In community after community, interview after interview, I experienced a gap between the clean and simple narratives and priorities of the UN Clusters (and the news media reports based on them) and the complex, diverse, and highly local perspectives of people on the ground. This gap forced me as a humanitarian to make ethically and professionally difficult decisions about whose perspective would be prioritized in our response.

As a field-level humanitarian in a smaller NGO, I had the rare perspective of seeing this discordance in perspectives play out in real time and in person. I would sit at the tables of the Cluster System one day and be out in the fields of individual farmers and riding in the back of aid delivery trucks the next. While most big organizations have separate staff playing these roles, MCC was small enough that I was part of both worlds at once. While feeling torn, I tried to stay engaged with both worlds, to serve as translator and bridge builder to get the best work done that we could. In some cases, we bridged this gap by doing both what the Clusters were proposing and what the communities were prioritizing. In several areas we worked with local community-based partners to provide both short-term food aid as recommended by the Clusters (in our case, in the form of canned meat and locally sourced rice, beans, corn, oil, salt, etc.) as well as the longer-term investments in sustainable livelihoods that communities were requesting (often assistance with rebuilding gardens with seeds, tools, and communal labor-sharing mobilization).

In other cases, we took the community's perspective even when those went against a Cluster's recommendations. This was an awkward position to be in, both personally and professionally, but it felt ethically necessary to side with the community when given the choice. An example was following the advice of our senior Haitian staff to source all the food we could locally in food-to-seed convertible formats, giving participants the maximum flexibility in how they used the resources. When we provided beans in food rations, we sourced locally adapted types that could also be planted successfully in that area. Similarly, when providing locally adapted and sourced seeds we ensured they were chemical free (even if this marginally increased spoilage), so that these seeds could also be safely eaten if needed. The warning from the Cluster against using this type of food-to-seed convertible format was that people would just eat or sell the seeds – sacrificing long-term investments to meet short-term needs. Conversely, the Cluster argued that providing food in a format that could be planted would encourage people to sell it and would be more difficult to cook and use efficiently (compared for example to pre-ground grain), reducing its nutritional value to participants.

However, we found the opposite of both these fears in projects where we took this approach. Families by and large followed the priorities they had given us in the interviews and focus groups that informed project design by consistently sacrificing short-term food security, going down to less than two meals per day in some cases, in order to plant as much as possible and share seeds with non-participant neighbors who were equally suffering. We found no significant evidence in any of our projects of participants eating or selling their seeds or selling food rations. One older man in the mountain village of Wopisa (Figure 15.1) explained this unexpected dynamic to me this way:

> Small farmers in Haiti, we have seen too much suffering to eat the egg in front of us. No, we have the patience to watch that egg grow into a chicken. If you give us a cooked egg, we will eat it and be grateful, but we would prefer an egg that could grow into a chicken.

Six months after the storm, an older woman in the southern commune of Saint Jean du Sud explained why she had preferred these longer-term investments over the larger short-term distributions of most coordinated NGOs.

> The other big NGOs came and gave food and tarps, and people were very happy for a day or a week. The markets were very busy … everyone bought and sold what they needed after the distribution. But now all that is gone. We were too far away to get any of that help. It all went to the cities. All we had was this small project, but now I am fat from my garden, and they are still begging for food … gifts that leave you poorer are not gifts.

Similarly, in the water, sanitation, and hygiene (WASH) sector, the bulk of Cluster-coordinated resources went towards short-term interventions to prevent disease outbreaks immediately following the storm and to repair infrastructure in the cities. These were valuable investments, but they did little for the nearly half of Haitians who live far from cities and for longer-term sustainable change. When asked what they most wanted, communities we worked with that prioritized WASH consistently asked for long-term investment over short-term aid. Some asked for the external assistance necessary for every household in the village to build safe durable latrines. Others asked for us to work with households to secure water treatment options they could sustain without additional external inputs. Still others asked for community water sources to be expanded and protected, for example by repairing community cisterns and protecting springs.

In some cases, these community requests were in direct contradiction to what the central government and UN agencies claimed were best practices. Officially, the central government and UN actors backed the model of "community-led total sanitation" (CLTS), which is a community-level behavior change strategy focused on shame and disgust to mobilize community action against open defecation. CLTS offers minimal external resources to support change, for example providing financial assistance for latrine construction for the poorest households. This insistence on CLTS as official national strategy by the government aligns with donor priorities but goes against growing local evidence of its failure to create lasting change in Haiti or to fit respectfully within a cultural context that prizes dignity. Local government officials and communities knew how few resources it took to mobilize and support wide-scale latrine construction, and they had seen examples of it working locally, despite a donor-driven consensus that this was bad practice. The Cluster System tightens alignment between major donors and the NGO and governmental actors who depend on their funding, making it very hard as an organization or an individual professional to go against a Cluster's consensus position. In WASH this meant that it had become nearly impossible to get national-level approval or donor funding for large community latrine-building projects in Haiti. NGO, government, and community leaders would privately admit the failures of CLTS in Haiti but did not want to challenge the system's consensus on the issue.

Thankfully, with 60 years of on-the-ground experience in Haiti, confidence in the validity of our local assessments, and deep local connections and experience in a variety of WASH-related programming, MCC was able to find a creative path forward. By working entirely at the local level with local governments and water and sanitation authorities we were able to partner with local communities in achieving their goals on this issue. We could not build latrines for people, as this was in violation of a national government directive and would have been prohibitively expensive for our small budgets. However, we could facilitate communities and local governments working together to ensure everyone in the community could build one (including those that required small subsidies to do so). By leaning into local priorities, community groups, and local governments as leaders in the process we were able to accomplish work that bigger centrally directed groups were not. When you monetized the local contributions to these latrine-building efforts, MCC's external contributions represented a small fraction of the cost of construction – accomplishing the government's desire to not create dependency while still allowing universal latrine coverage. Within six months of these projects, cholera had been eliminated for the first time since 2010 in all participating communities in the hard-hit communes of Verrettes and La Chapelle. When we scaled it up to the whole commune of Verrettes, the same thing happened at the commune level in 2018. The results have been durable, with some latrine construction and community mobilization and education efforts being sustained with local resources for over four years after funding stopped.

The push for stronger humanitarian coordination through the Cluster System came from disastrous examples of how badly uncoordinated responses can go. The necessity of coordinated response has been demonstrated globally again during the COVID-19 crisis. In Haiti, the critical need for coordination was evident in the massive humanitarian outpouring after the 2010 earthquake. Despite some high-level efforts at coordination, such as the Interim Haiti Recovery Commission (co-chaired by former US President Bill Clinton and Haitian Prime Minister Jean-Max Bellerive), the reality on the ground was often chaotic and dysfunctional. Even humanitarian insider Chelsea Clinton reported back in confidential emails to her parents that on the ground,

> the incompetence is mind numbing ... The UN people I encountered were frequently out of touch ... anachronistic in their thinking at best and arrogant and incompetent at worst ... There is NO accountability in the UN system or international humanitarian system ... [there was a] proliferation of ad hoc efforts by the UN and INGOs to "help," some of which have helped ... some of which have hurt ... and some which have not happened at all.

Precious resources were wasted, projects were needlessly duplicative, needs were poorly prioritized, NGOs competed against each other, and Haitian community groups and governments were undermined and silenced. The response was plagued with scandal and waste. The sector was right to push for reform, especially in Haiti. The Haitian government was right to demand more authority in setting direction. Donors were right to insist that humanitarian actors cooperate, coordinate, and pay attention to the growing literature about what works in humanitarian response. At this point, it would be counterproductive to return to the often-anarchic laissez-faire humanitarianism of the past.

The more meaningful question is not whether coordination mechanisms in the humanitarian sector are good or bad, but how they can be adapted to better recognize and support the value of deep localization and prioritization of local voices in decision making. It is frustrating to feel caught between a Cluster's consensus and the communities we are trying to serve. Coordination mechanisms by their nature are designed to simplify and streamline priorities and action plans at the level of their coordination (usually nationally). This can be critical to mounting a rapid effective response and having a clear narrative for the media and politicians, but coordination and central direction will always flatten the complexity of local realities, wisdoms, perspectives, and priorities. Cluster consensus is generally driven by the most powerful voices in the room, usually the major donor agencies, UN representatives, big NGOs, and government actors. In my experience, there is little room for groups closer to the ground (e.g., small-scale community-based organizations, more locally rooted NGOs, and local government actors) to contribute meaningfully. As just one sign of this in Haiti, all Cluster meetings I attended were held in French or English, never Haitian Creole; the language that all Haitians speak, and the only language of people without elite education. Most expatriate heads of humanitarian agencies never bother to learn Creole, meaning they could not meaningfully engage at the community level with actual participants in their projects even if they wanted to. As someone more comfortable in Creole than French, I often found myself literally at the back of the Cluster meeting rooms with the few Creole-speaking frontline staff in attendance getting half-hearted translations from a peer.

When I would get back to the field with our partners and staff after a Cluster meeting, they would always ask me: What had happened? What had I learned? What was decided? All too often my only response was that they must have been talking about another part of the country than we were working in because what they were saying did not match the reality in front of us. The broadly defined needs identified by the Clusters were real, and generally had some data behind them. However, they rarely reflected the nuance at the local level required to translate this big-picture need into effective programming response. Yes, broadly speaking, food insecurity was rising as livelihoods were destroyed and prices were increasing. But without deeply localized assessments, this was not useful in targeting or strategy. Similarly, when the guidance did get detailed, such as in prioritizing emergency food rations that were not convertible to seed, this was more based on broad "best practices" from the sector rather than a detailed assessment of the realities in specific parts of the country and alignment with community prioritization and values. Despite the frustrations, I continued to attend Cluster meetings because I did not want to be replicating the chaotic free-for-all of past eras. The Clusters did help us know who was working where, and generally which areas were under served. The Clusters also provided helpful surfacing of relevant best practice recommendations that can usefully be considered as a starting point in project design. But I can understand why most actors that did not have to participate in the Cluster system (e.g., those with independent external resources such as mission groups and independent philanthropists) do not usually do so. If Clusters are to meet their potential, they will need to find a path forward that better prioritizes local voices, knowledge, and accountability over simple narratives and donor priorities.

## Coordinated localization

The Cluster System has improved on the chaotic anarchy of the past. From the perspective of people on the ground who saw both responses in Haiti up close, the tight coordination by the Clusters after Hurricane Matthew made that response faster, more thoughtful, and less wasteful than what was experienced after the 2010 earthquake. However, from my experience, I believe that the central control of current coordination mechanisms is insufficiently balanced with the deep localization necessary to make humanitarian aid both responsive and effective to what are always ultimately highly local contexts, values, and priorities. Without putting intentional priority on localization, the balance of power in coordination will always favor the most powerful voices (generally those in the capital cities at the highest levels of government, major international donors, and the biggest NGOs). When conflicts in prioritization or approaches emerge, the nature of these coordination mechanisms will give preference to those already around the table in positions of authority. It is primarily the perspectives of top-level powerbrokers that are being coordinated into a consensus position, not the complex cacophony of thousands of local perspectives. National governments and their top-level officials, even in the most robust democracies, have limited understanding of the highly local and diverse realities in the places where projects will actually touch the ground. Without deliberate and time-intensive methods of prioritizing local voices, these central actors cannot know the complexity of the local contexts they speak for, and most do not. Similarly, UN and donor agencies and the directors of large international NGOs with massive programs should not be presumed to understand the highly local dynamics and diverse preferences of the places their work touches.

Haiti is not a geographically big or demographically complex country by global standards, with less than 12 million people in 11,000 square miles of territory and no major ethnic or linguistic divisions. If national or even department-level coordinated response plans do not meet the diversity of local needs and priorities in Haiti, it calls into question where exactly the model as currently conceived does work. There is value in these top leaders coordinating their actions and setting shared big-picture priorities, minimum standards, and structures for avoiding duplication and waste. However, this top-level coordination cannot substitute for the deep local knowledge, relationships, and local accountability that is required for good practice at the point where high-level priorities translate into concrete action.

Very few people during a humanitarian crisis are in a position to see this gap up close and in real time. Almost none of the people sitting in Cluster coordination meetings are the ones on the ground in their organizations talking directly to the impacted people and watching project implementation unfold. It is usually top-level executives, too often expatriates who don't speak the local language, who manage Cluster coordination, while only lower field-level staff, usually locals, are actually "*atè*" as we would say in Haiti ("on the ground"). Likewise, no one from any of the communities being discussed at meetings I attended had their voice heard in these elite coordination sessions beyond statistical representations from survey responses. Even within Cluster meetings, a strict hierarchy exists with the biggest players (major funders like USAID, Global Affairs Canada, and the EU's ECHO, national government officials, UN system officials, and the biggest international humanitarian agencies) sitting literally and figuratively at the head of the table leading the conversation and setting priorities. While local community organizations, local government officials, and small NGOs like MCC with more granular awareness of local realities are relegated to sitting along the margins with little opportunity to shape decisions, if allowed to be there at all.

It is in crises that coordinated action is most urgently needed, but also when its inherent weakness in overlooking complex local realities is revealed. An international "best practice" is not best if it does not fit the local context, culture, and priorities. Coordination is not efficient or effective if broad strategies are not adapted to meet diverse local needs and learn from local wisdom about what will work and what will not in each community. As the mango seller said the night before Hurricane Matthew hit, "The big men talk, but they don't understand … Their plans are not for people like me." If the plans of coordination groups are not for people like her, who are they for? Whose voices are being heard? Whose perspectives are getting prioritized, and why? "It is when the wind blows that you see a chicken's backside," she said. It is only when you get on the ground in a humanitarian crisis that you truly see where the humanitarian machine touches the ground and where gaps exist between clean Cluster narratives and diverse local realities.

I believe this is where we as humanitarians on the ground have the responsibility to act as a bridge between these different worlds, and to use our positions of privilege to tip the scales back towards localized perspectives as we are able. Organizations like MCC, who are less dependent on major donor agencies, have an opportunity to have a foot in both worlds and challenge the Cluster consensus when appropriate. As a development and public health professional and expatriate leader, I was comfortable speaking up in Cluster meetings and would be given a seat at the table. At the same time, since I represented an organization with long-standing local partnerships and personally had on-the-ground experience in every community we served, I could contribute something that many leaders around the table with more power and experience could not. If those of us with the power to speak into this gap do nothing, if we say nothing, the top-level coordination consensus will determine the response. That may be better than the chaos of pre-coordination eras, but it will leave most local voices unheard, local priorities disregarded, and local wisdom ignored. The consequences of this are not only wasted opportunities to do good cost-effective work, but as we have seen recently in COVID-19 and Ebola responses, it can also lead to outright hostility from local communities who feel unheard, disrespected, and overlooked. In Haiti, after Hurricane Matthew, aid trucks headed to Cluster-prioritized communities were looted as they passed by equally impacted communities who were being neglected by coordination maps and prioritization plans. Expensive imported foodstuffs were sold in markets at bargain prices to buy the things people really needed – and would have said they needed if they had been asked. In Ebola and COVID-19 responses, treatment centers set up without local input or support in communities whose priorities and perspectives were never understood have been attacked. Scarce humanitarian resources literally going up in flames. Centralized coordination has a vital place, but it is also inherently biased and must be balanced with localized understandings, priorities, wisdoms, and concerns. We need to find better ways of getting local voices and priorities into those conversations. As field-level humanitarians straddling the worlds of coordination Clusters and local realities, we are in a unique position to advocate for change in the system and to amplify the perspectives of those not being heard. Pushing the system in this way is not only ethically important but also a critical step to improving the impact and effectiveness of the sector.

# Extending the conversation

Modern humanitarian action was born when Henry Dunant witnessed the bloody battle of Solferino, where the forces of France and its allies fought Austria in 1859. After seeing more than 23,000 dying and wounded soldiers on the battlefield, he argued for the need for a neutral organization, capable of avoiding the parties at war, to help prevent unnecessary suffering. And so the Red Cross was born. In today's humanitarian action, those organizations that take a neutral stance in their work are classed as Dunantists. In contrast, Wilsonian organizations take a different approach. They believe that aid is essentially political and defend the benefits of taking a stand.[1] The two philosophies have the same goal – to deliver humanitarian aid in the best way possible – but come out of different philosophies[2] and influence the humanitarian sphere in different ways. Consequently, they also play an important role in world politics.

Humanitarian action as we know it today has roots in 18th- and 19th-century missionary efforts. It may have started as a good faith impulse to aid people in need, but since its origins, it has been deeply attached to the Western world's colonizing project. Humanitarianism thus represents the best of human intentions, but it is snuggled inside a flawed political effort that was originally designed for dominant countries to exploit the world's resources and civilize its peoples.[3] These historical roots help make up the structural factors that shape the humanitarian machine, along with the global political and social environment and the particular practices and norms that humanitarian sectors' members know and follow.

This history rankles humanitarian workers.[4] Many of our writers express the discomfort that is felt across the humanitarian sector when it encounters power imbalances that run counter to its principles, and is to some extent openly or implicitly stated in all chapters in this book. For more than half a century, probably since World War II, the humanitarian project has tried to throw off this colonial legacy of its roots. The machine has come to acknowledge the heavy weight of history and tried to replace the unidirectionality in the flow of power with a multidirectional model in which power flows with similar strength among donors, humanitarian organizations, and relief recipients. But just as in a real machine, larger gears move smaller gears. The structural gears of the humanitarian machine are designed to move energy from donors through INGOs, on through local NGOs, to the people in need.

Sometime in the latter decades of the 20th century, humanitarian agencies came to terms with the idea that implementing humanitarian projects by themselves in lands far away looked a lot like colonizing practices of the past. In an attempt to distance themselves, and give more control to local people, Western organizations looked for local partners to be in charge of implementing projects on the ground. It seemed like a win–win solution. International agencies would provide outside funding to local partner groups, who would distribute those resources to meet the needs of their people. Partnering with local NGOs has been, ever since, one of the most visible strategies to get rid of old-fashioned colonialist practices.

This strategy did not come free of challenges. To affect the power balance, you need to affect the source of that power, something that this strategy did not do. Humanitarian organizations and donors continued holding the power simply by virtue of enforcing the way that resources would be distributed. Under this new scheme, INGOs force the implementation of specific management practices that are designed to measure the work that was being done[5] and increase the level of accountability to donors. By doing so, INGOs demand that their local partners do things in a certain way, thereby restricting their freedom of action.

The tension between an ideal of egalitarian partner relationships and the inherent power granted those who control the funds is what Elbers called the partnership paradox.[6] The partnership paradox highlights one area where power colors the workings of the humanitarian machine. There are plenty of others. As Andrew Cunningham observes, "the aid environment is full of … power dynamics and assumptions built into these complicated engagements." Part III has reports of humanitarian agencies' license to choose which information they will listen to in order to make their decisions, international workers' privilege to leave high-tension situations to local workers who may not be able to leave, and a reminder that decisions about how and where to distribute aid inherently carry power questions.

Even everyday decisions like which language humanitarian workers choose to use has power imbalance implications. Humanitarian workers need to communicate with one another to coordinate work across sectors like logistics and WASH (water, sanitation, and hygiene) and to work with other groups within the same sector. They usually talk to one another in a European language, say English or French. If local people do not speak those languages, they cannot participate as fully in planning and coordinating efforts.

In the spirit of taking an unblinking look at the structural barriers in the humanitarian world, we were confronted with social hierarchy challenges as we put this book together. As we were planning and inviting potential writers to contribute, we decided that we did not have the resources to translate contributions. All our authors, therefore, were required to write in English, which automatically left out the stories of a good chunk of humanitarian workers who do not speak or write in English. The decision prompted us to promise ourselves that we would work on a second issue that tells the stories of non-English speakers.

Power differences are difficult issues to confront. When power is embedded in social structures the individuals and institutions who possess it sometimes are barely aware of the influence they have; rarely do they like to be reminded that they might be missing an important element in their relationships. Because the humanitarian sector is a human institution, it is forced to work within the world's social structures, including its power dynamics. It needs to live and work within the tensions created when ideals and practice do not align. But it can chip away at the sector's structural faults. Sometimes it might even be able to go around them. The "Do No Harm" principle that many of our writers emphasize reminds us that power dynamics present in the humanitarian machine need to be made as explicit as possible. It is one step in the process of ensuring that no harm is actually done.

## Notes

1  Stoddard, Abby. "Humanitarian Policy Group." *HPG Briefing* 12 (July 2003): 4.
2  Stoddard observes that Dunantist organizations tend to be European, while Wilsonian NGOs are likely to come from the United States.
3  Rieff, *A Bed for the Night: Humanitarianism in Crisis* (New York, NY: Simon & Schuster, 2002), p. 60.
4  Thomas Davies, *NGOs: A New History of Transnational Civil Society* (Oxford University Press, 2014); David Rieff, *A Bed for the Night: Humanitarianism in Crisis*.
5  David Lewis, *Non-Governmental Organizations, Management and Development*, 3rd edition (Abingdon, Oxon; New York, NY: Routledge, 2014); Willem Elbers, *The Partnership Paradox: Principles and Practice in North-South NGO Relations*, 2012, www.researchgate.net/publication/254882712_The_Partnership_Paradox_Principles_and_Practice_in_North-South_NGO_Relations.
6  Ibid.

# Conclusion

This book was born as a simple idea. All we wanted was to share the reflections of humanitarian leaders without intermediaries. It did not take us much time to notice that, with a little bit of extra effort, we could also educate our readers about the current conversations that are taking place in the humanitarian sector. Once the first drafts arrived, we started to wonder if the way that humanitarian workers feel and interpret their own work is in contradiction with the way it is presented in academia. The more we explored the depths of each chapter, the more real this possibility became.

To understand or even confirm these discrepancies is critical because, presently, international humanitarian action seems to have become some sort of social expectation. When the media projects pictures of crumbled buildings or lines of refugees over our phones and TV screens, we expect humanitarian workers from all over the world to get on planes and converge in distant places to provide valuable support. Some of them have experience navigating unknown lands, but oftentimes they suddenly find themselves in a strange environment, where local customs, laws, and general ways of being are completely unknown. And still they are charged with delivering services, a task whose success depends on having a profound knowledge of the local context. This is, by definition, extraordinarily difficult, if not impossible.

To resolve this dilemma, humanitarian organizations try to assess the needs of the people. The idea of "need" thus drives humanitarian action and justifies the relationship between disaster survivors and humanitarians. In a sense, it has been the force behind the creation of this giant "needs satisfaction" global humanitarian infrastructure. Western humanitarian workers are trained to believe that their actions must be based on objective, accurate, and verifiable evidence of the needs of the affected population. This is an important contradiction that puts humanitarian workers in a difficult position and creates tensions that weigh on their daily lives.

The dichotomy of local understanding of need, and external need assessment and diagnosis, continues to harken back to a time when humanitarian action was conceived in a more linear fashion. Some individuals who were in the know, and capable, delivered basic life-saving resources to those who needed it.

Humanitarian action does not understand itself like this anymore. It has evolved into a more complex and sensitive sector which believes in the knowledge and agency of local people. Still, the chapters suggest that humanitarian organizations too often continue to act like success in a "post-disaster" context depends on clues, and collecting bits and pieces of information.

Luckily, the humanitarian community has evolved. As several of our contributors make clear, it has acknowledged that the response it provides does not always meet the basic requirements of affected populations, and it could even unknowingly and unwillingly harm the very same people it serves. Our writers also make clear that the humanitarian community continues to do its best to fulfill its pledge to work for the benefit of people and is deeply invested in finding new ways to improve the work it does and to confront the challenges it faces.

There are inherent limitations in its quest, however. We have already discussed many of the tensions and contradictions intrinsic in the humanitarian machine, simply by virtue of the way it is constructed. Most of the humanitarian sector's strategies are bounded by principles and norms that originate in specific contexts with assumptions about societal values and helping behaviors. The focus on enhanced management mechanisms, for example, tends to emphasize coordination and efficient collaboration among organizations, but is designed primarily for the good of the humanitarian machine, rather than focusing the attention on the wellbeing of the people being helped. At some level, it appears appropriate and pertinent, but it is mostly humanitarian providers who find it valuable. If the trend is to continue, this approach, or any alternative approach, for that matter, needs to be challenged not on the basis of the objectives it pursues, but to ensure that it is not constructed solely on the basis of how it will benefit the aid provider. Rather, approaches to giving aid should be infused with enough flexibility to be able to consider the understanding of end users.

Our awareness of the importance of the meaning that humanitarian workers give to their work was one of the reasons why we decided to put this book together. It is why we wanted to give humanitarian workers a chance to speak for themselves. We wanted to merge the world of academia and abstract ideas with the practical, down-to-earth reality that is at the heart of the humanitarian experience. And so, almost unknowingly, we created a new space where we were able to reflect ourselves on the written word of humanitarian leaders. And we did so, in an academically rigorous manner, relating to all authors in the systematic way that good research demands.

These final pages bring the book to a conclusion by asking humanitarian actors, as well as anyone else who is interested in this work, a critical question. How is it possible that, while humanitarian workers have the wherewithal to affect and shape their own work, the humanitarian field itself looks like it is defined by something other than the interpretation of its individual workers? Our writers make many noteworthy observations, reflecting on standards and how to balance them with the need for flexibility, the challenges of crossing the gulfs between the world where aid originates and the world of the aid's users, the tensions of dealing with the realities of hierarchical power and an ideology of egalitarian actors. And yet, in spite of these observations and so many others like them, the humanitarian machine itself so often seems to be off marching to the beat of its own drummer.

The divergence of opinion across and within the chapters confirms an ongoing debate about the role of individual interpretations in determining how humanitarian work is carried out. A prime reflection for us as editors was that the individual parts of the humanitarian machine do indeed have the power to be the source of change. There are constant and ongoing improvements in the sector, but the essays in this book have helped us realize how important it is that the system as a whole does not disregard the potential negative effects of major discrepancies between the fundamental beliefs of humanitarian leaders and the unvarnished pragmatism of the larger system to which they belong. To ignore how humanitarian workers with their "boots on the ground" interpret their work is to lose a depth of knowledge, not only about how to deliver humanitarian aid, but also how to cultivate healthy relationships among peoples across the whole world.

The reflections of our contributors show a deep commitment to the abiding human desire to help those with need and their dedication to make it happen. Their thoughts also point out how very complicated it is to act out the responsibility they feel. Perhaps, most importantly, this book shows that the humanitarian system itself must openly, and constantly, acknowledge the inherent contradictions in how it is set up. It then has the obligation to pay attention to the individual voices of the humanitarian leaders, ordinary workers, and humanitarian aid users. In a sense, the stories in this book represent a call to rethink what it is that informs the ongoing development of the entire humanitarian machine. Focusing attention on these people may constitute a paradigm shift of some sort; as Kuhn said, "if a paradigm is ever to triumph it must gain some first supporters,"[1] people who will play with it, mold it, develop arguments around it to the point where they can be created and then multiplied.

We hope that other readers of this collection of stories, will, like us, be challenged to rethink how the humanitarian system is built and operates. We hope you will read through this group of essays thoroughly and seriously, reflecting on its content and the connections between the multiple experiences of the authors. We hope that it will stimulate some of you to engage in further research, and some others to convert this knowledge into a manageable whole that can point toward new theories on how to understand the humanitarian world and how it functions. We certainly hope that it will spur on others to become humanitarian workers and complement the amazing work that continues to be done.

## Note

1 Kuhn, Thomas S. 1970. *The structure of scientific revolutions*. Chicago: University of Chicago Press (p.158).

# Index